DEATH
OR
GLORY

THE DARK
HISTORY
OF THE
WORLD CUP

For the 'Spurls girls' – Helen and Phoebe

DEATH

OR

GLORY

THE DARK
HISTORY
OF THE
WORLD CUP

BY JON SPURLING

VSP

Published by Vision Sports Publishing in 2010

Vision Sports Publishing
19-23 High Street
Kingston upon Thames
Surrey
KT1 1LL

www.visionsp.co.uk

ISBN 13: 978-1905326-80-8

A CIP record for this book is available from the British library

Design: Neal Cobourne
Copy editing: Ian Turner
All pictures: Getty Images

Typeset by Palimpsest Book Production Limited,
Grangemouth, Stirlingshire

Printed and bound in the UK by CPI Mackays,
Chatham, ME5 8TD

© **Mixed Sources**
Product group from well-managed
forests, controlled sources and
recycled wood or fibre
FSC   www.fsc.org Cert no. TT-COC-002341
© 1996 Forest Stewardship Council

CONTENTS

ACKNOWLEDGEMENTS

This book wouldn't have been possible without the cooperation and assistance of many people over the last ten years.

The following fans, players and journalists gave of their time freely and generously: Essam El Khabar, Alaa Maihoub, Emad Al-Khidir, Alberto Villalta, George Male, Alan Ball, Simon Anstell, Juan Peroto, Sir Bert Millichip, Sir Neil Macfarlane, Mike Langley, Kenny Sansom, Daniel Gordon, Denis Barry, Luis Galván, Fritz Plantin, Roger St Vierre, Roger St Vil, Mwepu Ilunga, Claude Fevre, Ilunga Mwepu, Paulo César Lima aka "Caju", David Voares, Dadá Maravilha, Manuel Kalmes, Elza Simone, Hugh Johns, Albeiro Usuriaga, Juan Carlos Metiche, Pierre Dierdiste, Raul Gorriti, Freddy Rincon, Emmanuel "Manno" Sanon, Bob Lemoine, Mehdi Minavand, Atefeh Aghili, Che Bum Hohn, Berti Vogts, Luque, Wolfgang Blockwitz, Prine Felipe, Constantin Stanciu, Carlos Aquiem, Denis Silva, Manuel Molares, Joe Namphy, Jean Antoine, Daniel Blume, Diego Vasquez, Dieter Lehmann, Juan Derada, Martin Hoffman, Georg Buschner, Wolfram Loewe, Fritz Polster, Enzo Meifredi, Guiseppe Meifredi, Mario Perazzolo.

For those of the above who are no longer with us, I hope I've accurately recorded their conversations with me.

Special thanks to my fixer/translator in Rio, Carlos Marinez. Without his tenacity and extensive contacts, the Brazil chapters would be devoid of any joie de vivre. He told me that he'd convince me that Rio is the world's most vibrant city. I didn't need a great deal of persuading. Thanks to Hector Nunez and Celso Edmundes in Colombia and Juan Voares in Buenos Aires for putting me in touch with such passionate football fans and players. Jaime Marena — my Central American spy — I never knew where you were from one month to another. Now I don't know where you are at all, but thankyou for helping me hack back the conjecture surrounding 'The Fútbol War.' Jean Samou in Port au Prince; I hope that you and your family are safe and well.

Thanks to Alex Bellos, David Winner and Jonathan Wilson for guidance and assistance over the course of writing the book.

Thanks to Hugh Sleight, Matthew Weiner, Jon Crampin and Louis Massarella, who have commissioned Four Four Two articles so regularly over the years. Likewise to Andy Lyons at When Saturday Comes, Mike Berry at Backpass and Richard Lenton at Football Punk. Thanks also to Anthony Teasdale and Stu Messham for all their encouragement and help back in the days of Maxim and ICE.

Big thanks as ever to my mates. I finally wrote a non-Arsenal book. Maybe more of you will read beyond the acknowledgements this time! Barry, Phil and Tatiana, Seb and Marnie, Jo and Gareth, Louise B, Adam and Nicky, Brummie and Ruth, Ian and Anita, Tim and Lucy, Steve and family, Si and Sandra, Si Barrick, Charlie and Natalie, Louise C, Catherine, Grant, Sam and Simon, and Paul and Vicky, Clare and William. Brendon – thanks for your wit and wisdom at games and The Auld Triangle and for discovering The Trevi. A real find!

At work, thanks to other Cornwallis "fixtures and fittings" Helen (for putting up with my mess in our office), Vicky ("Shut up Spurling, you talk too much") and Olivia, who has been there with me from the off. Thanks also to Chris aka Jonesy, and to Hannah in the Department. Bally, of course I read your emails. Cheers to Rob Wilkinson, Emma Fuller and to Matthew "El Gaucho" Spall for their lightning quick translations and to Paul and Geoff for all the Arsenal conversations about Baptista's shoulders, Bendtner's finishing, and how much we all loathe international friendlies.

I owe a massive thanks to my agent David Luxton, who made the book possible, and to Jim and Toby at Vision Sports Publishing for their faith in the book. Thanks to Ian Turner for his careful copy editing.

ACKNOWLEDGEMENTS

Thanks as ever for the support ("Not another bloody football book!") provided by my Mum and Dad, Helen Murray and Stuart.

And to Helen and Phoebe, thanks for all your patience and support. The book is finished now. Time for a Spurls hug!

INTRODUCTION

In 1928, when Jules Rimet finally convinced his crusty FIFA colleagues that the idea of a football World Cup might just have some mileage, he couldn't have imagined what a monster he'd unleashed. The Frenchman spoke of a tournament which would "unite nations," revolve around "rules, comradeship, and fair play," and "encourage mankind to be one due to football." The reality has been somewhat different, and although a number of iconic images burn brightly in the memory there are a raft of edgier and darker stories lurking behind the gold, glitter and confetti. Several national team's journeys have been exploited by despots, others simply reflect the fraught state of play in the country at that time; sometimes both.

As an eight year old I was impressed by my Dad snorting derisively at Argentina's victory in '78 and claiming: "Their military has fixed that." The World Cup has always fascinated me, especially the seamier side. In the latter part of last century I dusted down my passport (by March 2010 I will have travelled to nine countries purely for the sake of football writing) and began to crowbar contacts at *Four Four Two* and *When Saturday Comes* into opening up their address books to help me compile a truly unvarnished history of the tournament. On my travels I've been beaten in an arm wrestle by a 95 year old former juvenile delinquent in a Buenos Aires bar, met the original rebel of Colombian football in Medellin – and it isn't Higuita or Asprilla – and interviewed the long forgotten architect of East Germany's finest hour at the 1974 World Cup, who insisted his team drove Trabants to keep them away from the prying eyes of the STASI. My research has brought me into contact with a huge array of remarkable people, each with their tale to tell. Their testimonies throw up scandals old and new, destroy a few well established urban myths and reveal dozens of heroes and villains; some of those interviewed could even be categorised as both.

The majority of stories have dictators, killers, and societal upheaval either lurking in the background, or screaming at readers in the foreground. It's most certainly not a balanced approach to the history of the World Cup, and it's not intended to be. Many of the tournament's pivotal incidents, due to the globalisation of football culture, are so enshrined in the collective consciousness and have been analysed so remorselessly that they have reached a kind of saturation point. When I was in Rio, former Brazil striker Jairzinho nixed my interview requests, explaining: "The problem is that I'm not sure what else there is to say about what the team achieved in 1970. I think all the stories have dried up." It's a fair point; just how many revisionist arguments can there be on why England have consistently screwed up since 1966? How many more superlatives can be deployed to describe the swashbuckling French in 1998, or Brazil in 1970? There's nothing in this book, for instance, about Gazza's tears, or Marco Tardelli's crazed celebration in 1982. I figure that those events and images are well covered elsewhere and will appear in numerous montages on TV throughout the summer of 2010.

What interests me is the darker underbelly to the World Cup. Just how do footballers and football followers cope in the presence of turmoil, social upheaval and downright evil? What does their reaction tell us about a nation and its society? In South and Central America, oft replayed footage of Mario Kempes tiptoeing through the tickertape or Pele orchestrating his side's destruction of Italy in the 1970 final reveal precious little of how Brazil's General Medici meddled with the team selection for the 1970 World Cup, or what the atmosphere was like in Argentina in 1978 as the military junta pulled out all the stops to ensure the national team won the trophy. Fleeting glimpses on YouTube of Colombia's 5-0 thrashing of Argentina in a 1993 qualifier, and Haiti's fifteen minutes of fame against Italy in 1974 unearth little of the sense of foreboding which settled on both camps prior to the start of the tournament, or the dire events which followed.

A spot of digging around can shed new light on events though. An afternoon drink on Ipanema beach with the anti hero of Brazil's 1970 team, Paulo César Lima, reveals something of the extent to which the military controlled the national team. Over the border in Argentina, a political prisoner recalls what it was like listening to the shouts and cheers from the '78 Final from his cell with a bag on his head and a gun cocked in his face. In Medellin, once Colombia's most lawless city, a former city policeman explains how Andres Escobar's murder still provokes demonstrations in Medellin and why Asprilla's and Higuita's mutation into gangster stereotypes makes their former '94 teammates despair. Sweating it out (quite literally) in Haiti's capital Port Au Prince before the earthquake – risking muggings and kidnap threats – amidst stories of voodoo and Secret Police involvement in the '74 World Cup side demonstrates how football in the region has a unique dual ability to illuminate lives, and to destroy them.

South and Central America continues to teem with World Cup rumours and counter rumours, and conspiracy theories old and new. Former Argentina defender Luis Galván confirms that football brings "sunshine and shadow" to the region and that it remains "a religion to many millions of people." Such intensity of feeling is reflected in the revelations of Honduran and Salvadorian players and veterans who fought in the streets and on the pitch prior to the 1970 qualifier between the two nations, and subsequently became part of the infamous "Soccer War."

In Europe, with the continent rapidly hurtling towards the Second World War, fascism and football often appeared intertwined during the 1930s. Benito Mussolini may well have engineered the 1934 Finals in Italy's favour, and one former disciple of "Il Duce" explains the mood in Rome as Fascist Italy won the World Cup. In Berlin's bustling Checkpoint Charlie district, veterans of the remarkable Cold War match between East and West Germany in '74 finally open up about whether *Ostalgie* (nostalgia for the Soviet era) extends to football, and why Erich Honecker's Government mistrusted the sport and the power that it wielded. Journalists and players recall how the blood feud between England and Argentina worsened against the backdrop of a nationalist surge at the time of the Falklands War, and how the wedge between the two nations had existed for decades.

When João Havelange took over from Sir Stanley Rous as FIFA President in 1974, one of his principal aims was "to expand the tournament beyond the European/South American axis." Over the last 36 years, the more global and expansive World Cup has opened up a raft of stories from the planet's distant outposts. Mwepu Ilunga, entirely miscast for decades as the Zairian buffoon who kicked the ball away as Rivellino prepared to unleash a trademark free kick in 1974, sets the record straight. The incident was voted the fourth most memorable World Cup moment by Channel 4 viewers in 2006, but as Mwepu explains, his actions might just have saved his life, and those of his teammates.

I hope the book is a testimony to football's extraordinarily universal power. The tournament can divide nations and continents, and threaten and even cost lives. Yet it can also mean that footballers are deified in a way that some unscrupulous politicians could only dream of, and, every four years, it can draw together millions of people from different backgrounds. Jules Rimet would have approved of that, at least.

Enjoy the book.

Jon Spurling, March 2010.

1

THE BATTLE OF THE RIVER PLATE

Far removed in time – if not distance – from his moment of infamy on Buenos Aires docks, 98-year-old Diego Vasquez, once a teenage delinquent with a string of convictions for arson and violence, is still doing his level best to cause mayhem. In a spit-and-sawdust, nicotine-stained bar perched a hundred yards from the River Plate, Vasquez regularly challenges men a quarter of his age to arm-wrestling contests, whisky-drinking competitions and bare knuckle fights, proud of his reputation as a hell-raiser of the highest order. On Tuesday 29th July 1930 he nearly sparked a riot as he barked threats at dock officials to allow him, and thousands of others without boarding passes or tickets to the match, to board the flotilla of steamers and tug boats and set sail for Montevideo to go and watch the inaugural World Cup Final, where Argentina would take on hosts Uruguay the following day.

No one really knows how many sailed across the River Plate from Buenos Aires to watch that first ever final – estimates suggest anything up to 20,000 – and as Vasquez later added, "If you believed everyone you spoke to at that time, it was around 200,000. Everyone later claimed to have made that trip, and hundreds were stranded on the water when the fog came down. It became a badge of honour amongst the youth of Buenos Aires." Vasquez reveals that he was stranded in his native city on the day but it soon becomes clear that if I want any more information from him about the chaos which surrounded the match, and his claim to having attempted to torch the Uruguayan embassy after it, I am going to have to fight him, or at least arm-wrestle him, under the watchful gaze of Marlon Brando and James Dean, whose photographs adorn the walls above our heads.

With his drinking buddies egging him on he proves a match for me and anyone else who wishes to risk humiliation in a competition of physical strength against a near centenarian.

The Estadio Centenario stadium in Montevideo, the venue of that historic first final between two of the greatest rivals in international football, is now more akin to a crumbling mausoleum, its reinforced concrete blistered and disintegrating due to the corrosive salt air. Occasionally, when Brazil or Argentina visit, it throbs once more, living up to its original billing as 'the Latin American Colosseum.' Too often it lies deserted and rubbish strewn, even on match days. Eighty years ago, with Uruguayan football's star in the ascendancy, it represented the crowning glory of the nation's centenary celebrations; a statement of modernist intent if ever there were one. For the six months prior to the 1930 tournament, an army of stone cutters and masons worked around the clock to complete the 90,000-capacity stadium. The late 1920s saw a building boom in the city, with a plethora of ultra-modern offices and public buildings springing up. Although Wembley and Hampden Park, capacity-wise, were larger, the Estadio Centenario was in a different league architecturally. The economy was booming, due to overseas investment and a flourishing meat and wool export trade. With a population and land mass similar to that of Scotland, Uruguay's moment in the sun was inevitably brief, but uniquely unforgettable.

Since gaining her independence from Britain in 1830, Uruguay had spent much of the 19th century fending off the aggressive sabre-rattling emanating from her noisier and heftier Latin neighbours, Argentina and Paraguay. Montevideo slowly gained a reputation as South America's most forward-looking city. In the late 1920s, Latino modernism burst into life around the seafront ramblas and the central parts of the city. Uruguay's architectural elite became the envy of her neighbours. In 1927, Juan Antonio Scasso was awarded the responsibility of building "a sporting Colosseum to reflect the glory of a centenary of independence." The entire project was given extra impetus by the fact that in May 1929, Uruguay was awarded the first ever World Cup. FIFA had decided that it would earmark ten per cent of the revenues for the tournament itself, while all costs, risks and losses would be borne by the hosting nation. Interested European would-be hosts, including Holland and Italy, withdrew their candidature and interest in playing in the tournament, leaving Uruguay as the only nation willing to finance the World Cup and pay all the participants' travel and accommodation expenses. The Roaring Twenties would come to a grinding halt in the aftermath of the Wall Street Crash, but this gesture – personally endorsed by President Juan Campisteguy – guaranteed the hosts a huge amount of international exposure, even in the pre-TV era.

Daniel Blume was 15 years old when the World Cup came to Uruguay. He remains immensely proud of the Estadio Centenario and as we trudge around the perimeter of the stadium its faded grandeur permeates the drizzly gloom. It was the world's first reinforced-concrete football stadium and its four double-tiered stands fan out like the petals of a giant flower. "All Uruguayans recognised the symbolic nature of this," explains Blume. "Uruguay was ready to bloom and prosper. It summed up the moment perfectly." Two stands were named after the national team's Olympic football triumphs in the 1920s and another was called 'Montevideo' in anticipation of Uruguay's World Cup triumph. On the north side of the ground, a nine-storey tower reaches 150 metres into the sky on the top of which fluttered the national flag. "For its time this was a bold and extreme symbol of national optimism," explains Blume. Yet, constructed in a park, it has managed to retain a partly rural, quaint feel, unlike the distinctly chaotic, urban experience of the Maracanã in Rio.

Later we enter the stadium to watch Uruguay's biggest team, Peñarol, labour to victory against "a small provincial outfit," as Blume puts it. From our seats high up in the stands we can see other satellite stadia and the university hospital. Once the pride of South American medical care, its external walls are also crumbling. The 25,000 crowd is occasionally raucous but, dampened by the rain, there are long periods of hush and it's nigh on impossible to imagine that in June 1930 this was the epicentre of world football.

"The moment here passed a long time ago," explains Blume. "Young Uruguayans know little or nothing of what happened here and those of us who do are dying off. Before Brazil or Argentina won anything, we were there first. Before Brazil v Argentina became the continent's biggest game, it was Uruguay v Argentina. At one time you could cram one fifth of Uruguay's population into the Estadio Centenario. No wonder the 1930 World Cup evoked such passion. My father used to say that our underdog status is reflected even in city's names. Buenos Aires means 'Good air' and Rio is often referred to as Maravilhosa – the 'Marvellous City.' Montevideo means 'the sixth hill from the East.' Understated, you see? Of course, we won the trophy again in 1950, but the 1930 tournament was our time, before the Depression, and we triumphed on home soil. Now Uruguayan football only occasionally splutters into life and sometimes it feels like there is nothing. But once we had everything."

THE BATTLE OF THE RIVER PLATE

In June 1930, the luxury Italian liner *SS Conte Verde* set sail from the French Riviera, bound for Montevideo. It was a state-of-the-art vessel and its cargo was precious. On board was FIFA President Jules Rimet, all of the French delegates, the four European sides who deigned the new World Cup competition worthy of taking part (France, Romania, Belgium and Yugoslavia) and the solid silver and gold plate Goddess of Victory Trophy – later renamed the Jules Rimet Trophy. The boat was palatial, a pleasant surprise for several of the players who were dreading the thought of the two-week voyage. The last survivor from the Romanian squad, striker Constantin Stanciu, has fond memories of the trip. "It was a once-in-a-lifetime experience," he recalls. "There was excellent camaraderie between all of the teams, although a large number regularly dashed off due to seasickness. I remember that the French were fitness fanatics and that some of our squad would join them for fitness training to ensure that we kept ourselves in good condition. We often saw Jules Rimet, who regularly spoke with our coach, and he was very charismatic. Our coach told us that Rimet was disappointed that so many European sides had opted not to travel because he believed the football World Cup could only be a force for the better. Speaking as someone who lost relatives in both World Wars, I completely agreed with Rimet's philosophy that sport should break down political and cultural barriers. It's a shame that hasn't always been the case."

Greeting the arrival of the *SS Conte Verde* in Montevideo docks was 15-year-old Daniel Blume, who was allowed to skip school and attend the momentous event with his father. "All the passengers, headed by Jules Rimet, came down a ramp," he recalls. "I was impressed by the grandeur of the delegates' arrival, but less so by the puny appearance of the European sides. They looked as white as sheets – it was probably the effects of being at sea for so long. But we'd heard about the might of the Germans and the Italians and the English and we still hoped that they'd changed their minds about participating and sailed across anyway."

The Germans and the Italians – the two European nations hit most harshly by the Depression – had cited cost as their reason for staying at home; the English FA, protesting at FIFA's refusal to adopt a fixed definition of "amateurism," also declined to travel. On Montevideo docks the expectant crowd waited for the European teams to disembark. "My father told me that the Europeans didn't have the stomach to come across," recalls Daniel Blume. "'They are cowards,' he was telling me and anyone else who cared to listen. 'Europe is in decay; they have no fighting spirit. Only the Latin male has the stomach for the fight,' he was screaming. He was really on his high horse. I reminded him – probably in my overconfident teenage manner – that both his parents were French immigrants and that most of the population had come from Europe within the last 50 years. 'Nonsense, boy,' he insisted, and clipped me across the back of the head. 'Only South Americans have the stomach for this.'"

Broadly speaking, Blume's father was almost correct; from the start the 1930 tournament was a battle of wills between Uruguay and Argentina, two deadly football rivals who regularly spat poison at one another, buffered only by the River Plate. In terms of sheer size and population, Argentina clearly had the ascendancy, but in the 1920s Uruguay riled her neighbours through a double Olympic success, which made them masters of *fútbol rioplatense*.

The English had introduced the game to South America in the late 19th century and the locals quickly added a Latin flavour, embellishing it with dribbling, shimmies, backheels and pirouettes. Matches between Argentina and Uruguay began to dominate proceedings in the region and the Uruguayans won the first official South American Championship in Montevideo in 1917, 12 months after ticketless fans had set fire to cars outside the Gimnasia y Esginia ground in Argentina, causing the game between the two to be abandoned. It was Uruguay's astonishing victory at the Paris Olympics in 1924 which stoked the fires of dissent between the pair. As Blume points out, "The International Olympic

Committee marked the eighth Olympiad by producing a silk scarf covered with the flags of all the competing nations. Unbelievably, they forgot to add on Uruguay. They just missed us off, and this insult really whipped up the team."

In the final, Uruguay swatted away the Swiss, winning 3–0. A new, thoroughly unexpected force had arrived in world football, but it was the manner of their play which made observers sit up and take notice. French journalist Gabriel Hanot wrote, "The principal quality of the victors was a marvellous virtuosity in receiving the ball, controlling it and using it. They created a beautiful football, elegant but at the same time varied, rapid, powerful and effective . . . perfection towards the art of the feint and swerve and dodge . . . Before these fine athletes, who are to the European professionals like Arab thoroughbreds next to farm horses, the Swiss were disconcerted."

Uruguay's triumph was greeted with consternation in Argentina and the new Olympic champions were immediately challenged to a two-legged play-off. In Montevideo Uruguay hung on for a 1–1 draw but in the return leg, after several ticket kiosks were upturned by supporters desperate to gain entry to the already packed stadium and the crowd invaded the pitch, the game had to be replayed. This third match was notable because it was the first time a fence was deployed in world football to keep spectators away from players and officials. Uruguay eventually lost 2–1, having resorted to brute force in the face of a hostile 35,000 crowd. At one point the Uruguayan players were showered with pebbles by the crowd and play was halted when the visitors lobbed them back. The next day, when Uruguay boarded their ship to sail home across the River Plate, Argentine fans and the departing Uruguayan players threw coal at each other.

At the 1928 Olympics in Amsterdam, both Chile and Argentina joined Uruguay as South American competitors and the two nations from opposite banks of the River Plate swept into the final, with Holland and Belgium complaining about "South American rough-house tactics." The interest

7

in the final was huge. The chain-smoking arm-wrestler Diego Vasquez, now drinking shots using both fists and having finally beaten the "gringo weakling" not so fairly and squarely (he smashed my arm down on the table when I turned away, sending the glasses jumping in the air on the bar tables and spilling beer everywhere, much to the delight of his friends), finally declared himself ready to talk. Expressive, booze-fuelled, and a compelling storyteller, it's clear the former teenage firebrand has lost none of his ire. "In Buenos Aires, thousands of us gathered in squares outside radio shops or bars which had loudspeakers fitted. In those days there were no radio commentaries, so you had a guy barking out descriptions based on information received by cable. I now prefer the TV, I must say, but the tension was unbearable nonetheless. I stood outside the newspaper offices of *La Prensa* and I remember it well at the end, the grimmest news of all – 'Uruguayos dos, Argentine uno.' Most of the reports admitted that Orsi, our left-winger, was the best player and that we were unlucky to lose. But we had lost regardless. The mood was more of sadness at the time, although later one of my friends fired a pistol at the Uruguayan embassy. To me, though, it had happened a long way away and it didn't have the impact of what happened two years later."

The streets of Montevideo, by contrast, were a jumble of colour, noise, and celebration, and Daniel Blume recalls, "My father treated us all to a meal out, which was a rare example of him in a lighter mood. Everyone was feeling jubilant and there was a strong feeling of nationalism sweeping through us. Even though I was quite young, I understood what it was like that night to be a proud Uruguayan." Within two years, the smouldering rivalry between the two nations would be much closer to home, and distinctly more edgy.

Argentina made the short hop across the River Plate to the 1930 World Cup Finals with Buenos Aires sports newspaper *El Gráfico* boldly announcing, "The World Champions arrive in Montevideo." Future Uruguayan coach Ondino Viera later claimed, "That announcement was a declaration of war, and in a sense the 1930 Finals turned into a Great War." By this time life in Argentina had turned ugly. A military junta had taken over as the country, brought to its knees by the Crash, suffered a collapse in its coffee and beef exports. The cities teemed with anarchists and communists, shanty towns mush-roomed in size and the working classes grew increasingly fractious. Not for the last time an Argentine government looked to the national team to deliver salvation via World Cup success. Diego Vasquez recalls, "It's crass to suggest that people automatically forget their problems when football is played. It's a temporary distraction – no more than that. It was to be the same in '78. But it is nonetheless a big distrac-tion. For the weeks the tournament was in progress, football was the sole talking point amongst everybody. It consumed us in a manner which you wouldn't have thought possible. I imagine the government rubbed its hands in glee: it bought them precious time."

El Gráfico sold a staggering 100,000 copies in Buenos Aires every day of the tournament, highlighting the vibrancy and uniqueness of fútbol rioplatense. Edited by a Uruguayan, Lorenzo Borocotó, the paper asserted that the South American style was intrinsically more pleasing on the eye than the more direct European game. "The football that the Argentineans, and by extent the Uruguayans' play is more beautiful, more artistic . . . skilful dribbling and delicate passes are key to the style," read Borocotó's editorial. He added that the style of play emanated from the urban experience of young Buenos Aires children, where the pibe – typically a scallywag from the slums – played with a rag ball and, physically assaulted and forced to avoid bumps and holes, he would invent new modes of play. The guile and trickery came from the street. By 1930, football in Argentina was as much a national obsession as it was in England. I put it to Diego Vasquez and Daniel Blume that given Borocotó's angle on the development of fútbol rioplatense and historian's Felix Luna's claim that "Uruguayans and Argentineans are the same people expressed in two different nations," that there's virtually no discernible cultural difference between the two nations. Both men, having first cited hearing difficulties ("What can you expect from someone who is nearly 100?" asks Vasquez pointedly), dodge the question.

A day before the 1930 tournament began, El Gráfico further lit the blue touch paper, asking, "Which version of the fútbol rioplatense will prevail: the authentic Argentine version, or the version adopted and pilfered by Uruguay?"

"Word leaked out that the Uruguayan team had read that article," recalls Blume, "and it incensed them. They were double Olympic champions, and hosts. It was belittling nonsense, and written by a Uruguayan too. Journalists and others were unwise to underestimate us. Most of us believed that war had been declared."

The foot soldiers in this Latin American conflict may have been fêted as superheroes in their respective countries, but they were paid little more than the fans who parted with their hard-earned wages to watch them play. The Uruguayans' most famous player was the black right back José Leandro Andrade, who'd gained fame in Europe at the Olympics in 1928 for his ball-juggling ability. A shoe shiner by trade, Andrade's teammates included Héctor 'El Divino Manco' Castro, the dashing striker who'd lost his right hand in an electric saw accident when he was 13 and Hector 'El Mago' ('the Magician') Scarone who practiced by knocking bottles off the crossbar from 30 yards.

"During the Finals," explains Blume, "all the Uruguayan players trained in and around Montevideo. They took a morning stroll sometimes in the city centre and crowds thronged to see them. There was often a ripple of applause, and sometimes just respectful silence. We were in awe of them – and they were at such close quarters! There was none of the hysteria you'd get today."

For Argentina, the centre half Luis Monti – nicknamed 'Double Ancha' ('Double Wide') due to the amount of ground he covered during matches – was his nation's talisman. With his Desperate Dan jawline Monti, who had broken rivals' noses and legs over the years, had a well-justified reputation for being a fearsome opponent. He was also a skilful and gifted passer of the ball who could dispatch ferocious free kicks. For Diego Vasquez, Monti rapidly acquired demigod status and his often contradictory persona encapsulates perfectly Argentina's often turbulent World Cup history.

"Monti represented all that is both good and ugly about football in this country," he says. "He wasn't the *pibe* in the manner of a Maradona, or a matador like Kempes, but his pragmatic approach to the game flew in the face of how the purists would have you believe our game was in 1930, and was a more accurate reflection of what the Argentinean game is really like. He wasn't averse to hurting others, but he was also supremely gifted. There were often reports of him mixing with supporters in Buenos Aires bars, and he could drink. He was the working class's representative on the pitch. To me he was a hero, just as Maradona became to my grandson, albeit in a different kind of way."

"In the Montevideo air, there is the sensation of football," wrote a Uruguayan sports journalist just before the tournament kicked off. "You can breathe in shots and when the coastal wind blows, one thousand balls fly through the air looking for a goal to score in." The first World Cup match took place at 3pm on 13th July 1930, amidst some confusion. Snow had fallen on Montevideo the night before and the Estadio Centenario wasn't quite finished, so the opening game between France and Mexico took place in front of a crowd of 4,444 in a satellite stadium, with Lucien Laurent having the honour of scoring the tournament's first ever goal in France's 4–1 win. In their next game, Europe's brightest prospects came predictably unstuck against the immovable object that was Argentina. It was a match laced in controversy, although not of Argentina's making.

In the 81st minute of a tight contest Luis Monti rifled home a free kick. "It was a juddering thump and the Argentines in the crowd went wild," recalls Blume. "In those days players didn't overcelebrate, but the players went mad. The crowd went into a frenzy because most of us were cheering for France. Now they were losing." Three minutes after Monti struck the inexperienced Brazilian referee blew for time just as the French centre forward Marcel Langiller bore down on goal, sparking a near riot from furious French players and irate Uruguayans who invaded the pitch. The game was eventually restarted and Argentina clung on for a 1–0 win. After the match the visitors' team bus was pelted with rocks by home fans and the Argentine Football Association threatened to withdraw from the World Cup altogether, claiming, "The affair might gravely affect our country's fraternal feelings with Uruguay." Only a last-ditch plea from the Uruguayan press convinced Argentina to stay put.

In their next game, Argentina thrashed the hapless Americans (nicknamed 'the Shot Putters' due to their heavy physique) 6–1, displaying a combination of ruthlessness and guile. US trainer Jack Coll, who'd previously claimed to be more concerned about "who we will be playing in the final," was so outraged by Argentina's physical approach that he ran up to Belgian referee Langenus to remonstrate with him, but in the process dropped a bottle of chloroform which smashed and caused him to faint.

Uruguay's passage to the final was more serene. They defeated Peru in the Estadio Centenario's inaugural game and then hammered Yugoslavia 6–1 in the semi-final. The Europeans later withdrew from the third-place play-off after claiming they'd had a perfectly good goal disallowed against the hosts which would have tied up the scores at 2–2. The River Plate showdown would take place on Wednesday 30th July.

The atmosphere in the respective capitals during the days leading up to the final bordered on the hysterical, and both cities effectively ground to a halt. Firms and offices closed on match day and the gigantic General Motors plant in Buenos Aires declared a paid holiday for its workers. Vasquez recalls, "Argentina is a nation in which emotion frequently runs very high. It's well used to political and economic upheaval, but the nationalist fervour which swept through

THE BATTLE OF THE RIVER PLATE

Buenos Aires during the 1930 World Cup was on a par with Eva Perón's death and the '78 World Cup. It was all so local, you could taste it in the atmosphere around town. All the talk turned to how you could get tickets for the boats across the river. It didn't matter at that stage about tickets for the final – just getting across to Montevideo was important. Money was crucial. If you had it, you could get access to the boats which would take you across, and if you were wealthy, you could queue jump. Many of those who eventually made it were middle-class followers who jumped on the bandwagon at the last minute." There were clear cases of money and wealth buying access to the boats. The six national deputies made the crossing in a government barge towed by a tugboat. The very rich hired their own private yachts and other businessmen went by plane.

For many others, it was nigh on impossible to leave the city. Approximately 15,000 had originally booked their places on overnight steamers, once it was known that Argentina were in the final. Those who still wanted to make the journey across the River Plate descended on the docks and besieged the shipping offices, hoping against hope for a golden ticket to Montevideo. Vasquez recalls, "It didn't necessarily follow that if you had a match ticket you had a boat ticket, so there was a lot of confusion, and anyone with a slight interest in football, it seemed, descended on the South Basin. It was absolute carnage. Incredibly dangerous. My friends and I confronted one official – there was a huge amount of pushing and shoving – and told him to let us on a boat or else we'd throw him off the quay. The crowd surged forward. There was testosterone in the air. We were horribly aggressive. If my father had seen how I behaved, he would have disowned me. Looking back it could have led to hundreds drowning, but at that point a policeman pushed through the crowd and told us he'd shoot us if we didn't back away. As the ships sailed off the crowd grew even more frenetic. There were people who'd climbed up on the giant cranes. There was community singing "Argentinos Si, Uruguaya No." There was such fervour as the steamers departed. My brother leapt off the quayside and got on the back of one of the boats, but he didn't actually make it to the match as his vessel was marooned in fog the following morning."

Across the water the atmosphere was equally all-consuming. Blume explains, "There was a ferocious sense of national pride. We have a phrase which sums up the indomitable Uruguayan spirit – '*Garra Charrua*' ['Victory in the face of certain defeat']. It sums us up, we love a David against Goliath challenge. We never give up in the face of what seems a greater opposition. We'd heard stories of fights and discord at Buenos Aires docks amongst people clamouring to travel to the game. We felt that reflected Argentina's lack of discipline."

On the day of the match, an estimated 150,000 people descended on the Estadio Centenario, although around 65,000 of those were left outside, forced to listen to the roars of the crowd. Blume made his way towards the ground with his father. "You couldn't help but feel the sense of grandeur and occasion. On the way to the stadium we walked past fellows selling grilled meats and that smell mixed with the plumes of cigarette smoke – it was an unforgettable mix. Yet the atmosphere was also tense. Anyone who shouted 'Argentinos' was punched and there were major scuffles along the route. We knew that many Argentina supporters had been searched for weapons at the docks – you could hear them grumbling about it and when they got to the stadium some fairly intimidating looking guards searched them again. The atmosphere was hardly cordial. At the gates to get in the verbal insults became louder still."

After a sleepless night in their Santa Lucia hotel (Uruguayans had hurled verbal abuse and rocks in order to keep the Argentine side awake), Luis Monti complained that he'd received death threats against him and his mother that would be carried out by Argentines if his team lost and by Uruguayans if his team won. Only the late intervention of San Lorenzo officials stopped their player from withdrawing from the match altogether. Both sides were accompanied by police and soldiers along the route to the Estadio Centenario amidst rumours that snipers had been hired to assassinate leading players from both sides. Even the referee, the Belgian Jean Langenus, got in on the act, insisting on special protection for his officials and family and a getaway boat afterwards. The Uruguayan government even readied a vessel in Montevideo harbour which would depart with the Argentine team on board an hour after the final whistle.

"Monti certainly wasn't at his best during the match," recalls Blume. "Unlike the force of nature I saw against France he was subdued and played well within himself. Lots of people claimed responsibility in Montevideo for issuing the death threats, but I always suspected that the Italian mob were at the heart of it – trying to make his life difficult in Argentina so that he would depart to Europe. It never struck me as a Uruguayan way of doing things." Years later it does indeed seem more likely that Juventus, anxious to lure him, used their contacts in South America to unsettle him. It worked. At half time, Monti would admit to his teammates that he didn't want to become a martyr due to football.

Before the game began, a row ensued over the match ball. "The Uruguayans wanted to use their bigger ball, and we were expecting to play with ours," recalled Francisco Varallo, the last surviving player from the 1930 Final who recently celebrated his 100th birthday. After a coin toss, the Argentines got their way in the first half, and after agreement from the referee, a Uruguayan ball was used in the second half. Meanwhile, on the River Plate, a boat full of Argentina fans drifted aimlessly around in the heavy fog; it wouldn't get back to Buenos Aires until the following morning.

The match sparked into life after only 12 minutes, Pablo Dorado rifling the hosts into the lead. Eight minutes later the Argentines drew level and, just before half time, they took the lead after Monti's through ball put Stabile in, although he appeared yards offside. The vast majority of the crowd grew restless and at half time, with the hosts trailing 2–1, Blume recalls "a crescendo of boos and everyone glancing nervously at one another." Argentine midfielder Jose Della Torre told his teammates "this crowd will kill us if we win," and the Uruguayan coach urged his men to "get stuck in" after the break.

In the second half Uruguay turned on the style. Cea put the hosts level with a simple tap in and Irlate struck from 25 yards to reclaim the lead for the hosts. When Castro directed a clever header past the keeper to make the score 4–2 there was a cacophony of noise from the home fans and the travelling supporters tried to leave, only to be blocked by jubilant Uruguayans. "There were some punches thrown again," explains Blume. "Rather than celebrate, some of my countrymen wanted to fight Argentines. When the national anthems were played at the end of the match, things calmed down slightly. These days, the presentation of the trophy is the key moment of triumph but the biggest roar came when the national flag was slowly raised up the tower on the opposite side of the stadium. For me, and I suspect tens of thousands of others, it was an indescribable moment of joy." Later that evening, Blume and his family joined the floodlit processions through Montevideo, amidst the sound of klaxons and ships sounding their horns. The 15-year-old was happy to discover that he'd have the following day off school as the government declared a national holiday.

In Buenos Aires, a disconsolate Diego Vasquez, who'd been listening to the match on loudspeakers in a city square, recalled how the desolation of the crowd quickly turned to fury. "The day before the match there was a call to arms from the city's newspapers who urged football fans to bring the national flag, so that when victory arrived there would be a huge outpouring of nationalistic fervour. The sight of those fans trudging away, with their flags still furled up, haunted me for a long time. Inevitably, though, matters turned unpleasant. We went drinking and there was a feeling that somehow we should try and exact some revenge. So we made tracks towards the Uruguayan embassy and on the way picked up rocks and bricks. When we arrived we threw rocks at the building. An associate of ours fired pistols at the windows. Elsewhere there were tales of people being abused and spat at for shouting 'Uruguayos'. Eventually the police turned up in the early hours, told us to grow up and go home. The next day it was like a funeral across the city. Buenos Aires was in mourning." A few days later the Argentine FA broke off diplomatic relations with Uruguay. The two nations didn't meet on a football pitch again for two years.

The aftermath to the final was dramatic for both nations. Argentine newspaper La Prensa set the tone by not simply blaming Argentina's "lady players . . . who are in danger of fainting at the first onslaught," but also "those leaders who manage, speculate, and deal in football as if it were a purely commercial affair." Other publications wrongly pointed out that before the second half the hosts had persuaded the referee to allow them to use their own – slightly bigger – ball ignoring the fact that the referee agreed to the share beforehand. Italian writer Berrara insisted, "Between the two rioplatense national teams, the ants are the Uruguayans and the cicadas are the Argentines."

The seeds of self-loathing and paranoia which have been an integral part of Argentina's World Cup history were sown. Eight Argentine players never represented their country again. Luis Monti opted to ply his trade in Italy with Juventus, and the man dubbed a coward by Argentina's feisty press corps would subsequently play for Italy in the World Cup finals four years later.

In Montevideo the effects of the Crash were catastrophic: a military junta seized control in 1933, sweeping away any lingering sense of nationalist optimism from the previous decade. The World Cup triumph, in a sense, was the nation's last hurrah for many years. Uruguay wouldn't compete in the next two series', amidst allegations that they were exacting revenge for the partial European boycott of 1930. And in the long term neither River Plate nation was ultimately able to prevent the dramatic rise to prominence of Brazil, who'd been virtually anonymous in the inaugural Finals.

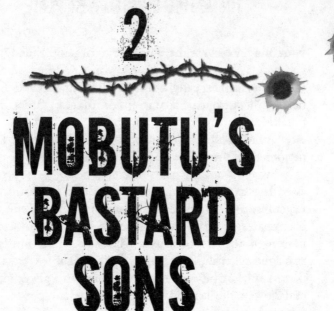

2

MOBUTU'S BASTARD SONS

After playing a leading role in helping Africa's first sub-Saharan country reach a World Cup Finals, Zaire full back Mwepu Ilunga had every reason to be pleased with life in the early months of 1974. The Leopards reached Germany after seeing off the cream of African talent, and the parade through the capital city of Kinshasa to celebrate the qualification was, in Mwepu's words, "stratospheric in terms of its importance."

Kinshasa, in its former guise as Leopoldsville, was once the centre of slavery during the Belgian occupation of Zaire (now the Democratic Republic of the Congo) and reaching the finals "asserted the power of black Africa and helped erase the stain of slavery, to a degree at least," says Ilunga. "To think that Kinshasa had been the centre of such misery, and then for this parade to happen with so many elated countrymen there was a memory which will never leave me, despite everything which happened after that. All the players were very much looking forward to playing in the Finals. We felt that we could then have great pride in ourselves, our country and that more than anything else, it would please Mobutu."

As the 1974 World Cup approached, the all-seeing, all-powerful President Joseph-Désiré Mobutu became increasingly interested in the fortunes of the Zaire football team. Mobutu had taken control of Zaire (formerly the Belgian Congo) in a CIA-backed plot in 1965 and, after years of ethnic and regional conflict since independence from Belgium in 1960, he looked on football as a way of uniting the disparate population. He often cited the example of Ghana, whose African Nations Cup victories in 1963 and 1965 had boosted President Kwame Nkrumah's prestige. He was also aware that he had been presented with a potentially golden publicity opportunity at a time when he was trying to push a pro-Africa culture programme. A year after the World Cup he would organise and host the famous Rumble in the Jungle world heavyweight boxing match between Muhammad Ali and George Foreman.

In the run up to the 1974 Finals Mobutu forbade any players from Zaire signing for foreign clubs, despite huge amounts of interest in his "national treasures." "Zaire must not become the cradle in Africa for Europe's mercenaries," was Mobutu's slogan. "But what that really meant was that too few of the squad had any real experience of playing non-African sides," recalled Ilunga. "It was a disaster for the team."

After they had qualified Mobutu lavished gifts and praise on the team and treated his players like sons, recalls Ilunga, although he admits that several members of the team already had grave misgivings in the event that the team's fortunes went awry in Germany. As it turned out, things went far worse than any of them ever imagined possible. Zaire's 1974 World Cup performances were so shocking, and Mobutu's wrath so harsh, that for a while the players' lives appeared to be in grave danger.

Tracking down the 1974 Leopards is a daunting prospect. The surviving members of the squad were so scarred by their World Cup experience that few remained in the game and many simply refuse to discuss what happened. Now renamed the Democratic Republic of the Congo, their London-based embassy can't help locate any of the World Cup stars and seems positively reluctant to help me in my quest. "I can't imagine anyone wants to revisit that," one employee says. But just as the trail seems set to go cold, The Independent puts me in touch with Kinshasa-based French journalist Claude Fevre, who has recently been in contact with two members of the team.

"There's so much bullshit swirling around about them," explains Fevre, "you wouldn't believe it." In fact I would, having been led down several dark alleys and heard numerous urban myths about the players over the past few months. "I've heard it said that that the defender Lobilo was killed by the Mobutu regime because of his poor displays in Germany, which isn't true," explains Fevre. "Two other players were said to have fled to Uganda to escape Mobutu and were later killed by Amin. One of them was the defender Kabasu. The problem is that as soon as someone disappears in some-where like Zaire people assume they have been murdered. There's no evidence to support this but three of the players have subsequently died. One is the midfielder Kilasu. The goalkeeper Kazadi died prematurely in poverty. The fact is that many of the team now live like tramps. Mobutu saw to that. The Congo is a big country and people simply vanish, which gives rise to these spectacular stories. It's the same with several members of Mobutu's government. They were rumoured to have died and suddenly they reappear."

In a 2008 When Saturday Comes article, Matthew Barker revealed how centre forward Ndayé Mulamba, whose nine goals at the 1974 African Cup of Nations remains a record, was proclaimed dead at the 1998 African Cup of Nations, only to later turn up destitute in South Africa. In 1994 he'd been awarded the National Order of the Leopard at the Cup of Nations in Tunisia only to be stabbed in the leg on his return by thieves looking for the cash they assumed he'd been awarded. Now a recovering alcoholic, he still walks with a pronounced limp.

Some of Zaire's other players fared slightly better. Midfielder Kidimu came from a wealthy background and his family was able to pay for his plane ticket to the USA, where he studied at the University of Michigan before launching his own business and winger Etepé Kakoko became the only 1974 player to play outside Africa, in the West German lower leagues. Adelard Mayanga, the skilful striker, now lives in the Matonge district of Brussels, often known as Little Zaire, which contains a raft of iconic '70s images, including giant photographs of Mobutu and, on the walls of cafés and shops, pictures of defender Mwepu Ilunga.

Ilunga is arguably the World Cup's most unlikely cult hero. His moment of infamy arrived in the dying minutes of Zaire's match against Brazil when, with the Leopards already trailing 3–0, he broke from the wall as Jairzinho and Rivellino prepared to launch a thunderbolt free kick and booted the ball upfield. As the crowd hooted with derision and the Brazilians shook their heads in disbelief, Ilunga bowed to the stadium as the referee booked him. In 2002, Channel 4 viewers voted it the fourth most memorable World Cup moment ever and a similar poll conducted by Brazil's prime sports channel in 2006 placed Ilunga's bizarre intervention in sixth place – an astonishing feat considering Brazil's rich World Cup history. BBC commentator John Motson asked, "What on earth did he do that for?" before describing the incident as "a bizarre moment of African innocence." In the mid-'90s Ilunga recreated the moment on Frank Skinner's and David Baddiel's *Fantasy Football League* show, as part of the Phoenix from the Flames section. The mood was one of ridicule and a raft of C-list celebrities have continued to laugh at the incident in a similar vein on satellite channels in the last decade. The story behind the moment is far more complicated than any of them imagine.

Fevre informs me that Ilunga views his moment with decidedly mixed feelings. "He's eaten out on it on several occasions," Fevre claims. "Yet he also feels he's been made the scapegoat for the whole campaign." Mobutu later commented that Ilunga's intervention against Brazil, "heaped shame on the country of Zaire," but I've also heard bizarre stories that he kicked the ball away deliberately in an attempt to gain his five seconds of fame. Fevre tells me that Ilunga is "willing to tell you everything you want to know for £100." The only slight drawback is that he wants the money wired to Fevre who will then convert it into Congolese currency and pass it onto Ilunga. Fevre will also need to translate Ilunga's French responses via a two-way link in the Congo. Suddenly, Claude goes all mercenary on me too and demands £100 for himself, to be wired immediately. I nearly refuse but, to my knowledge, Ilunga has never told a Western journalist what really happened before or after the 1974 World Cup so I accept. Although Ilunga is a diffi-cult interviewee, frequently complaining about his financial position, Mobutu and his knees, the story he tells is both fascinating and horrifying.

He explains that shortly after Zaire reached the World Cup Finals, Ilunga and his teammates received a telegram from Mobutu inviting him to his residential compound in Nsele, on the banks of the River Congo. "I can remember receiving the telegram like it were yesterday," recalls Ilunga. "It said 'Mobutu Sésé Seko Kuku Ngbendu wa Za Banga [loosely translated this means 'The all-powerful warrior who, because of his endurance and inflexible will to win, goes from conquest to conquest leaving fire in his wake and arising from the blood and ashes of his enemies like the sun which conquers the night'] invites the victorious Leopards to his home to meet with him to revel in the glory of the national football team's amazing achievement.' The letter was beau-tifully written by hand. You have to remember that for many of us, who'd been raised in poverty, meeting Mobutu was like meeting a god. He was a super-being to some. I look back on that day as one of the most amazing of my life. To me, Mobutu was someone who was proving to the world that Zaire could be a dynamic and forward-moving country. It showed that an African leader could rule without white man's interference."

But not all the Zaire players regarded Mobutu as a demigod. Several of Ilunga's teammates' families had been adversely affected by his pro-African cultural awareness campaign, which entailed them wearing traditional African dress, and using only traditional African names. Defender Boba Lobilo's brother had been a highly rated presenter on Zaire's daily news bulletin (which was preceded by Mobutu's image descending through the clouds from the heavens) before he dared to mention, live on air, the name of the former finance minister Emmanuel Bamba, who had been exectuted by Mobutu in 1966. By the early 1970s Mobutu had banned the media from mentioning the names of any government officials apart from himself.

"Boba Lobilo's brother should have described Bamba as a disgraced former finance minister. Mentioning him by his first name meant his career was ended. He spent some time in jail." Ilunga claims that two other teammates had also been threatened because they were initially unwilling to drop their Christian names and adopt African ones.

With a sense of understandable trepidation, the Zaire team approached the Nsele compound dressed identically in abacosts – Mao-style tunics which Mobutu ordered that all men in Zaire should wear on formal occasions in place of shirts and ties. And once inside Ilunga claims that even those with axes to grind were open-mouthed in wonder at the luxury of life inside Mobutu's lair. "He had his own zoo. For some reason I remember the snow tiger more than anything else and beautifully manicured gardens, a fleet of Mercedes Benz cars and minibuses, and the buildings were all made of amazing white marble. They reflected the sun and if you looked at them for too long you were almost blinded. It didn't seem to occur to us that whilst he was living a luxurious life many Zaireans, including some of our families, were starving. He was very much the African chieftain." What also impressed the Zaire team was the fact that on the river, two ships were moored side by side. One was the President's yacht – called President Mobutu – and next to it was a hospital ship named Mama Mobutu.

Finally, it was time for the team and their President to meet. The players were ushered by burly guards towards his luxurious steamer and told to wait. After a few minutes they were summoned and there, surrounded by "advisers and absolute luxury," sat Mobutu, sporting his trademark leopardskin toque and glasses. "My sons," he beckoned, "please come in and allow us to talk."

Zaire's footballers had been instructed not to shake Mobutu's hand, not to speak unless spoken to by the great leader and not to make any sudden movements in his presence as he was paranoid about assassination. Instead they gathered around in a semi-circle as Mobutu lavished praise on Zaire's new sporting icons.

"He spoke of how the World Cup would be a showpiece for the new Africa and how proud he was that Zaire would be the first ever team from black Africa to appear at a Finals. Even Boba Lobilo – whose brother had been so badly treated by Mobutu – admitted that he was beguiled by the Zairean President. What really impressed us was when Mobutu started speaking about our yellow shirts. 'Yellow looks beautiful on black skin. You'll feel like 11 Pelés when you play football,'" he said.

Mobutu had actually helped design the team's kit, and his insistence that a large leopard's head was prevalent on the front meant that along with Holland's brilliant orange shirts, and arguably Haitian tangerine, his country's shirt from that year remains the most memorable from the 1974 Finals.

"Somehow he convinced all of us that we could do very well at the Finals. He had this incredible galvanising influence," explains Ilunga. The other way in which Mobutu was able to win over the team was through lavishing gifts on them. "He promised each of us a brand new car, a new house and $20,000. He also told us that we'd get a generous amount of expenses in Germany and more money when we came back after the Finals. To be offered wealth like that was unheard of in Zaire. Most of us left Nsele feeling giddy. It was the most astonishing day of our lives. We did, though, notice how his guards shifted uncomfortably when he was

making his promises and this later became a big problem.
The other thing we hadn't considered – maybe not even
Mobutu had – was what happened if the team didn't play
very well in Germany."

The signs weren't good on the playing front. After a series
of disastrous friendly defeats against Swiss and Italian clubs,
Yugoslav coach Blagoje Vidinić admitted that his players
were ill prepared for the rigours of a World Cup. Never-
theless, there remained a giddy sense of optimism
surrounding the team, misplaced or not. Mobutu's contacts
in Europe, allied to his phenomenal wealth (he had an estimated $50 million stashed in Swiss bank accounts by 1974),
meant the Zaire team travelled to and around Germany in
style. They arrived at Frankfurt airport on a Boeing 747 char-
tered by the President. "The food on the plane was, literally,
fit for kings. It was a feast, with all sorts of meats and exotic
fruits," explains Ilunga, "and to follow there was Courvoisier
and cigars. It was a different world for most of us and, we
thought, a taste of things to come." The team was then
whisked from the airport in a brand spanking new Mercedes
Benz minibus to their hotel.

"The facilities and the surroundings were amazing," recalls
Ilunga. "Many of us had never been to Europe before so
the neon signs and the sheer affluence of Germany took
our breath away, as did our training centre."

Zaire's arrival in their natty minibus certainly went down
well with the locals and prior to their opening match against
Scotland there was a giddy sense of optimism surrounding
the team. The only downside was that the promised expenses
for the team had not yet been approved by Mobutu, so the
players were starting to grow restless inside their hotel. But
with Zaire's first match at the Finals approaching, financial
issues weren't exactly uppermost in the players' minds. Not
yet, anyway. Ilunga recalls the atmosphere in the dressing
room prior to the Scotland game.

"It was overflowing with nationalistic zeal. That's the only
way you could describe it. We felt we were doing it for

Africa, for ourselves, and for Mobutu. Shortly before we went out onto the field Vidinić pulled out a telegram from his pocket. It was from Mobutu. 'Go out onto the field and move with the speed and stealth of the leopard. Go out and bring glory to your country. Become heroes. Become legends.' And then the bell sounded, and out we went."

On the eve of the game the Scotland boss Willie Ormond had commented, "If we lose to Zaire I will send the team home" but for the opening half hour the Africans' one-touch passing bewitched the Scottish defence and delighted the watching Frankfurt crowd but, crucially, they failed to score. Then a trademark Peter Lorimer thunderbolt and Joe Jordan's soft header gave the Scots an unconvincing, stuttering victory. Goalkeeper Kazadi had made a howling error after his defence's ineptitude at deploying the offside trap had let Jordan in, but the crowd still sportingly applauded the Zaireans off at the end.

"The feeling inside the dressing room was still fairly upbeat," says Ilunga. "We felt we'd acquitted ourselves quite well." They had been, as one Belgian newspaper put it "a breath of fresh air."

Although he accepts that Willie Ormond's side played the better football on the day, Ilunga claims that the Zaire team was horrified by the racist abuse meted out by one member of the Scottish team in particular. "He was respected as a world star. 'Hey nigger', he was shouting. 'Go back to Africa, darkie.' It was terrible, and the referee did nothing to stop it. I suppose some of us were naïve, as few of us had ever been outside Africa. It was designed to put us off our game."

As well as experiencing European gamesmanship for the first time, the Zaire players were quickly realising that Mobutu's promises of wealth were empty ones.

"After the game a few of us wanted to go out and sample the nightlife," explains Ilunga, "so we asked the coach if we could have some of our money which had been promised to us." The answer was to forget it. 'Stay in your rooms and behave like professionals,' he told us. I couldn't believe what I was hearing, because I liked Vidinić. I thought he was a good coach and a good person. It was only when I saw Mobutu's people hovering around that I realised what was going on. His security service had pocketed the money. They sent us to our rooms and told us that we weren't in Germany to socialise."

From that point onwards, other than venturing out to train, the Leopards were held under virtual house arrest, watching TV in their rooms in a language they didn't understand and smoking and drinking more than was good for them. Two nights prior to the second game against Yugoslavia, Ilunga's club teammate Kazadi, the goalkeeper, told all the players at dinner to go to his room directly afterwards. There he suggested that the team should strike and refuse to play, thus conveying the message to Mobutu that his own security forces were not to be trusted. "The atmosphere was very tense and I think that eight of the players, including Kazadi, voted against playing, but the rest felt that they'd be betraying their country if they decided not to turn out." So the Zaire players took to the field against the Yugoslavs in a state of some disarray.

The Zaire v Yugoslavia game has passed into the annals of World Cup infamy. With Mobutu watching on closed-circuit TV back at home (he rarely attended live events for fear of assassination), he saw Kazadi let in three goals in the opening 15 minutes. The keeper wasn't to blame for any of them, but coach Vidinić opted to substitute him immediately and later claimed that the reasons for the switch "must remain a state secret." It was rumoured that replacement goalkeeper Dimbi Tubilandu was a favourite of Mobutu's, a fact confirmed by Ilunga. Just after Tubilandu had taken up his position between the sticks, the Yugoslavs rattled in a fourth.

As Zaire's shambolic defending contrived to gift Yugoslavia five more second-half goals (they eventually ran out 9–0 winners), Mobutu looked on with a growing sense of fury. Early in the second half the cameras panned to the Zaire bench. They showed an estimated 100 million worldwide audience a huge argument (Ilunga claims players from rival clubs Mazembe Lubumbashi and AS Vita Kinshasa had never really got on), with some of the substitutes sharing a none-too-crafty cigarette. At one point, two of the substitutes turned to Vidinić to remonstrate with him. "They were accusing him of taking a bribe from his countrymen," claims Ilunga. "That story did the round for years, that the Yugoslavs reckoned pretty quickly that their World Cup fate may well rest on how many goals they scored against us, and they had words with Vidinić. We lost because we played dreadfully, though. I don't think our coach could have done anything about it. We trooped off feeling what? Embarrassment? Shame? Fear of Mobutu? It's hard to say, really. I couldn't honestly see how he could regard us as his sons after that, though. Maybe bastard sons."

Later that evening, after the players had eaten their dinner in virtual silence, the full ferocity of Mobutu's temper was vented on the players. "We were told to sit tight in the dining room," recalls Ilunga, "because the lobby was being cleared of journalists. We knew it was going to be bad, and we were absolutely terrified. Then, after a few minutes, in walked these three serious-looking officials, with faces like death. They'd come with a message from Mobutu. 'He says you have all brought shame on to the country of Zaire. You are scum, and sons of whores. The great leader says that if you concede more than three goals against Brazil in the final match, you will never see Zaire or your families again. Your leader is disgusted in all of you.' They ranted on at us for around 30 minutes, before leaving the room. There wasn't anyone inside that room who doubted that those men meant every last word of what they said."

When Zaire took the field in their final group match against the mighty Brazil the players knew that, quite literally, their lives depended on the outcome of the game. Yet Brazil had stresses of their own, knowing that unless they beat the Leopards by three clear goals, they and Scotland would draw lots to decide who joined Yugoslavia in the next stage of the tournament.

"We lined up and looked at guys like Rivelino and Jair-zinho and they were tense, you could tell. We knew we'd lose, but we could make sure that we went down fighting." Zaire did precisely that and, completely transformed from the side which capitulated against the Yugoslavs, harried and pressed Brazil. With just ten minutes gone Rivellino hit a thunderbolt shot which smashed against Ilunga's head and bounced down off the crossbar before Kabasu belted the ball clear. Ilunga even had the cheek to blast an early shot fractionally over the Brazilian's own crossbar before Jair-zinho rattled home Brazil's first goal of the '74 World Cup shortly before half-time. "At half-time the mood in the dressing room was positive, we were only 1–0 down," recalls Ilunga. "We thought that at least we could possibly deny the great Brazil a place in the last stages. That would have been something, anyway."

Midway through the second half, Rivelino belted home a trademark 30-yard shot for Brazil's second, much to the relief of coach Zagallo. But the game's most memorable incident occurred with Brazil marauding forward for the vital third goal. As Brazil's big guns lined up for a free kick, Zaire's defenders assembled their wall. Ilunga took up position on the end of the wall and his defensive colleague Kumombo nudged him and said, "Make sure there are no gaps in this wall or we're in trouble." Ilunga takes up the story. "I saw Rivelino snort and take his trademark five steps back. I remember it like it was yesterday. His moustache twitched and he looked all of us in the eye. His legs were like the trunks of trees. I panicked. Everyone knew what he was capable of from that distance and I thought that if we went 3–0 down now we were massively in trouble. I thought I could waste some time if I kicked the ball away before the referee instructed Brazil to take the kick. So I kicked it away. Immediately I felt foolish because the crowd started to laugh and so did the Brazilian players. I bowed to the crowd and shouted 'You bastards' at them but it was hard to deny that I looked like an idiot."

I'd heard rumours that Ilunga kicked the ball away as a

publicity stunt, which he strongly refutes. "Do you think I'd deliberately make myself look like an idiot?" he asks. "You have to remember that we were playing for our lives. Stupid pranks weren't uppermost in my mind."

When Rivelino finally unleashed his free kick it blazed into the defensive wall – "It crushed someone's balls, I think," chuckles Ilunga – and this time he hoofed the ball away legitimately. With Brazil searching for the elusive third goal and the crowd baying for the final whistle their full-back Valdermirro scampered down the right and unleashed a hopeful cross-cum-shot which goalkeeper Kazadi helpfully spooned into his own net. The final whistle went almost directly afterwards and, as Brazil's stars celebrated scraping into the last eight, Zaire's players – whose World Cup record read 'Won 0, Drawn 0, Lost 3; Goals For 0, Goals Conceded 14' – consoled themselves with the knowledge that, for the time being at least, they could get back home. The question remained, though, how would the Father of the Nation respond to the return of his wayward sons?

Mobutu's retribution was predictably swift and typically harsh. The Zaire team flew home and arrived back in Kinshasa at the dead of night with no one there to greet them. The lavish promises of wealth never materialised.

"Our father," recalls Ilunga bitterly, "decided to take his presents back. We were later told that his guards had got so jealous of his promises to us that he had been forced to give them the cars, houses and money. We ended up with nothing and began to find that doors were slammed in our faces because of what happened. Mobutu began to destroy our careers. Our contracts at our clubs were cut and when some of the more experienced members of the squad tried to get coaching jobs they were turned down. Mobutu's contacts saw to that. I heard it rumoured that Mobutu reckoned the team had set the perception of African football back by 20 years. I suppose that if your sole purpose is to promote a more positive image of Africa then we had disgraced him."

Mobutu's attempts to use football to raise his country's profile for the better had failed, but he was already planning an audacious attempt to show Zaire in a more positive light. In 1975, the Rumble in the Jungle between George Foreman and Muhammad Ali took place in Kinshasa's national stadium and he attracted leading black American performers such as James Brown and the Spinners to perform in a pre-fight concert. The national stadium had played host to several of the Zaire football team's qualifying matches and underneath the stadium there were rumoured to be dungeons where political prisoners had been kept. Shortly before the fight an American tourist was murdered in Kinshasa and Mobutu, fearful of the impact the murder would have on the tourism industry, decided to act. He rounded up 100 of Kinshasa's most high-profile criminals and, at random, had one in ten of them murdered. "Mobutu was saying, 'I am Jehovah. I decide who lives and dies,'" wrote Norman Mailer in his famous book, The Fight. Some claim that the extent of the slaughter was exaggerated and that the Zaire President used it simply as chance to settle old scores but it is true that the lives of his footballers, like the fortunes of the nation, were hurtling towards the abyss. "Nothing Mobutu did was without forethought," claims Ilunga.

As my time with him draws to a close, it's obvious that the financial plight of Zaire's 1974 Leopards is in stark contrast to the promises of super-wealth promised by Mobutu prior to the tournament. "Many of us live like tramps," explains Ilunga. Fevre claims that two more members of the team were killed during the uprisings which finally saw Mobutu ousted in 1997. He lived in exile in Tanzania before eventually dying from prostate cancer in 2000.

Many Congolese still remember the 1974 team fondly, as a reminder of a relatively prosperous and stable period in the country's history. Not long after after the Ali v Foreman fight a sharp decline in the price of copper, Zaire's main export, combined with Mobutu's unparalleled looting of the country's wealth, signalled the onset of social and economic collapse. The Leopards' fall from grace was equally rapid; in 1978 the team withdrew from the World Cup qualifiers after the regime pulled the plug on football funding. Along with the rest of the population, the aftermath of the '74 tournament marked the beginning of decades of hardship for the players and the people of Zaire, and in turn, the Democratic Republic of the Congo.

Other African nations who have qualified for the World Cup have succeeded in the face of enormous civil strife. In 2006, after their decisive victory against Sudan in the qualifiers, Ivory Coast players, led by Didier Drogba, dropped to their knees in front of an Ivorian TV camera and made pleas to their civil war-ravaged nation to stop the fighting. "Ivorians, we ask you to forgive one another. We can't let things carry on like this." Yaya Toure later expressed a wish that, "through football, the nation can find peace." Things did subsequently calm down, but it had little to do with the influence of football.

Angolan players, for whom memories of a ten-year civil war remained painfully fresh, also expressed the hope that World Cup qualification for the same tournament in Germany would start to heal the country's gaping wounds.

Yet somehow the tale of Zaire in '74, with its contributory elements of hope, betrayal and disaster, continues to resonate loudly, some 36 years later. Along with Roger Milla's jig of delight after his goals in Italia '90, Illunga's intervention against Brazil is probably sub-Saharan Africa's most famous World Cup moment. Twenty-eight years later, how does he view his five seconds of fame? "If I could do it all again, I'd rather have worked hard at becoming a farmer," he responds.

3

THE UNFORGIVEN

Complexity lies at the heart of Rio de Janeiro. The super-rich live virtually cheek by jowl with the desperately poor, often separated only by a busy highway. Iconic landmarks like Sugarloaf Mountain, the Christ the Redeemer Statue and, of course, the Maracanã Stadium, provide a towering sense of excitement and breathlessness in this almost unfathomably large country. And then there are the famous white sanded beaches. Yet just yards away from the (somewhat) faded glamour of the Copacabana, children work the streets in the evening and even in the more upmarket Ipanema, it's unwise to venture onto the beach after dark. Brazil's World Cup history is similarly complex. My fixer Carlos explains, "The two-dimensional way of looking at Brazil's great players and great teams doesn't really get to the root of the story. Anyone can buy a DVD and see all the classic goals by Pelé or Zico or Ronaldo, normally with some bossa nova in the background. And that's great – if that's all you want. But you only scratch the surface if you look at things that way."

There are those in Rio who are painfully aware of the seamier, edgier underside of Brazil's World Cup experiences. Some even appear to revel in it. In June 2010, 30 fans are to lobby the Argentine government in an attempt to obtain a formal apology for Brazil's controversial exits from the

World Cups of 1978 and 1990. A lawyer, Marco Venerto, is anxious to extract a confession which accepts that not only were Peru bought off during the '78 tournament (which saw Argentina progress to the final at Brazil's expense) but that when the old enemies clashed at Italia '90, Argentine doctors handed Brazilian midfielder Branco a bottle of water drugged with tranquilisers during a late break in play. Branco later claimed to have felt dizzy and nauseous for the last ten minutes and failed to close down Diego Maradona as he set up Claudio Caniggia for the winner. Despite former Argentine manager Carlos Bilardo telling *Veintitres* magazine "I'm not saying it didn't happen" – Bilardo, known simply as 'Big Nose' in South America, has since backtracked on his statement, saying, "Not this again. These magazines always put in what they want" – and the Brazilian Football Confederation preparing a dossier, most have given Marco Venerto a wide berth, labelling him an extremist, and claiming that his efforts will ultimately prove fruitless.

During that same month, a gang of veteran supporters will hold an unofficial wake to mark the 60th anniversary of *Maracanazo* ('the Maracanã blow'). They will be joined by others who weren't even born when Brazil lost to Uruguay in the 1950 World Cup in the decisive final match of that tournament, a result often referred to simply as 'the Defeat' in Brazil. Such behaviour isn't considered unusual; indeed, there are likely to be other less high-profile wakes across the country.

That loss, and its aftermath, is still regarded by some as the greatest tragedy ever to befall the nation. Brazilian writer João Maxim claimed, "Its strength was so great, its impact so violent, that the goal seemed to divide Brazilian life into two distinct phases – before it and after it." Writer Nelson Rodrigues said, "Every country has its irredeemable catastrophe, something like a Hiroshima. Our catastrophe, our Hiroshima, was the defeat by Uruguay in 1950."

Down in Argentina, the mere mention of *Maracanazo* brings a wry smile to the face of my translator in Buenos Aires. "They [Brazilians] seem to think that when the national team loses it's like defacing the Mona Lisa," he argues. "They are even worse than us when it comes to looking for scapegoats. They turn on their own. In a different kind of way, their World Cup history is almost as controversial as Argentina's."

There are morbid interests, and then there are unfathomable, deep-seated obsessions. For all Brazil's myriad triumphs on the world stage and the aura which surrounds the national team, the loss to Uruguay in 1950 still swims inside the national consciousness like a determined bacillus. Some in Brazil keep an obsessive hold of the events that day; others have been driven to an early grave by the bitter memories. According to popular legend, two fans overcome by grief hurled themselves from the top tier of the Maracanã immediately after the game and, around the country, others ended their lives shortly afterwards. Although newspapers reported that a 58-year-old man in Rio collapsed at home during the match and three Uruguayans suffered cardiac arrest during the game, those Maracanã suicide stories (mentioned in Brian Glanville's masterful The Story of the World Cup) are apocryphal but the fact they have become enmeshed in the whole tragedy shows the depth of football fervour in Brazil. The sense of loss is no less acute with the passing of time, but many are still willing to bare their soul on the subject. There is nothing quite like it in world sport.

Writer Roberto Muylaert compared the defeat with the assassination of John F Kennedy. The black-and-white film of the goal is the equivalent of Brazil's Zapruder footage. Muylaert claims the goal and the gunshot which killed Kennedy both have "the same drama . . . the same movement, rhythm . . . the same precision of an inexorable trajectory." There were even clouds of dust present at both events, one from the assassin's gun, the other from the foot of Uruguayan goalscorer Alcides Ghiggia. Another comparison mooted by my fixer Carlos was that of the sinking of the Titanic. When I retorted that it was somewhat crass to compare the loss of a football match with the deaths of over 1,500 passengers (and for that matter Kennedy's murder or the instant incineration of 150,000 Japanese citizens), he looked at me with a mournful expression, shook his head sadly, and said, "You really don't understand, do you? There are many similarities [with the Titanic disaster]; the sense of expectation, the overconfidence, and the feeling of total invincibility. Then there came the sudden shock, the grim reality, the blame shifting, the revisionist arguments, and the raft of books and films which take different angles on the subject. The *Maracanazo* was our *Titanic*." Melodramatic it may seem, yet the defeat to Uruguay almost 60 years ago still haunts the sleep of millions of Brazilians of a certain age and bothers quite a few who weren't even born. As with any story, it's the human angle which makes it so compelling a tale.

In a smart apartment 200 yards away from Copacabana beach lives 74-year-old Elza Simone. After her son hands me a glass of beer, she starts to show me her huge collection of Brazilian football memorabilia, much of which is filed in gigantic scrapbooks, pigeonholed neatly on heavy oak bookcases. There are nick nacks everywhere in Elza's flat, and a yellow and blue parrot occasionally squawks as we chat. As she leafs through the scrapbooks all the usual suspects are present and correct. Pelé is there with the Jules Rimet Trophy in 1970, Jairzinho crosses himself after having scored in every match of the competition that year and Rivellino loses the plot after netting in the final against Italy. She also has a gallery of photographs on the wall. On the left, bleached by the sun, are '80s stars Zico and Careca and, going back in time, there are sepia-tinged shots of Leonidas, Brazil's first bona fide black star.

The entire right hand side of the gallery is devoted to snapshots from 1950. A group of men, holding picks and shovels, stand proudly on a mound of earth with the half-built Maracanã towering above them. Pointing to the middle figure Elza explains, "He's my father, and with him are his two brothers, and one of his sons." There are signed photos of two thirds of the Brazil's three man strikeforce from the 1950 tournament nicknamed the 'Trio of Death', Zizinho (Pelé's idol) and Ademir. Only Jair, the final member of the Holy Trinity, is missing. Perhaps most remarkably of all, there is a giant still frame of the dashing Uruguayan Ghiggia, the ball in mid-flight, peering expectantly towards Brazil goalkeeper Barbosa. A split second after this picture was taken, in this most fateful of football matches, Brazil's hearts were broken after Barbosa was beaten at his near post and somehow, despite all that has come since, they have never quite been mended.

Elza's puffy eyes widen with incredulity when I ask her why this photograph takes centre stage on her living room wall. "Because I view football as something from which I can learn about my country, and you learn much more from defeats. In victory, everyone is united. Divisions appear when you lose. I learnt a great deal about Brazil – much of it concerning – in 1950." Elza shows me a quotation from Carlos Heitor Cony, a writer who was later persecuted by the Brazilian military junta in the 1960s. "Survivors of that cruel afternoon believed they would never be happy again," he says. "What happened on 16th July 1950, described a collective moment, like the Tomb of the Unknown Soldier. These are things that build nations, a people drenched in their own pain." Elza simply taps the book and nods.

The Simone family emigrated from Salvador, capital of the Bahia region and the centre of black Brazil in 1948. Elza's father Joares, the great-grandson of sugar plantation slaves, heard that skilled labourers were required in Rio to build the Maracanã in time for the 1950 World Cup. In the latter part of the 1940s Brazil, under General Eurico Dutra, had drawn up a democratic constitution after a decade of dictatorship under General Vargas. Painfully lacking in industry and a solid transport infrastructure, the nation had slowly started to modernise, and social tolerance appeared to be improving at the same time. In the Jornal dos Sports the influential writer Mario Filho argued that the construction of an ultra-modern stadium in Rio would demonstrate

Brazil's emerging economic and social power. What was needed were thousands of workers who were willing to put their hearts, souls and backs into the project, around the clock.

In *Futebol: The Brazilian Way of Life*, Alex Bellos likened the whole programme to "Egyptians building a modern day pyramid." Elza Simone suggests that the experience bordered on the spiritual, "For my family, it was the start of a new life. The work which my father, uncles and brother were involved in at the Maracanã enveloped them and they gushed about how it fulfilled them each day. It was mainly migrants who built the Maracanã and my father would tell me that he was now part of a more open-minded, tolerant Brazil. He always approved of the name given to the Maracanã – 'The Cathedral of Football' – because it symbolised that life and football should be all about tolerance and embracing everybody. As the stadium took shape, the workers would test the strength of the terracing by stamping their feet and cheering imaginary goals as they flew in. The sense of giddiness in the air was amazing. There was a genuine feeling that football was about to transport us to a new world. This was all backed up by the media and the headlines couldn't have been more gushing."

One newspaper, *A Noite*, claimed, "Today Brazil has the biggest and most perfect stadium in the world, dignifying the competence of its people and its evolution in all branches of human activity. Now we can have a stage of fantastic proportions in which the whole world can admire our prestige and sporting greatness." With its 360-degree flat concrete roof and high internal arches, the elliptical design was indeed space age. Critics argued that the money would have been better spent on schools and hospitals, but they were drowned out by those who claimed that football could heal the nation. "I'm not against your request! I'm in favour! But I want you to be in favour of stadiums. It could well be that hospitals will become less necessary," argued Vargas Neto in *Jornal dos Sports*.

A strong connection between the players and construction workers heightened the feeling of nationalistic fervour in Brazil. "Some of the players, particularly the black stars like Barbosa and Bigode, took the time to speak with the workers, because they spotted kindred spirits. I'd imagine that kind of relationship is unique. Some became very close. From that point on, Barbosa and my father kept in regular touch. Another reason why the team was taken to the hearts of the people to such a degree was because it was truly a rainbow squad which appealed to people from all walks of life and ethnic backgrounds. It reflected how diverse Brazil was," explains Elza.

Back in 1938, Brazil's playmaker Leonidas had illuminated the World Cup to such a degree that he was the undisputed star of the tournament, even though Brazil were defeated in the semi-final by Italy, after he was rested for a final which they never reached. Writer Armando Nogueira later reflected, "We Brazilians said, 'Finally, Europe is seeing us in a different light. Not for the good nature of its people, not for art, nor for music, but because we had the best footballers, and they were black.'"

In part, the unique Brazilian style of football was borne out of the Capoeira, an African martial art with an emphasis upon dance and physical dexterity. "From this came the fact that many black Brazilians were excellent at dribbling, better at going around men, using the body more than the ball," added Nogueira. "The Brazilian footballer is the ultimate entertainer, a dancer." Elza Simone recalls, "Leonidas was my father's first idol. Yet in some ways, he also fitted a stereotype, that black Brazilian stars were mercurial, unpredictable, off the cuff. He sometimes played barefooted. That type of off-beat style is not what you want, ideally, from defenders and in 1950, the three black players, Barbosa, Bigode and Juvenal, were all defenders. The media, and most people within the game, expected attackers to be black, not defenders. That caused issues later on."

In the months leading up to the 1950 tournament the Cold War began to seriously heat up. As the situation in Korea worsened (war was officially declared on the day the World

Cup kicked off), US Senator Joseph McCarthy began his witch-hunts against "the God-damned reds" and Vietnam officially split in two in a portend of things to come a decade later. Milder ripples were caused by the news that Scotland wouldn't be competing, as they'd vowed to sail to Brazil only if they won the Home Championship that year. They finished second to England, who would now appear in their first World Cup, and Scotland declined to participate. India's refusal to take part was down to FIFA's reluctance to indulge them in their wish to play barefooted. Little of this was dubbed news-worthy in Rio. The talk was only of football.

Posters were displayed in shops, bars and restaurants. Floats advertising the World Cup cruised through the streets during the Rio Carnival. Most enthrallingly of all, the Jules Rimet Trophy was placed on show in the windows of a down-town shoe shop on Avenida Rio Branco. "Thousands of us went to see the trophy. It was tiny, but magnificent. Like a Holy Grail. It was like a pilgrimage. There was such a hunger for football," recalls Elza Simone.

In the Brazilian team, the Trio of Death would be anchored by a strong midfield and the athletic Barbosa in goal, who didn't wear gloves because he liked to feel the ball with his bare hands. On the opening day of the tournament, 5,000 pigeons were released into the clear blue sky, and the Mara-canã shook as a 21-gun salute thundered out. English official Arthur Ellis, who had been invited to the ceremony and would later become a minor celebrity in England for his appearances on It's a Knockout, recalled being showered in plaster dust as the blank cartridges hit the Maracanã's new roof. Flares and fireworks rocketed into the sky and the military band pumped out songs with a nationalistic fervour.

The hosts began in unstoppable form, crushing Mexico 4–0. After a 2–2 draw with Switzerland they cruised past Yugoslavia on a sweltering day in Rio in front of 160,000. There were numerous cases of sunstroke, the beer ran out and the first aid posts were overrun. Brazil were even aided by the (partly) unfinished stadium, when Yugoslav player Miti smacked his head on an iron girder before the match, resulting in medical treatment and his team starting the match with ten men. Brazil then proceeded to destroy Sweden, 7–1, and Spain, 6–1, in front of over 150,000 paying customers, meaning that a victory against Uruguay at the Maracanã in the final group match would see them crowned World Champions.

Elza Simone recalls being amongst the Maracanã crowd for the match against Spain. "It was the most beautiful day of my life up to that point," she insists. "Our play was beautiful and after the fourth goal went in, we sang 'Olé' every time a Brazilian touched the ball. The band joined in and, quite literally, the matches were played to music. The crowd waved white handkerchiefs in the air and we shouted '*Adiós*' to the Spaniards. It was cruel but beautiful. All in unison. It was like the crowd was an extra player. The whole team was in on it. Ademir scored four against Sweden and Jair and Chico starred against Spain. Writers described it as, 'ballet on a football pitch' which was bordering almost on the supernatural. The feeling was that no one could live with us."

At that point the problems for the hosts began, and they mainly revolved around the weight of expectation on the team. One member of the Trio of Death, Jair, explained the growing pressure on his team mates to my Rio fixer in 2000, when Carlos was in the early stages of a career as a freelancer. Cast out into the international wilderness for six years after *Maracanazo*, Jair was often overshadowed by the wizardry of Zizinho and Ademir, but later went on to become a successful coach and businessman. Although slightly less showmanlike than the other two on the pitch, he was frequently outspoken off it. "Although we'd played magnificently in the early stages of the tournament, there was an enormous burden on us," said Jair. "Before the World Cup we'd lived like monks and had been told when to eat, sleep and piss. Eat, sleep, piss. On it went, day after day. Some days it drove you mad. Then after we beat Spain and Sweden, the whole thing went totally mad. At that time there were municipal elections in Rio taking place and all these politicians (me and Zizinho used to call them 'the leeches') suddenly wanted to get to know us. It was crazy. Zizinho said to the coach, 'I want to eat my dinner, I don't want to meet them,' but suddenly we were dancing to their tune. Yet for weeks, none of us had been allowed to see our wives or kids. We didn't like it. We were being taken advantage of. Some resentment set in at that point, I think, and we weren't as focused on the match against Uruguay as we'd have liked. The coaches have to shoulder some of the blame for that, I think. Before the 1950 game against Uruguay this was clearly in evidence and it backfired on us. The worst case I can remember was that we were all presented with gold watches which said, 'For the World Champions' on the back. Talk about tempting fate. Again, me and Zizinho looked at each other and said, 'But we haven't won yet.' We were told to wear the watches anyway."

There were just two days between the victory over Spain and the decisive match against Uruguay. During that time a million T-shirts with the slogan 'World Champions' were sold. The day before the match, São Paulo's *Gazetta Esportiva* predicted, "Tomorrow, we will beat Uruguay!" The *Diario Carioca* boasted, "World Football has a new master. Brazil is the name of the new star."

"It was all total blustering bullshit," sneered Jair. "It was absolute bullshit. None of the players were overconfident, I can assure you of that. Not one. We knew that kind of nonsense from the mouths of people who didn't play the game was ridiculous. Some of us couldn't understand the position of the coach, Flavio Costa. On the one hand he was telling journalists about how we shouldn't underrate the Uruguayans and how back in '38, Leonidas had been rested in the semi-final and how that had cost Brazil. So in one sense he was aware of the pitfalls. Yet Costa also stood as a candidate in those Rio elections and was part of the circus around us. It made us tense. Barbosa was the tensest of all. The goalkeeper's position is the most exposed and he knew that. As he used to say, 'If you guys miss an open goal, you can redeem yourself. If the goalkeeper makes an error, it's never forgotten.' Never was a truer word spoken. The goals we let in against Spain and Sweden were soft, but all that was ignored, because we eventually won so easily."

On the day of the match against Uruguay, an estimated 200,000 people, many of them without tickets, forced their way in to the Maracanã with Brazil needing only a draw to be crowned World Champions for the first time. Elza Simone's brother went and he later told his sister, "I'm amazed no one died on the way in. There were tens of thousands of ticketless fans and with the pushing and shoving inside and outside it was almost hysterical. You could feel that there was almost too much riding on it from the outset."

Before kick-off, the Mayor of Rio, Ângelo Mendes de Morais, spoke to the players and fans via 254 loudspeakers, telling them, "You, players, who in less than a few hours will be hailed as champions by millions of compatriots! You have no rivals in the entire hemisphere! You, who I already salute as victors!"

The Trio of Death soon got to work against the Uruguayan defence, but their opponents were well marshalled. La Celeste ('the Sky Blues') defended to the last man and a telling moment arrived in the 28th minute when Uruguay's captain Obdulio Varela clouted Bigode, Brazil's black left half. Both players later downplayed the incident but the press later cited this as an example of Brazil's defence, and Bigode in particular, lacking moral fibre, as he was slow to recover from the knock.

Nonetheless, a minute into the second half, Friaça scored for Brazil to give them a lead which they just about deserved. Fireworks exploded inside the Maracanã. Fedoras were thrown into the air. "Although the crowd roared, there wasn't joyous celebration amongst the players," recalled Jair. "It was more relief, to be honest. You'd have thought that the pressure would have been lifted, but that wasn't the case. The goal should have spurred us on but suddenly we got cautious. We did. That is the truth. Suddenly the noise seemed overwhelming and the Maracanã preposterously big. Nerves set in. We stopped attacking like we knew how to and, for the first time that tournament, relied on our defence, which hadn't really been tested, to see us through. I hit the post, which would have settled it there and then, because Uruguay would never have come back from 2–0 down and even if they had all we needed was a draw. It was the wrong tactic, but we weren't the last great Brazilian side to make this error: Telê Santana's side was undone by poor defending against well-organised opponents in '82. It was Uruguay who emerged as the stronger side."

In the 66th minute, Uruguay's Varela nudged the ball to Ghiggia, who dribbled past Bigode like he didn't exist and crossed the ball for Schiaffinio, who fired past Barbosa to make it 1–1. "You could have heard a pin drop, but still, a draw would have been enough," recalled Jair. With ten minutes left, Ghiggia's exchange of passes with Perez took both Jair and Bigode out of the game and instead of crossing the ball, Ghiggia fired the ball towards Barbosa's near post. Voted the tournament's best stopper before the final, Barbosa was caught off guard and the ball sneaked past him and nestled in the back of his net. Inside the Maracanã the crowd was in stunned silence. On the official footage, middle-class white women with pearls around their necks cover their mouths in disbelief and black men with open collars stand dumbfounded. Radio Globo commentator Luiz Mendes repeated the fateful words "Gol do Uruguay" seven times consecutively, with completely different intonation – surprise, shock and resignation.

Years later, Ghiggia famously commented, "Only three people have, with just one motion, silenced the Maracanã: Frank Sinatra, Pope John Paul II, and me." The final few minutes were played out in an almost surreal atmosphere. Jules Rimet, who'd left his seat high up in the grandstand seconds before the Ghiggia goal, had previously noted that the stadium was "like a sea in a storm with a loud and tempestuous voice." Now it was eerily quiet and when

English referee George Reader blew the final whistle a disorientated Rimet surreptitiously handed the trophy to Varela, and by the time *La Celeste* eventually embarked on their lap of honour, most of the crowd had silently dispersed.

"My brother told me it was like a funeral outside," recalls Elza Simone. "People were either stunned into silence or they were just sat in the streets crying, or shouting in pain, or wandering aimlessly, lost in their own thoughts." The posters were consigned to the dustbin, Brazil's gold medals were melted down and Brazil's victory song, *Brasil os vencedores* ('Brazil the Victors') never made it onto the airwaves. The stone statue of Rio's 'Victory' Mayor outside the Maracanã was shoved off its plinth and smashed on the pavement. In one fell swoop all of the hosts' coruscating attacking play in the other matches counted for nothing. The first postwar World Cup, often seen as the first modern tournament, may have been notable for its joie de vivre and from FIFA's angle it made a tidy profit, but history has virtually written out such irrelevances. The opportunity for redemption arrives once more in 2014 but, to date, Brazil, unlike Argentina, Uruguay, Italy, England, France and Germany, are the only major footballing power to host the World Cup and fail to win on home soil. Brazil didn't play at the Maracanã again for four years.

Over time, various theories have been put forward for the defeat. In *Futebol: The Brazilian Way of Life*, Zizinho explained to Alex Bellos the pitfalls of the 'WM' formation which the hosts opted for, and in *Inverting the Pyramid: A History of Football Tactics*, Jonathan Wilson provides a forensic examination of the tactics deployed by Flavio Costa. Wilson concludes that the formation left Bigode, more of a left-winger than an orthodox left back, fatally exposed to Ghiggia's pace. Critics closer to home claimed that the team's white shirts with blue collars weren't sufficiently nationalistic and had a "psychological and moral lack of symbolism." From that point onwards Brazil's players would wear yellow tops in World Cups after a competition was held for the people to design a new strip. Even the crowd didn't escape blame. "When the players needed the Maracanã the most, the Maracanã was silent," explained musician Chico Buarque.

Amongst the Brazil players, especially in the years that followed, there was a widespread acceptance that Uruguay's guile and refusal to adopt the role of the sacrificial lamb in the Maracanã had been overlooked. Skipper Obdulio Varela's influence proved crucial. La Celeste had been chronically underrated by their own FA President Dr Jacobo. On the eve of the final, he'd said, "What's important is that these people [Brazil] don't make six goals. If they score only four goals our mission will be successful." Some of the Uruguayan officials had even headed for home before the match, fearing the worst.

On the morning of the final, Varela had spotted O Mundo on sale in the lobby of the team hotel, with the front page headline, under a picture of the Brazil team, "These Are The World Champions." After buying as many copies as possible, Varela told his teammates to urinate on them. Prior to the match, legend has it that he also told his team to disregard the instructions of coach Juan Lopez and to attack Brazil down their right-hand side, rather than opt for a purely defensive approach.

"Me and Zizinho got to know Varela quite well," explains Jair. "Zizinho and him got on really well and he used to call him 'the Old Bastard' in an affectionate way, because we knew that his influence was massive on Uruguay. More than anyone or anything else, it was Varela who did for us. Even when we scored, Varela argued about whether it was offside with the referee. He genuinely led his team that day. Sometimes, a stroke of inspiration like that is what wins you World Cups." Varela became a recluse afterwards and wore a Humphrey Bogart-style trilby and coat to hide from journalists.

Uruguay's top brass visited several Rio nightclubs after the final to celebrate but told the players to stay in the hotel and avoid trouble. Varela was given a brand new Ford as a reward for his efforts but it was stolen in Montevideo a week later. Jair explains: "At that point, Uruguay had won both the World Cups they'd played in. They knew what was required of them. They had a great side in 1950. Many of them played for Peñarol, who were invincible in those days. Our coaching staff should have done more homework on them. Varela felt terribly guilty about it all. Years later, he'd still talk about his guilt. He was too humble. I told him, 'You were the better side.' The Uruguayan captain defied orders and went on a bar crawl that night in Rio, and he was hailed by Brazilians. There was no anger towards Uruguay. The hostility was aimed at those closer to home." Within a few days the media, despite acknowledging the collective grief within Brazil, would find a convenient scapegoat, and at the same time, dismantle the perception that their nation was united, tolerant and multicultural.

The press swiftly rounded on defenders Bigode, Juvenal, and Barbosa in the aftermath of the 1950 final. "Guys like myself and Zizinho shrugged it off to a degree," claims Jair, "because we answered back and there were some rational reasons why we lost. When anyone had a go at me about it, I'd just say, 'It just didn't work out,' and either walk off or change the subject. Zizinho and Ademir did the same. But the media piled right in on top of Barbosa in particular. His life became a living hell. They said the three black guys were cowards and lacked the stomach for a fight. The press disgusted me and I told journalists that it was wrong. I'd say to them, 'Uruguay had four black players in their team and won.'

"The country, of course, went on to idolise Pelé, so where did that leave their argument? But Barbosa was hounded until his death. The problem was that, in public, he was a deferential guy. If you knew him he was funny and good company. But outside his group of friends he'd clam up and avoid confrontation. Zizinho did his best to protect Barbosa. He'd remove anyone from his house parties who dared to speak to Barbosa about what happened in 1950. Juvenal and Bigode moved around a lot too, always trying to avoid talk of the *Maracanazo*." A few years after the defeat, when Barbosa walked into a baker's shop, a woman told her son, "Look, there is the man who made all Brazil cry." Writer Carlos da Sylvia viewed Barbosa's treatment in quasi-religious terms, fulfilling the ancient role of the scapegoat, sacrificed to restore balance to a ruptured society.

Elza Simone recalled, "Barbosa kept in contact with my father after the final, and was never the same again. It wasn't too bad when he was still playing for club sides, because he had something to focus on, although he never played for Brazil again. He was viewed as an albatross. Everyone avoided him. He'd come around to see us and tell us that people still spat at him and that others would cross the street to avoid him even 20, 30 years later. The last time I saw him was the time after the 1994 World Cup squad refused to meet him because they thought he might curse them. The legend goes that he later burnt the Maracanã posts (a groundsman apparently smuggled them out) in a bid to cleanse himself of what happened and invited his friends around to eat the meats cooked on the embers of the wooden posts. I don't know if that's true but he never rid himself of the memories of that day. I'm convinced that much of the treatment was down to his skin colour and my father would get into lots of arguments defending him. My father was more cynical after 1950 because we saw how things really were, and so was I. This was supposed to be the start of the decade of the new, confident, multicultural Brazil. In the 1950s and 1960s, Brazil became more industrialised. The Ford plant opened in São Paolo and Brasilia was built. Pelé became the best player in the world and yet this treatment of Barbosa went on and on under our noses. It was hypocritical."

Gradually, all of Brazil's class of 1950 are dying off. Juvenal was the most recent to pass away, dying from a lung infection in October 2009, and Friaça, Brazil's goalscorer against Uruguay, died eight months earlier. Barbosa died in poverty at the turn of the century. Zizinho went onto a football discussion programme on TV shortly after Barbosa's death and told a gaggle of journalists, "You killed him. You harried him to his grave." Barbosa's last public utterance was, "In

Brazil, the most you can get for any crime is 30 years. For 43 years, I've been paying for a crime I didn't commit." The history of football is littered with scapegoats, but Barbosa's treatment, along with that of Colombian Andres Escobar's in the wake of the 1994 World Cup, is the most extreme. It was 45 years before another black goalkeeper, Dida, was selected for the Brazilian national team and in the meantime mediocre stoppers (like Félix in 1970) won World Cups.

In June, Elza Simone plans to go around to a friend's house in Ipanema, and in the garden she and her friends will talk about their health, their children, their grandchildren, how much longer they might live and Brazil's prospects in the World Cup. Talk will then inevitably drift on to the subject of the *Maracanazo*. As a mark of respect to Barbosa, Elza will raise a toast to 'the Unforgiven' and pray that he has now found peace. To lighten the mood slightly, guests will then watch the quirky *The Day on Which Brazil Lost the Cup* where the film's narrator, in an attempt to change the outcome of the match, travels back in time and shouts a warning to Barbosa as Ghiggia approaches. The plan backfires and, momentarily distracted, Barbosa allows Ghiggia to score anyway.

Referring to the film, Elza explains: "It suggests that somehow we were fated not to win the World Cup. I view football as a mirror on society, culture, and race. The defeat against Uruguay revealed several unpalatable home truths." Sixty years on, will the wake finally represent closure for Elza? "Of sorts, but to forget is to stop learning from the mistakes of the past and all those injustices. That's a dangerous state to be in."

4

TIPTOEING THROUGH THE TICKERTAPE

Thirty years after Argentina lifted the World Cup on home soil in 1978, a raft of iconic images continue to burn brightly. "The sheer passion of the crowds, the sight of Kempes in full flight, the confetti storms, Passarella lifting the prize . . . the intensity of that month still remains with all of us," explains former Argentina defender Lius Galván, a member of the team which beat the Netherlands in the final. Former ITV commentator Hugh Johns described to me "the pure theatre of the tournament, which led to you feeling that Argentina had to win the World Cup. It was South American football at its most raw." After the hosts triumphed in the final, an estimated two million fanatical Argentines took to the streets of Buenos Aires for a riotous three-day celebration. According to journalist Juan Peroto, who was based in Buenos Aires throughout the tournament, they only dispersed "once fatigue and alcohol poisoning took hold."

Yet beyond the fiestas lay several unpalatable facts. More controversy surrounds the 1978 World Cup Finals than any other football tournament. Far from clearing as time passes, the murky waters become more muddied the deeper one digs.

Peroto likens the far-right Argentine junta's attitude to the 1978 World Cup to "the Nazi regime's approach to the 1936 Olympic Games. The relentless propaganda, the hiding of painful home truths, including concentration camps, and the high profile of the dictatorship . . . Goebbels couldn't have organised it better himself." The conspiracy theories are relentless: rumours of match fixing, substance abuse, assassination attempts and direct junta intervention have swirled around for 30 years.

Given the political turmoil which existed in the country (inflation and unemployment had spiralled out of control and the inner cities were in advanced states of decay) and the outside pressure placed upon the military dictatorship that was running the country, it was a miracle that Argentina got to host the 1978 tournament at all. The military had seized power two years before, ousting the ineffective President Isabella Perón in the process and waging a policy of terror against those suspected of opposing the dictatorship. Coups were de rigueur in South America but this new regime was altogether more vicious. The junta, led by the moustachioed General Jorge Videla, was responsible for the illegal arrest, torture and murder of thousands of Argentines as part of the notorious 'Dirty War' waged against opponents of the new regime. With the population living under such a tyrannical cloud, Videla saw distinct advantages to be gained from hosting the World Cup: the feelgood factor, he hoped, would unite Argentines under one flag, raise the country's profile abroad and silence the dissenters at home.

Even some of Argentina's players had mixed feelings as the tournament drew closer. Defender Alberto Tarrantini admits, "I can only speak for myself, but Videla's plea to unite behind the flag left me feeling completely cold. It was about football, football, football as far as I was concerned and making Argentines feel better. It was not about boosting the regime's stature. The junta and Argentine culture were different entities."

As preparations gathered pace (Videla hired leading American public relations firm Burson-Marsteller to launch a propaganda regime to publicise the tournament), Juan Peroto saw at first hand that Videla was determined to sweep away the seamier side of Argentine life. In Rosario, a wall was built alongside the main road into the city to hide the tens of thousands of slums which lay behind it from visiting fans and journalists. The *villas miseries* were simply bulldozed and the shanty-town inhabitants bussed to cities which weren't staging World Cup matches. Rosario's 'misery wall' was decorated with the colourful facades of beautiful houses and the policy went hand in hand with Operation *El Barrido* (the Sweep), in which hundreds of citizens disappeared in the months leading up to the World Cup. Videla would later say, "They're a different entity. They are neither alive nor dead. They are disappeared."

Peroto recalls, "I remember reading George Orwell's *Nineteen Eighty-Four* at that time, although it was banned in my country. To me, it was a very powerful period in my life, as people – in their thousands – disappeared along with whole villages. They simply ceased to exist, like in Orwell's book. The junta had a rallying slogan which was '25 million Argentines will play in the World Cup.' This was popularised to '25 million Argentines will pay for the World Cup' and I started to see what was really happening."

Two of Alberto Tarrantini's friends disappeared shortly before the World Cup. "I went to the authorities and asked what had happened to my comrades but I was met with a wall of silence. They wouldn't even acknowledge me. I firmly believe that if I hadn't been a player with the national team I'd have suffered the same fate as my friends." The Dirty War grew in intensity as the World Cup got closer.

As word of the oppressive Videlan regime spread abroad, various European countries were put under pressure by Amnesty International and other groups to boycott the World Cup. Paolo Rossi and Sepp Maier signed petitions against the torture of political prisoners but the European no-show failed to materialise. Dutch star Johnny Rep recalls,

"Many players were aware of what was happening in Argentina but in the end I suppose the lure of the World Cup was simply too strong." Only West German defender Paul Breitner refused to travel on political grounds, although Sweden's Ronnie Hellström would later protest alongside the Mothers of the Plaza de Mayo during the tournament.

Argentine journalist Ezequiel Fernandez Moores has recently shed new light on European countries' attitudes towards events in Argentina and suggests that business interests remained paramount in governments' decisions to send teams to South America. Amnesty International was vocal in Germany, for example, but Mercedez-Benz, Siemens and Telfunken, amongst other companies, stood to lose millions of Deutschmarks in sponsorship and advertising in the event of a German boycott. Moores insists the story that the Netherlands nearly pulled out of the tournament is an urban myth. Despite receiving detailed information about the atrocities which went on in Argentina, not a single member of the Dutch side refused to play on humanitarian grounds. Wim van Hanegem, who withdrew from the squad on the eve of the tournament after a row over wages, became increasingly frustrated with the Dutch humanitarian organisation SKAN. Van Hanegem informed SKAN member Freek de Jonge that he would pass the phone to his dog if he called again. Moores points out that during the tournament the Dutch government gave the Argentine dictatorship millions of dollars in credits via ABN bank and sold weapons to the junta, as well as Fokker planes.

As Amnesty International's anti-World Cup calls intensified, FIFA President João Havelange allowed General Omar Actis to take charge of planning. Known for being the most outspoken member of the junta, in 1977 Actis announced to Videla that he planned to speak out against a FIFA-sponsored plan to build a new stadium at Mar del Plata and install a new colour television system in Argentina to tie in with the World Cup, claiming that in Argentina there were more worthy issues upon which to lavish money. Days before he was due to deliver his speech, Actis was murdered. His death was blamed on the Marxist Montoneros rebels, 30 of whose supporters were discovered mutilated in a run down Buenos Aires district the following day. Yet rumours persist that Actis was disposed of by the junta. Within a day he'd been replaced by Captain Carlos Lacoste, a minor FIFA official who was known as the junta's hardman. Within a year he'd spent an incredible US$700 million on the World Cup; the cost had originally been estimated at US$100 million.

Lacoste pressed ahead with installing the new colour-television system. ITV commentator Hugh Johns recalled the state-of-the-art facilities that the media encountered on arrival in Argentina, "The plush surroundings when we arrived were absolutely spectacular – far better than most facilities which you'd find in Europe. Only when you drove past the shanty towns on the outskirts of the cities did you stop and consider that the money could have been better spent. It made me feel very uneasy about being in Argentina. Other journalists felt the same." The cavernous Mar del Plata stadium was built, too, in Buenos Aires. During his trial in the 1990s Lacoste was found guilty of diverting public funds meant for the project into the pockets of several of his junta cronies (he denied this, although he was later found guilty) and of profiting from the organisation of the tournament to the tune of around US$4 million. As part of Lacoste's defence, FIFA President Havelange claimed he'd lent his old pal Lacoste huge sums so that "he could buy himself a nice property in Uruguay."

Under Lacoste's beady eye, an organising body known as Ente Autuartico Mundial (EAM '78) was tasked with the process of readying Argentina for the tournament. It made numerous disastrous errors, the most infamous of which was watering the freshly laid Mar del Plata pitch with seawater. In Buenos Aires I met a twinkly-eyed former groundsman at the stadium, Juan Derada. Rich in anecdote and blessed with an ear-shattering laugh, he explained that in 1978 the EAM's influence was enormous, "Suddenly you had a group of people with no experience of dealing with this type of thing pushing us around. It was ridiculous. It was all about the pressure of time. The reason the seawater incident happened was because the junta hijacked what we were doing, pushed out experienced people and decided to bring in their own people. You should have seen their lacky's face after they found out that seawater had been used on the pitch. He was like a new version of Hitler. He went around blaming us, telling us our legs would be broken, but we just laughed in his face because we knew he'd be for it when the grass started to die. I didn't really feel too much sympathy for him when I found out that he disappeared shortly before the Finals."

At the opening game between holders West Germany and Poland on 1st June, Jorge Videla spoke of "harmony and friendship" amongst competing nations, a message endorsed by guest speaker, the US Secretary of State Henry Kissinger. The junta promised a "World Cup of Peace" and Videla instructed "all patriotic Argentines to unite behind the national flag." His people did just that, as Videla ensured that free flags were available on the streets. The confetti storms which made the tournament unique reflected the riotous, carnival-like flavour of Latin American football. Argentinian striker Luque recalls, "The fans seemed to forget the poverty and the deprivation in the big cities. Most days we'd have fans running alongside our team bus, praying for us and holding rosary beads. You could see in their eyes just how much it meant to them. We laboured under a huge responsibility to win the tournament for our people and help them to forget their suffering. How could we not win the World Cup for these people?"

After scraping through 2–1 against Hungary, Luque received a none-too-subtle warning from the junta about what could happen if they slipped up in their qualifying group. As well as Hungary, Argentina had been placed with France and Italy in a difficult-looking section. Luque recalled, "France and Italy were very highly rated teams, and would go on to do very well four years later at the 1982 World Cup. After the Hungary match, one of the military men warned me that this could easily be a 'group of death, as far as you are concerned.' He said it with a smile on his face but I had no reason to believe that he was joking. After all we knew how important the World Cup was for the junta. Uppermost in my mind was that earlier that day the brother of a close friend of mine had disappeared. His body was later found by villagers on the banks of the River Plate with concrete attached to his legs. At that time opponents of the regime were sometimes thrown out of planes into the sea."

Against France, the team struggled to stifle Michel Platini's creativity and were pegged back in their own half. The notoriously combustible Buenos Aires crowd booed the team incessantly until shortly before half-time. Recent allegations by members of the French team have suggested that this game was rigged. After winger Didier Six was denied what appeared to be a certain penalty in the first half, an unnamed French player claimed the referee informed Daniel Passarella, who'd bundled over Six, "Don't do that again please, or I might have to actually give it next time." In the second half Six was bundled over by Luque in the opposition box and TV pictures appeared to show the referee winking at Luque afterwards. "That never happened – no way," claimed Luque. Just to add to French fury, Daniel Passarella scored from the spot to put the hosts 1–0 ahead after Marius Tresor slipped over and brushed against the ball – a clear case of ball to hand.

The rumours surrounding the Argentina v France match took a strange twist in 2003. During a French radio phone-in on military dictatorships a caller – claiming to be a former French football international – deliberately muffled his voice and said he'd seen "several high profile Argentine players take a couple of blue pills" prior to kick-off. French websites later speculated that the caller was Marius Tresor, although this has never been proved. The caller then alleged that Argentine players were so high on amphetamines that "you could hear them screaming in their dressing room and they had to warm down for two hours after the match." FIFA officials, the caller alleged, also excused Argentine players the obligatory drugs test after the game. "A very well-known Argentine player was on the list to have his test but when the FIFA guy walked in an Argentine official gave him an envelope and he just walked off," insisted the caller. When two French players protested, the caller alleged, they were informed by the FIFA official, "Come on, you know the score around here."

Galván vehemently denies any wrongdoing amongst his teammates. "It's total nonsense. FIFA officials couldn't be placed under that kind of pressure by any member of the team, or the government." The team's water boy – Okambo – had a vital role to play during the World Cup, as it was his job to hand over the player's urine samples for tests. Galván does however confirm the story that one FIFA representative was flabbergasted to discover that one of the Argentina players was pregnant. The game remains shrouded in doubt but there was none surrounding the quality of Luque's scorching winner, a dipping half-volley which flew in from 30 yards. "The noise," according to Luque, "was like a jet engine. It must have carried for miles."

It certainly travelled the kilometre or so to the detention and torture centre at the Argentine Navy Mechanical School. In a building as close to the stadium as Wembley Park tube station is to Wembley, government agents routinely castrated men, raped women and used dogs and electric batons. The depravity continued apace during the Finals. Even by the standards of Latin America in the 1970s, the junta's actions in Argentina were virtually off the scale. Chained up inside during the match against France was Manuel Kalmes, incarcerated for spreading anti-junta literature. "I'd been there for several weeks and a bag was placed over my head because my guard was fearful that I'd talk to other prisoners about plotting an escape. My cell was on the side from which I could hear the crowd and when Luque scored the noise hit the prison like a tidal wave. You could hear the crowd chanting "Luque, Luque" and we prisoners joined in. Why not? The guard's reaction was curious. We heard him run around the cell, yelping like a dog after the goals. But then he went quiet again, lent in close to us and whispered, 'That's the last goal you'll ever cheer you sons of whores.'" Kalmes admits, "At that point, I had no reason to disbelieve what the guard told us."

Argentina finished second in the group, behind Italy, and qualified for the second stage, where they were grouped with Poland and South American rivals Brazil and Peru. It was at this point that manager César Luis Menotti came into his own. The chain-smoking doctor, an avowed Marxist, was forced to work under increasing pressure. "You'd see Menotti talking to junta men in corners of rooms and he'd come away with a frown on his face," explains Galván. "But the way he told us to express ourselves on the pitch flew in the face of that pressure. Menotti gave us a great deal of freedom on the pitch and told us to go out and express ourselves as much as we wanted to. On a basic level he espoused traditional Argentine principles, namely treating the ball like it was our friend, and with great skill."

Manuel Kalmes explains, "The side at the time of the '78 World Cup embraced a typically Argentine way of playing. In Spanish, it's called *La Nuestra* – 'Our Way.' That buccaneering style of Kempes, and the skill of Ardiles and Luque is what Argentine football is really about." Galván chuckles at Kalmes's assessment of the team. "There were also a few butchers and hatchet men in there too, like Larossa and Tarrantini," he explains. "We were pragmatic: all of us could treat the ball as our friend and our rivals as enemies. We had to be like that. We were Argentina."

The hosts played their next round of games in Rosario. Mario Kempes recalls, "It brought back a lot of happy memories for me as it was where I'd started out as a player. The other guys liked it as the crowd was almost on top of the pitch. It was a really intimidating atmosphere inside and could freeze opposition players." First of all there was a routine 2–0 victory over the Poles, followed by a face-off against deadly rivals Brazil, but despite the pumping atmosphere the match was a damp squib and ended 0–0. "Both sides were just too afraid to lose," admits Galván. "It was like a game of chess but we checkmated each other." With Brazil defeating Poland 3–1 the hosts knew that they had to beat the Peruvians by three clear goals to reach the final. Along with Cassius Clay's first encounter with Sonny Liston and the 1988 Olympics 100 metres final, the Argentina v Peru game is arguably the most controversial sporting event of modern times.

Kempes, his beard and moustache now shaved and with his hair flying in the wind and his socks rolled down, was transformed from the anonymous striker of the '74 World Cup, and he destroyed the Peruvians. Galván recalls, "All of us were used to the explosive atmospheres inside Argentine grounds, but this was quite unlike anything else. The noise and the colour was special. I glanced up at the dignitaries' section when we ran out. There were Videla and Lacoste, lords of all they surveyed. Although you try and just focus on the game, you realise that it's more than that when the junta is there and everyone discovered that soon enough anyway. Mario scored after 20 minutes and we went in at half-time 2–0 ahead. It's always the perfect score, I think. You've enough of a lead to be confident in what you can do, but not so that you can sit back and relax. In the second half we pulverised Peru and scored four more. Did I detect anything remotely wrong with Peru's performance? No. Not for one minute. I honestly felt that they simply suffered from stage fright. I'm still sceptical when people say they were bribed. There's no evidence. Nothing. Just some rumours." Tarrantini claims, "It couldn't have happened. No. There's no way a whole team can be bribed to lose 6–0." Other Argentine stars simply refuse to comment.

Some insiders began to have suspicions almost immediately. As Luque dived to head the vital fourth goal, a huge bomb was detonated at the house of Juan Alemann, an official from the Economics Ministry who had questioned the cost of setting up the tournament. Alemann claimed that Lacoste was responsible for the assassination attempt, "If anybody ordered that bomb to explode simultaneously with the fourth goal it was because he really knew that in the match there would be a fourth goal," he said.

In 1986 *The Sunday Times* published Maria Laura Avignolo's article which claimed that a deal had been struck between Argentine and Peruvian generals, and that Argentina had shipped 35,000 tonnes of free grain to Peru, and possibly weapons too, while the Argentine central bank unfroze US$50 million worth of credit. Accused of "moral turpitude," Avignolo was put on trial in Argentina, although he was later acquitted.

Ever since the match the finger of suspicion has pointed firmly at eccentric Peru goalkeeper Ramón 'El Loco' Quiroga, who had been born in Rosario to Argentine parents. Not long after the match the Peruvian press reported that Quiroga had admitted accepting a bribe for deliberately conceding goals but he later retracted his statement. Quiroga refused to be interviewed for this book claiming he "has nothing further to add on the subject." Reserve keeper Manzo admitted to the fix a few days after the match whilst drunk, but later retracted his statement. Years later a FIFA panel ruled that without Quiroga's direct intervention, Peru would probably have conceded five more goals. One member of the Peruvian squad, who prefers to remain anonymous, but has a reputation as a 'storyteller,' according to colleagues, has recently told a well-known Peruvian journalist that the first XI received US$20,000 each in cash from an Argentine official after the match. "We had nothing to lose, we were out of the tournament, so why not?" he argued.

Perhaps the most plausible Peruvian account is that of reserve midfielder Raúl Gorriti, who reveals to me his version of events for the first time. "About 15 minutes before kick-off we were in our dressing room. The noise from the crowd was staggering and the walls were literally shaking. Many of the players were looking petrified. Then in strode Videla, with his security guards. "Remember who your Latin brothers are," he told us. "We stick together, don't we?" This statement somewhat ignored the fact that Argentina were doing everything in their power to eliminate Brazil and were on the brink of war with Chile. It had a strange effect on our players. He came around and shook our hands individually and had a few words with our coach in private. I do not think any of our players, or the coach, received bribes. We were a tight group and I would have found out," claims Gorriti. "The facts were that Peru is a poor country, which made us an easy target from Videla's point of view. So you had a young team, low on confidence, intimidated by Videla. That is why I believe we crumbled. It was stage fright." Galván insists, "A combination of the atmosphere and our self-belief beat Peru. For sure the junta was capable of huge crimes, but I don't think they could have fixed that game because it would have been too difficult. At least, that's how my teammates and I feel obliged to view it."

When Videla visited the Argentine players immediately after the final whistle in their dressing room, Alberto Tarrantini decided to exact some revenge for the unexplained disappearance of his friends. "Videla came in," Tarrantini has since explained. "I bet my captain Daniel Passarella US$1,000 that I'd rub soap on my balls and then shake Videla's hand. 'You're on,' Passarella said. Videla came to meet us and I was as good as my word. I'd rubbed soap all over my balls and he had to shake my hand. He made a face and with all the glare of the photographers and press there too! I'll never forget his expression afterwards. He just glared at me. But I don't regret what I did."

Manuel Kalmes awoke on 25th June 1978 to the screams of his cellmates as they were being tortured, but ended the day celebrating with hundreds of thousands of Argentines on the streets of Buenos Aires, after his country's 3–1 victory against the Netherlands. "It was the first time I'd been allowed in public for two years," he recalls. The final, played at the gigantic River Plate stadium, was staged on a blustery, grey day. As the confetti swirled across the pitch the Dutch players already had doubts over the likelihood of a victory. "It was difficult to see how we could win the trophy in Argentina," admits Johnny Rep. "Or to put it another way, I couldn't see how Argentina could lose the final on home soil. However, we'd made the decision not to accept our medals, or the cup from Videla afterwards." According to Galván the Argentine players, meanwhile, were advised by Menotti "not to look in Videla's direction before the match."

One of the more bizarre stories circulating about the Finals, and one which is repeated to me three times by separate sources in Buenos Aires, concerns Nazi war criminal Dr Josef Mengele, who fled to South America after the war. Heavily disguised, the 'Angel of Death' is strongly rumoured to have sat with the junta during the final. "Nothing would surprise me," says Galván darkly. "We knew the stories that the junta mixed with Nazis who were on the run."

The gamesmanship began before the kick-off. Argentina refused to accept the choice of referee, the Israeli Abraham Klein, arguing that the Netherlands' close political ties with Israel made him an unsuitable choice. FIFA caved in and appointed the Italian Sergio Gonella, instead. Then with the game due to kick off Daniel Passarella lodged a formal objection with FIFA officials over Dutch midfielder René van der Kerkhof's plaster cast and the host players walked off the pitch for five minutes leaving the opposition out on the pitch alone in front of a chanting crowd. Eventually Van der Kerkhof was ordered to wrap a bandage around the cast.

After spending the first 15 minutes hacking down the Argentines in revenge, the Dutch settled into their smooth-passing rhythm before Kempes sliced through the Netherlands' defence and slammed the ball past Jongbloed to put the hosts ahead. On the outskirts of Buenos Aires, as the crowd inside the River Plate Stadium erupted with joy, Manuel Kalmes's mother wept bitter tears. As one of the Mothers of Plaza de Mayo she'd demanded to know the whereabouts of her son but was met with stony silence. "I'd seen Videla's face in the dignitaries' section and immediately, for me, the final was tarnished," she explains. "It was wonderful to see Argentine men playing so well on a world stage but for me it was a beautiful but dirty World Cup."

Dutch substitute Dick Nanninga equalised with 10 minutes left, as he'd promised his native journalists he would, before

Rob Rensenbrink hit the post with seconds of normal time remaining. As Eduardo Galeano memorably explained in *Football in Sunshine and Shadow*, "The fact that post wasn't knighted in Argentina reveals much about the ingratitude of human nature." Extra-time goals from Kempes and Bertoni finally gave the Argentine people, and Videla, the victory they craved. Fittingly, the beauty of the celebrations — as Tarrantini and goalkeeper Fillol embraced, a boy with no arms flung himself on top of them, and the picture became known as 'the Hug of the Soul' — was tinged with political controversy. Several of the victorious Argentine players, including Galván, refused to shake Videla's hand. "It would have destroyed the experience and I wanted nothing to do with the junta. All I wanted to do was touch the trophy and celebrate with the fans." The Dutch team boycotted the banquet that evening after earlier blanking Videla. Even Menotti, the victorious coach, made a coded protest, explaining, "It is a homage to the old, beloved Argentine game . . . a belief that modern trends aren't always good for the soul."

As he appeared on the balcony of the Pink Palace in Buenos Aires with the victorious players three days later, Videla appeared to have achieved his twin aims of uniting the country behind the flag and delivering the World Cup. Yet as Dutch star Johnny Rep points out, "During the World Cup the media spotlight fell firmly on Argentina, foreign journalists got wind of the atrocities and started to ask questions, so a great deal of good eventually came out of it."

With the Reagan administration placing Argentina under intense pressure, Videla stood down in 1981 and he was later jailed for crimes against humanity. Admiral Lacoste did rather better. Under the patronage of João Havelange, he became a high-ranking FIFA official and lived out his days in luxury. Controversy still resonates. Last year, Ricky Villa met several of the Mothers of Plaza de Mayo and was repeatedly asked, "But why didn't you speak out at the time, Ricky?" Villa is not the only former Argentina player to be asked the same question.

The final word must go to Manuel Kalmes, whose recollections of the chaotic scenes on the streets of Buenos Aires that evening sum up the surreal contradictions of the tournament. "Our guard told us that we were going for an evening out," he explains. "At first I thought he was joking. I'd been banned from going on the streets for over a year. But he unchained us and, at gunpoint, we were led to a car outside in the forecourt. You could hear fireworks going off all around. When we got in the car there was another guard in there waiting for us. He had a gun. "We are going out to celebrate," they explained. "But if you try to run we'll put a bullet in you. With all the fireworks no one will notice." We cruised into the central district and our guard gave us a beer each. The old bastard even smiled for once. I was allowed to stand up and put my head through the open roof. I inhaled the air, which was thick with smoke, and looked around. It was one massive carnival. Everyone was there, supporters and opponents of Videla. There were people drinking, dancing and jumping up and down with joy. I thought about running and telling everyone what had really gone on at the Navy School. I was aggrieved that Menotti and the players, or the press, didn't speak out against Videla, because they must have known. I still believe that. Like in Nazi Germany, many people were complicit in what happened, but during the World Cup they submerged their feelings and pretended it wasn't happening. I didn't say anything that night, or try to run: I just soaked up the whole experience. The thing was that no one would have wanted to listen if I'd told them anyway. That night, fellow Argentines would have thought I was mad. And that was the greatest madness of all."

5

PHARAOHS AND DESERT FOXES

In truth, other than geographical proximity, there is no satisfactory historical explanation for the intense rivalry between Egypt and Algeria, which boiled over as the two vied for a place in the 2010 World Cup Finals in November 2009. The countries, sandwiched by Libya, do not even border each other.

Indeed, in the 1950s, Egyptian leader Gamal Abdel Nasser's regime gave support to the Algerian revolutionaries during the nation's long war of independence against France and, to this day, Nasser is regarded as a hero by many Algerians. In 1978, Sadat's Egypt did make a separate peace with Israel and, for some time, was ostracised by Algeria and the rest of the Arab World, but even this tension has faded with the passing of time.

Explaining the rivalry between the two nations Cairo resident Essam El Khabar, tells me: "There is the feeling in Algeria that we Egyptians are stuck up, and a bit aloof. We're a bigger country of course and over the years have played a greater role in the affairs of this region, and we have a rich history which Algeria doesn't have, but in many ways our governments and our peoples are very similar. The main reason, aside from some of the historical niggles, why these World Cup qualifiers are so heated is because of what happened back in 1989, during and after the 'Death Match.' No matter how much time passes, what happened in Cairo that night will never be forgiven, or forgotten, by us Egyptians. From that point on, it was easy to view the Algerian race as violent and mindless."

And the rivalry took on a sinister new twist as the countries faced each other in late 2009.

The 'Death Match' to which El Khabar refers occurred two decades ago when the teams met, in similar circumstances to the qualification campaign for the 2010 World Cup, in Cairo to decide who would grab the final African place for Italia '90. Egypt midfielder Alaa Maihoub played in the match and recalls the sheer ferocity of the encounter: "Algeria had played in the previous World Cups and were massive favourites to go through again with all their stars. But we got very tight on them throughout the game and gave them no space to breathe. The match was incredibly violent. The Algerians blew their tops – and I can't honestly say that we behaved especially well either. The Tunisian referee lost all control of what was going on but we scored the winner and reached the Finals. The Algerian players went mad. They surrounded the referee after the game and accused him of taking a bribe to fix it for us. Then they turned on us and battles were kicking off between both sets of players all over the pitch. Then the trainers got involved and our team doctor was blinded in one eye after one of the Algerian players shoved a broken bottle in his face."

Algerian legend and former African Player of the Year Lakhdar Belloumi, who scored his country's shock winner against West Germany at the 1982 World Cup, was accused of the assault by the Egyptian players, but Belloumi has always protested his innocence and pointed the finger at a former teammate in an interview with Algerian daily Echorouk.

Shortly before the two sides met in Algiers in November

2009, in a match which Algeria won 3–1, their President Abdelaziz Bouteflika intervened and requested that Egyptian fans move on from the Death Match. The game in Algiers passed almost without incident, save for the knot of travelling Egypt fans who, after smuggling in cardboard cutouts of Belloumi, proceeded to torch them in spontaneous bonfires on the terraces. "Wait until you get back to Cairo," they chanted, but the African champions knew they faced an uphill task. Only three goals would see them qualify outright, and a 2–0 victory would mean a one-off play-off in Omdurman, a Sudanese city on the banks of the Nile.

"The trouble is that both countries are desperate to put their domestic issues to one side and prove themselves on the pitch," explained Algerian fan Emad Al-Khidir, who bravely travelled to Cairo for the return match. "Economically things aren't working in either nation. As well as that, Egypt are obsessed with what has become known as 'the curse of the Pharaohs,' meaning that although they may be champions in Africa the real measure of a team's success is whether or not they play in the World Cup Finals, and Egypt haven't been there since 1990. The national team means different things to different people in Algeria. My father often reminds me that back in the 1950s the Algerian national team didn't even exist. It was banned under FIFA rules because the country was actively seeking a separation from the French Empire. So to men of a certain age like my father, the national team also represents political freedom. To my generation, we grew up hearing stories about the 1982 team. They beat West Germany 2–1 and Belloumi was the big star, but when it came to the crunch, in the final group match we came to call the 'Anschluss,' Austria allowed West Germany to defeat them 1–0 which enabled them both to progress to the next round. It was a pact which should have seen both teams expelled from the World Cup. It was shocking. Algerians waved peseta banknotes at the German players. We heard later that even German television described it as 'shameful' and that when German fans surrounded the team hotel to demand an explanation, the players threw water bombs at them. Such contempt, even for their own country-men. Later we heard that even before the game the Algerian players had been resigned to what was about to happen and gone shopping. As a nation, we were outraged. It was an affront to the whole of North Africa. We'd love to avenge what happened in 1982. It's why getting back there means so much to my people."

The Algerian players arrived at Cairo Airport 24 hours before the return match began. As the team bus nosed its way through the streets approaching their hotel, local hooli-gans threw rocks at the vehicle, which smashed the windows and caused head injuries to three Algerian stars. Striker Rafik Saïfi filmed the attack on his mobile phone and released the grainy images to the press. Within minutes the film had been uploaded onto the Internet. As Egyptian film crews gathered around the bus, Saïfi and his teammates posed with the rocks which were thrown, and sang "Viva Algerie, One, Two, Three!" into the cameras. One of the players, Khaled Lemmouchia, was left with glass embedded in his forehead and later suggested the match should be "called off for the benefit of both countries."

When Egyptian TV screened the footage, some viewers insisted that the windows had already been smashed before the rock attack and that as well as feigning their injuries with fake blood, the Algerians had put through their windows with hammers. A caller to the BBC World Service, Essam Marghani, alleged, "Egypt is a very peaceful country. We host our guests very well. I have seen that this [the bus attack] is some sort of provocation of the Egyptian people, which is something some North African countries are famous for. The attack was initiated from the inside of the bus."

The Cairo-based government newspaper *Al-Ahram* concurred and accused the visitors of foul play: "The bus carrying the team from the airport to the hotel was at the centre of a strange incident in which some players started to smash the vehicle's windows, claiming they were the target of stone-throwing." The Algerian team's bus driver later claimed that the glass was on the outside of the coach and that the players had made "a bad movie, because Algerians are bad people."

The online war was similarly fractious. Hackers on both sides caused chat forums and government websites to crash. An estimated 30 scam emails disguised with football imagery and containing viruses were sent to rival supporters in a bid to induce cyber chaos across the border in the lead-up to the showdown in Cairo. Facebook groups attempted to stoke the fires. One 'I didn't fight in 1989, but I will be there in 2009' group attracted 120,000 Egyptian members within two days and a rival 'Algeria rules Egypt' group (featuring an image of a burning Egyptian flag) garnered support from an estimated 250,000 Algerian supporters. Others used Facebook in an attempt to calm matters down. An 'Algeria and Egypt, hand in hand' Facebook group of a few hundred followers reminded any visitors that it was "only a game," and other members urged fans on both sides to remember the country's bi-national ties dating back to the 1950s.

As the countdown to kick-off in Cairo began, Emad Al-Khidir arrived at the ground in a bus full of Algerian supporters, surrounded by a police motorcade. "As we swung into the car park," he explained, "missiles came our way. Rocks smashed through the windows and the police presence suddenly disappeared. For five or ten minutes we literally hid underneath our seats until those who were throwing the missiles were stopped by officials around the stadium.

"Before kick-off, a rumour went around that two Algerian fans had been killed in the fighting outside the ground. Although the Algerian ambassador in Cairo later denied the accusation, with the war-zone which was going on around us outside I had no reason to disbelieve the stories I heard. Everyone we spoke to in Cairo was convinced that the stone-throwing against the team was a staged event by Algeria, designed to persuade FIFA to cancel the match and play it at a neutral venue."

In Cairo, the media appeared to have done its worst to

stoke the fires of discontent between the two nations. The best-selling Egyptian football magazine *Shoot* devoted an entire issue to the game, filling the pages with thinly veiled insults towards the Algerians. On the front cover was a scene from the film 300. The Egyptian team's faces were superimposed on those of the soldiers. The coach Hassan Shehata led the charge from the front (with obligatory Egyptian flag in hand), under the headline "Attack," written in Arabic and smeared in blood. T-shirts sponsored by a soft drinks company spelt out the message "I was there in 1989," and a mobile phone network dispatched a fleet of mopeds around the city with their drivers instructed to wear a sign proclaiming "Death Match" on their backs. Other riders bore the image of the country's idol Mohamed Aboutrika, on his knees, encouraging the nation to "Pray for us, all Egyptians." Swathes of Egyptian fans were furious about the arrangements for the game. Unscrupulous government officials (described colourfully in Egyptian fans' songs as "sons of whores") stood accused of selling bundles of tickets on the black market at 15 times the official price.

When Emad Al-Khidir finally forced his way inside the ground, his team endured the worst possible start. The din from the 100,000 strong crowd (female fans had been asked to stay away, the press expected "several heart attacks tonight," and some members of the crowd arrived an estimated six hours before kick off to create a wall of sound) drowned out the Algerian national anthem, and players from both sides offered silent prayers before the "Mother of all Battles," as the Egyptian press had labelled it, began.

After two minutes, former Wigan striker Amr Zaki scored for Egypt from close range, to the delight of the home crowd and at first it seemed that the visitors (three of whom were clad in head bandages after the bus incident) would go under. But a tit-for-tat encounter saw Algeria hold their nerve until the sixth minute of injury time when Egypt substitute Emad Moteab nodded home, sending the home side wild, and meaning the two teams finished level on points, goals scored and goals conceded.

The stadium, apart from the tiny wedge of silent Algerians in one of the corners, was in uproar. Inside and outside the ground, fireworks and flares were set off. The feeling was that Algeria had blown their chance and would be put to the sword in the play-off match the following week. Such was the intensity of the atmosphere inside the ground that Khaled Lemmouchia, who had played with shards of glass still inside his wound, admitted, "I scarcely dare think what would have happened if we'd scored tonight. We would have been in danger."

Both of the coaches tried to distance themselves from the nationalistic fervour surrounding the contest. "We play the game for fun, not to create a war," insisted Egypt's Hassan Shehata. But the shockwaves from the match in Cairo travelled far and wide. In Algiers, the homes of several migrant Egyptian workers were set alight. Ibrahim Mehleb, Chief Executive of the Egyptian Arab Contractors Company, announced that his company's employees in Algeria had been told to remain at home. In Marseilles, French police were forced to intervene as skirmishes broke out between Egyptian and Algerian immigrant youths.

The final act of the 2010 qualifiers was played out at the decrepit Al-Merreikh Stadium in Omdurman, Sudan, on 14th November 2009. More than 15,000 riot police were placed on red alert in an attempt to keep order, although due to the traditional sporting rivalry between Sudan and Egypt, Algeria were treated like the home side. Two thousand travelling Egyptian supporters, selected at random by the Cairo based travel company organising the visit, were provided with free accommodation courtesy of their government. The rest were dispersed to segregated campsites situated near the ground. In front of 30,000 fans, the game was settled by Algeria's Antar Yahia with a volley five minutes before half-time, but with an estimated 10,000 locked outside, riots and fires raged through the night before Sudanese police restored order in the early hours of the following morning. A few days later the police announced that an estimated US$3 million worth of damage had been done to shops and businesses in the city.

While the fires continued to rage on the streets of Omdurman the rival bloggers and the hackers resumed their cyber battle. A fresh Facebook group was set up in Algeria called 'Screw the 1989 Death Match.' "Egypt may have somehow earned themselves the title African champions," sneered one member, "but never let it be forgotten that we have now qualified for three World Cup Finals to their paltry two. Let us also celebrate the likes of Belloumi, who enshrined the spirit of that wonderful side of the 1980s, which was cheated out of the tournament by Austria and West Germany. We hope this Algeria team will emulate this in South Africa." In Cairo, the 'Champions of Africa' group's message on Facebook was clear: "Algerian sons of whores will be the first team sent home form the World Cup." Once again, a raft of football websites crashed across both nations, destroyed by rival hackers.

Egypt's President Mubarak urged supporters to remember "It's just a game," but it has gone way beyond that in this part of North Africa.

BALL DROPPING

It wasn't as if FIFA had a lack of time to prepare for the calamitous World Cup draw which took place in Madrid in January 1982. As far back as 1964 it had been decided that that the Spaniards would host the 1982 tournament, a fact officially confirmed two years later at the FIFA Congress in London.

This would be the first ever World Cup featuring 24 teams (recent previous tournaments had featured 16 countries). This was down to Brazilian João Havelange who, as part of his campaign to succeed Sir Stanley Rous as FIFA President in 1974, had pledged to increase the size of the tournament in order to strengthen his position with the numerous African and Asian football federations. With his glamorous wife alongside him, Havelange launched his charm offensive across far-flung reaches of the globe. Campaigning long and hard, he visited 83 FIFA affiliated nations in 1974 alone. It worked and, after he was appointed, he immediately set about modernising the World Cup.

The 1982 tournament would be the first to fully encompass Havelange's vision for the future. But with countries like New Zealand, Kuwait, Honduras and El Salvador now thrust into the melting pot along with the more established nations, there were fears that the newcomers would amount to little more than cannon fodder for the likes of Brazil,

Italy and West Germany. Ex-England manager Sir Alf Ramsey accused Havelange of "diluting the quality of the tournament in order to pursue his own self interest . . . the development does not really have the interests of these smaller nations at heart." But Ramsey's views were by no means shared by all those within the football community, and Havelange insisted, "The 1982 World Cup will be the first truly global football experience, in my opinion."

Around £40 million was shelled out on redeveloping Spanish stadia to FIFA requirements. Another £60 million was spent on organisational costs, of which £6 million was earmarked for the first ever televised World Cup draw. Havelange stated, "An estimated 75 per cent of the world's population now has access to colour television sets and it is now appropriate that they should now be able to witness such an event." The 500 million who tuned in endured the ultimate car-crash TV experience.

The first problem to dog the draw occurred several weeks before when Spanish police received an anonymous tip-off that Basque Separatist Movement ETA was planning to "seriously disrupt the event." Although it proved a false alarm, arriving dignitaries on January 1982 were greeted by machine gun-toting guards and sniffer dogs as they approached the building.

Another problem was the verbal hostilities which raged between several nations in the weeks leading up to the draw. The French, Scottish, Polish and Belgian FAs had lodged a joint protest with FIFA complaining about England, who hadn't played in a Finals since 1970, being selected as one of the six number-one seeds, along with recent winners Argentina and West Germany. With Anglo-French relations already strained (Margaret Thatcher and French President Francois Mitterand were locked in heated discussions about the logisitics surrounding the proposed Channel Tunnel project), French manager Michel Hidalgo claimed it was "farcical that a nation which hasn't played in the Finals for 12 years should be granted this privilege." His English counterpart, Ron Greenwood, did little to quell Hidalgo's anger, responding, "Continentals seem to get all sorts of complexes like this."

Tension also simmered between the major South American nations, with Argentina's Diego Maradona mischievously suggesting the draw would be arranged, "to ensure that everyone's sweethearts Brazil get the safest route possible to the final." The Brazilian media responded immediately, referring to the questionable events of four years previously, when Argentina's 6–0 victory over Peru saw them reach the 1978 final instead of Claudio Coutinho's team and suggesting that a ban on both César Luis Menotti's team and Peru, who they claimed had been compliant in the result, would be in order. Brazil captain Socrates also referred to the ongoing human rights abuses in Argentina. The feel-good factor that immediately followed the 1978 triumph in Argentina had evaporated quickly and the military junta, now led by General Galtieri, continued to murder political opponents by dropping them out of aeroplanes and helicopters into the River Plate. The 'Mothers of the Disappeared' set up weekly protests in front of the Presidential Palace and, as time passed, their demonstrations began to have an effect.

Manuel Kalmes's mother (whose son had been a victim of the junta) recalls, "There was a growing feeling that as time passed, we could chip away at their power. As the 1982 World Cup approached there were more and more joining the protests and it became clear that the government under Galtieri couldn't make us disappear. The '78 World Cup was all about good propaganda for the junta and four years on the government hoped that retaining the trophy, and winning the Falklands War, could buy them more time."

World Cup newcomers Cameroon threatened to withdraw if New Zealand, who'd recently played an international friendly against South Africa, refused to publicly condemn apartheid. The Kiwis' point blank declined to accede to the African nation's request and there were fears that, along with Algeria, Cameroon would boycott Havelange's party.

Ultimately there was no mass African boycott, although Cameroon goalkeeper Thomas N'Kono continued to protest bitterly throughout the tournament. Polish manager and Solidarity supporter Anton Piechniczek warned of "riots on the streets of Warsaw if my country is grouped with our Soviet oppressors" and Brazil manager Tele Santana (who had taken over after Claudio Coutinho had drowned a few months before) suggested that all competing finalists avoid importing Argentine corned beef. "You might as well feed your families raw sewerage," he claimed. Just for good measure, officials from El Salvador and Honduras mused what might happen in light of the 'Soccer War' 13 years before, should the two sides progress to and meet in the later stages. Given that the odds of this happening were approximately 5000/1, this issue didn't figure especially highly on FIFA's radar.

Doing his level best to sweep all this under the carpet, West German FIFA delegate and former FIFA Vice President Hermann Neuberger insisted, "The draw will prove that football can heal all wounds." In order to prove that this wasn't exactly the case, a raft of German newspapers re-ran the story that, four years earlier, Neuberger had allowed the famous German World War II pilot Hans Ulrich Rudel, holed up in Argentina since the end of the war, to visit the West Germans at their World Cup training camp, whilst at the same time banning former international star Gunter Netzer, working as a journalist, from speaking to the players. Neuberger had never forgiven Netzer for joining Real Madrid without consulting the German Football Federation (DFB), and the FIFA delegate was subsequently pilloried by his own press for this public relations disaster. "It's a greater crime to sign for Real Madrid than be a card-carrying Nazi on the run, apparently," boomed Der Bild Zeitung.

For the draw itself, FIFA enlisted the help of a group of boys from a Madrid orphanage "to show how football reaches out to the youth of the world." The boys were instructed to remove miniature plastic footballs (each of which contained a nation's name and flag) from four giant revolving metal cages and give them to the FIFA delegates. One of them, Prine Felipe, who'd lost his parents in a car crash months earlier, told me, "The atmosphere before the event was very tense. I recall Neuberger was really on tenterhooks. We had one lady instructing us on what we should do, but as boys we were quite high-spirited and didn't really listen all that well and you could feel the tension growing when we had the dress rehearsal. Even then, the cages didn't work properly. The balls kept getting stuck in them."

The draw began to fall apart – quite literally – when the balls containing the Chilean and Peruvian flags became jammed in the revolving cages and split open in full view of the cameras. To make matters worse, Prine Felipe accidentally pulled out the balls of third seeds Scotland and Hungary too early. For a few minutes, Jock Stein's side found themselves in Argentina's group, before the mistake was rectified. German delegate Neuberger was not best pleased, barking out on live TV, "Get it sorted out boy!"

Felipe continues, "You can see all of us boys smirking on the television footage. It was quite funny because it was actually the technology at fault, not us. The cameras and the lights were phenomenally hot and you could see Neuberger sweating profusely as he became more annoyed."

The hitches meant that the programme over-ran by five minutes, due to FIFA's insistence on 'cultural breaks,' which included national dances from the competing countries, and there was even a delay in the playing of the Spanish national anthem. Due to yet another technical hitch, it took a further five minutes after the end of the draw for Marcha Real to be played. As a result, the Spanish National Lottery – for the first and only time in its history – was delayed, and furious Spanish companies threatened to sue FIFA because there was no time for a commercial break. "If the national lottery was conducted along similar lines, we'd have another civil war on our hands," claimed Spanish daily ABC.

Neuberger was forced by FIFA bigwigs to formally apologise to the boys from the orphanage after his outburst. "He seemed quite contrite, so I was happy to accept his apology. I think he was embarrassed about the whole thing," explains Felipe.

Jimmy Hill, who'd presented a World Cup Draw special on BBC1, rounded off the BBC's broadcast of the event by concluding, "I know that our own FA have been accused of dropping a ball or two in their time, but I don't think we've ever seen anything quite like that farce." *The Sun* dubbed the draw *Game for a Laugh*, and England captain Kevin Keegan was quoted as saying, "I'd have walked out if I was that boy."

Some of the boys from the Madrid orphanage have an annual reunion in January to celebrate their 15 minutes of fame and clips from the error-strewn draw regularly make it onto the Spanish TV version of *It'll Be Alright on the Night*. "Despite a very difficult childhood, we've all gone on to lead fulfilling lives," reveals Prine Felipe. "Most of us now look back and laugh about that day. A Spanish satellite TV company recently got in touch and they are planning to make a documentary on us because everyone still remembers what happened so clearly."

When the next draw was made in 1985, FIFA insisted that delegates pull teams out by hand, but the cultural breaks remain an integral part of the draw ceremony. Yet even as the draws become more elongated, dramatic, and 'culturally profound,' they are unlikely to beat the '82 carve up for sheer farce. The closest, perhaps, came in 2006 when, after the draw in Leipzig, Germany, Matthias Blume, an interior decorator by trade, came across the 32 orange, FIFA-embossed country labels which had been thrown into a bin. Spotting a chance to make some money, he immediately set up an Internet auction and received an offer of €11,250 for the 'Germany' label, from a fellow countryman named only as 'Ralf'. Blume, who also received £1,750 for the 'England' label, described his entrepreneurial skills as "brilliantly unorthodox" and told the media he'd spent a portion of his earnings on "a top-quality skateboard."

7

THE FÚTBOL WAR

Both sides continue to blame one another for starting the six day war between El Salvador and Honduras in 1969 that has become known as the 'Fútbol War' (or 'Soccer War'). Honduras insist that their territorial integrity had been violated by El Salvador and Salvadoreans claim they launched a pre-emptive strike to ward off an imminent Honduran invasion. Debate still rages as to the role football actually played in the infamous conflict. The players lament that they were used as pawns by their respective governments, and although the title of Ryszard Kapuściński's masterful account of the conflict may suggest where his version of events lies, even *The Soccer War* suggests that money, power and plain old-fashioned xenophobia may well have been greater contributory factors than football. Yet just as the assassination of Archduke Franz Ferdinand and Adolf Hitler's invasion of Poland were the sparks which triggered off the World Wars of 1914 and 1939 respectively, the World Cup qualifiers between Honduras and El Salvador, who'd been firing bullets and insults at one another for decades, lit the blue touch paper for the nasty and occasionally farcical conflict between the two nations.

As Kapuściński's historian friend Luis Suárez, an expert on Central American politics admits, "the border between soccer and politics is vague."

79

In the late 1960s, the entire Central American region was bubbling with intrigue and political upheaval. Somehow football often seemed to be at the centre of it, either directly or indirectly. In Guatemala, Carlos Arana Guat assumed power in a 'non transparent' manner and immediately cracked down on law and order. My contact in the region, Jaime Marena, recalls a huge number of troops being sent to keep guard at football matches, because the authorities were convinced (rightly as it turned out) that left-wing opposition groups used matches as a meeting place to launch their insurgency movements. In Nicaragua, the Somoza dynasty regularly swooped on games in a bid to 'cleanse' the country of the Sandinistas. Further south, General Medici ordered his generals to monitor the movements of Pelé and the Brazil team. Uruguayan President Areco, who, after civil unrest, issued an emergency decree in late 1969, freely admitted to Medici that a decent showing by 'La Celeste' in the 1970 World Cup would buy him valuable time in power. Argentina's President Organia, on the other hand, having seen his team fail to qualify for that tournament, realised his time was nearly up and it wasn't long before the Peronists once again swept into government. In the host nation, Mexico, President Ordaz, whose troops had executed 250 dissidents on the eve of the 1968 Olympics, said, "The fact that we are hosting the 1970 World Cup now gives a chance for the other nations within the CONCACAF region to show their mettle. Given the size of our population – some 90 million – it is perhaps unsurprising that our neighbours and comrades are often in our shadow. Here is their chance – an opportunity to show their fighting spirit to the world." Apparently Ordaz – who cleverly organised the elections for the first week of the World Cup, when he knew nationalistic fervour would be at its height – wasn't deliberately attempting to be ironic or sarcastic.

At the time, the conflict between El Salvador and Honduras, which became known as 'the Fútbol War' was largely overlooked by the world's press, distracted by the Apollo 11 mission and the Chappaquiddick scandal that embroiled

Senator Ted Kennedy. In the midst of this, confusion reigned on the western side of Central America. As the war rumbled into action, El Salvador midfielder Juan Martinez told an American journalist, "Everyone's blaming each other for what is happening, and I've got a bad feeling that we'll all be damned to hell for all of this."

Several of the players from both teams remain scarred by the experiences of 40 years ago and continue to insist that they were merely trying to play football matches. "Some of my countrymen still walk up to me and say, 'It was your fault.' They should know better, but they don't," shrugs former El Salvador defender Alberto Villalta.

Like the experiences of the Zaire players four years later, the intrigue which swirls around El Salvador's 1970 World Cup adventure makes it a compelling story. "In 1969, the whole region was ready to explode," admitted Alberto Villalta in 2006. "You could feel it in the air. We were told to go and spill blood for the honour of our country. The message was reinforced by our families and the media across both countries. You couldn't avoid the incessant babble about fighting and warring anywhere. We were just footballers, who wanted to play sport. But there was no escape." Ongoing border disputes, murders, a high-profile suicide, a blood-thirsty media and – the unlikeliest cause of all – a teachers' strike gone horribly wrong . . . against this backdrop, both nations' footballers, with the eyes of Central America resting firmly upon them, prepared to lock horns in arguably the most infamous series of World Cup matches ever played.

One of the difficulties of investigating the Fútbol War is the singular lack of primary sources remaining. Much of what has been documented down the years are stories which have been passed down and football writers, understandably, have tended to rely on Kapuściński's book for first-hand evidence. In order to gain access to a disparate and, in several cases, impoverished group of players, only the likes of Jaime Marena, who has travelled widely in the region and who has built up a network of contacts, have the key. I was put in contact with

Marena by the University of Kent and warned by an intern that he was "mercurial." In other words, he was downright unreliable. Disappearing under the radar for months on end, he would then resurface and recount conversations which provided fresh insight on one of the World Cup's murkiest and most misunderstood stories. His mobile number changed with bewildering regularity but his irregular calls were unfailingly engrossing. All the interviews with the surviving players, residents of both countries and fans from that period were conducted by Jaime, wherever he is now.

Gathering information in Central America can be a time consuming, tricky and occasionally fractious business. Many of the Salvadorean and Honduran players from that era earned little from the game, and 40 years on they want their cut if they are to reveal anything of consequence. Marena told me that one of the Salvadorean players, having demanded $100 in advance to speak, then admitted his memory was so poor that he couldn't actually recall events with any clarity. Only when Jaime refused to leave his house did the player grudgingly give the money back two hours later. Chequebook journalism is risky in these parts, but a necessary evil nonetheless, particularly as other forms of evidence have mysteriously disappeared.

Although newspapers on both sides of the border are said to have fanned the flames of war, the back copies have vanished. In San Salvador, *Diario Co Latino* and *La Prensa Grafica* allegedly bandied around words like 'pigs' and 'scum' to describe the Hondurans, whilst over the border *La Preise* is supposed to have done likewise. Other forms of slander and verbal abuse included the countries calling one another 'Nazis,' 'dwarfs,' 'drunkards,' 'sadists' and 'thieves.' Following the well trodden example of the British Civil Service, fire, flood and multiple moves across town apparently account for why so much paperwork has disappeared into the ether over the years. Plus the occasional civil war and military coup . . .

The problems between the neighbouring nations of Honduras and El Salvador in the late 1960s all boiled down to living space. Honduras, with a population of about three million and 43,000 square miles, had plenty of it; El Salvador shoehorned her four million citizens into a mere 8,000 square miles. Statistically, Salvadoreans were the most densely packed populace in the entire hemisphere and, to make matters worse, there were thousands of acres of unused Honduran land lying just over the narrow river valley from El Salvador.

It was little wonder that year on year, thousands of Salvadoreans waded across the water in search of a scrap of land. In the early 1960s, Alberto Villalta's family took up the Honduran government's offer of temporary residency. "About 60,000 Salvadoreans were over the border at that time, and most didn't have any legal documents. The Honduran government gave them five years to obtain legal status, or get back across the river. According to official statistics, only about 1,000 bothered to go through the correct channels. My family didn't have the education or the willingness to do it properly. They thought the Honduran government would always turn a blind eye to the illegal travellers. They later described the Fútbol War as a peasant war, and to a degree, the El Salvador football team was a peasant team. Several of my teammates had families living illegally across the border. This was about to change."

By the mid-1960s, Honduras, now controlled by a military junta, instituted an agrarian reform programme, which saw land forcibly removed from the Salvadoreans who were illegally living there and given to Hondurans who were being relocated. After spending several years nurturing coffee fincas and other crops, the squatters decided they weren't going to give up the land without a fight.

"One of my cousins died in a machete fight along the border. I think that many of the players from El Salvador knew of someone who had died in such a way," recalls Villalta.

In the two months before Honduras and El Salvador clashed on the pitch in July 1969, there was plenty going on off it. Salvadorean policemen grabbed hold of Honduran politician Martinez Argueta who was visiting relatives across the border, and decided to lock him up for 20 years for illegal entry into their country. In retaliation, four Honduran soldiers rounded up 60 unarmed Salvadorean troops on the border and locked them up. Only direct intervention by US President Johnson resolved the situation, but in the year that followed machete fights and gunfights became de rigeur along the border.

It was hardly surprising, then, that when the El Salvador squad arrived in the Honduran capital Tegucigalpa prior to the first of their CONCACAF semi-final matches to decide who would progress to the final World Cup qualification play-off, the atmosphere was tense. In the group stages, the Salvadoreans had nudged out Dutch Guiana and the Dutch Antilles, and Honduras had cruised past Costa Rica and Jamaica.

Although an armed guard ensured El Salvador's safe passage from the airport into the city – which was then still relatively provincial – the visiting players' moods changed as the team coach headed towards their hotel. "The bus screeched to a halt and the driver suddenly began swearing. Two of the tyres had been punctured and immediately it happened, a crowd gathered around us. We were convinced we'd been targeted and we didn't learn the real truth until some months later," recalls Alberto Villalta. In fact an especially militant group of striking teachers, anxious to publicise their cause for improved pay, had scattered tick tacks and roofing nails along the city's main thoroughfares. Amidst the epidemic of flat tyres and punctures in the city, the Salvador *fútbolistas* were the most prominent victims of all. It took over two hours for the police to eventually disperse the crowds.

With the match scheduled for the following day, while the Salvador team attempted to sleep in their hotel a massive group of Hondurans gathered outside and created a cacophony of noise. This was common practice in the region when it came to big football matches, and the night before they played Brazil the England team would suffer the same fate at the Guadalajara Hilton, but the situation in Tegucigalpa soon spiralled out of control.

Alberto Villalta recalls, "It was a sweltering night and you had to keep the windows open. If you closed them, you'd melt. The abuse started from 11pm onwards. There must have been hundred gathered outside. *"Hijos de putas!"* ("Sons of bitches!"), *"La puta que los pario"* ("Sons of whores!") they shouted. Then you had car horns going all night, and guys clattering dustbin lids. I don't think any of us slept a wink and once the Salvadorean journalists who were staying in our hotel wired the news back home, we knew there would be a tit-for-tat situation for the return leg."

The game, which El Salvador lost 1–0, was by all accounts a bare-knuckle classic. Honduras's goal, scored by Roberto Cardona in the last minute, prompted home supporters to pick fights with visiting fans and impromptu bonfires were lit on the terracing. Hospitals reported that several El Salvador fans were injured and required treatment.

In isolation, such events were not unusual in Central America but matters had already taken an extraordinary turn for the worse. Eighteen-year-old El Salvador supporter Amelia Bolanios, who was watching the match at home, "could not bear to see the fatherland brought to its knees," wrote Salvadorean paper El Nacional on the day after the match and, having got up and run to her father's desk, she reached for his pistol and shot herself through the heart. Two days later, Bolanios's televised funeral was watched by 78 per cent of the Salvadorean population, in what was described by El Nacional as "a spontaneous outpouring of national grief."

San Salvador resident Carlos Aquiem lived two streets away from Amelia Bolanios and recalls, "It is always a tragedy when a young person dies and especially when a life is lost over something as relatively trivial as football. On the one hand there was a genuine outpouring of grief from some of the populace, but the government's exploitation of the whole thing was shameful. They ensured that an armed guard marched at the front of the procession and the President himself walked behind the coffin. The footballers, who'd just flown back from Honduras, also walked behind the cortége. It was very cynically done. Along the route, soldiers lined up and looked menacing. We were told they were there to stop people rushing forward with grief to throw flowers at the coffin. Many of us wondered if they were put there to stop people leaving the event. There were troops behind as well as in front of those watching. The onlookers were sandwiched between men with guns. There was an atmosphere of 'You are going nowhere.' In my opinion, the entire event besmirched the girl's memory, but if their purpose was to unite the population and to stir things up for the return leg, it worked. I'd have hated to have been one of those footballers – the pressure was enormous."

When the Honduran team arrived in San Salvador a few days later, they were caught up in a maelstrom of violence and racism. Striker Roberto 'The Rabbit' Cardona, so called because of his searing pace, immediately had placards of a large rabbit sodomising a smaller rabbit thrown in his face at the airport. "I could handle that kind of reception, but it upset others in the squad" he said. Of course there was also the obligatory chant of 'Hijos de putas!' resounding around the airport. Several of the baying Salvadorean mob had brought along toy golliwogs (unlike the El Salvador team, the Honduras squad contained several black players) with bones through their noses and proceeded to pour petrol on them and set them alight.

The entire situation was deemed so combustible that the army was summoned to take the visitors to their hotel. The vengeful Salvadorean mob surrounded the building and continued to wreak havoc. Trying unsuccessfully to grab some sleep was midfielder Manuel Molares. He recalls, "I guess we knew that something would happen. At about 11pm a huge roar went up outside and suddenly they pelted the whole hotel with rocks. It was only a three-storey building and they were able to smash every window in the whole place. We literally hid under our beds and before long dead rats and rags with shit smeared all over them came flying in. They threw petrol bombs in at ground-floor level. It was terrifying. Eventually, a contingent of policemen and our staff, came in and told us that we would be moved to another hotel. Armed policemen and soldiers held the crowds back but they followed us to our new accommodation, sang all night anyway and played drums. I think by then we were all so wound up that there was no way we could sleep anyway. When we went to the game the next day we went past our first hotel. It looked like something out of a war film, with shards of glass and blackened brickwork from the smoke."

The Honduran players were escorted to San Salvador's Flor Blanca Stadium in armoured cars, in order to protect them from the crowds lining the streets which held up pictures of the national martyr, Amelia Bolanios. A large contingent of the crowd had been present inside the ground since first light, in order to guarantee themselves a spot for a game, which even outdoes the Battle of Santiago in 1962 between hosts Chile and Italy for notoriety.

Carlos Aquiem arrived for the late afternoon kick-off shortly after 2.30pm and the scenes which awaited him, and the events which followed, still burn brightly in his mind: "There were soldiers everywhere, making sure that no one got through with weapons or anything else. You felt the whole thing was like a powder keg. Any Hondurans stupid enough to identify themselves were immediately set upon. I heard stories that three were ripped apart by the mob. It could be apocryphal, but such was the level of venom, nothing would surprise me.

"Once inside the ground there were regiments of the National Guard ringing the pitch with their rifles on full display. A lot of them were just kids. You could see them shaking and it concerned me to think about what might happen if things went wrong. Would they simply lose control? I actually started to feel sorry for the Hondurans when, after the playing of the national anthems, a dishrag covered in shit was raised up the flagpole, instead of the Honduran flag. Several of us discussed the fact that in order for this to have happened our own Football Association must surely have been in on the whole thing. It was mob rule."

Frozen by fear and fatigue, the Hondurans were crushed 3–0 which meant that – as this was in the days before the aggregate score counted in two-legged World Cup matches – a single play-off match at a neutral venue would be required. Before all of that, though, after the Honduran team had snuck back across the border under armed guard (their coach Mario Griffin admitting, "We're awfully lucky that we lost"), both capital cities descended into anarchy. Visiting Honduran fans who had gone to the game dispersed towards the border but in the mayhem that ensued, two were killed.

"The violence rumbled on until the early hours," recalls Carlos Aquiem. "Cars with Honduran number plates were overturned and burned and there were sporadic attacks on Hondurans afterwards too. There was looting of shops, mainly to obtain alcohol, and the police seemed to have lost any semblance of control."

There was a tit-for-tat aspect to the ensuing mayhem in Tegucigalpa. The returning Honduran players quickly told journalists what had happened across the border and as soon as the information became public resident Salvadoreans were made to suffer. Honduran midfielder Manuel Molares recalls, "Some of my neighbours were Salvadoreans, and they had their front windows put through. Their shops were smashed up. It was nasty and unforgivable. How could one think it was anything else when innocent women and children were hiding under their beds thinking they are going to die? I felt very depressed about the whole thing and it made me question what kind of society we lived in. My neighbours got away with a warning but the whole thing spiralled out of control. Given the type of situation we were in, there were reports of murders, pillaging and huge numbers of injuries. I don't think anyone has ever proved they happened but the stories continue to do the rounds about what our goon squads did to the Salvadoreans all those years ago."

In Mexico City, Luis Suárez, after reading the bile-filled reports of the first two matches, turned to his friend Ryszard Kapuściński, and said simply: "There is going to be a war."

The play-off match took place in Mexico City and, given the publicity surrounding the first two matches, it was unsurprising that an estimated 25,000 from both countries made the pilgrimage. The 60,000-capacity stadium was crammed to the rafters. On one side of the ground stood the Salvadoreans, and on the other their deadly rivals. Between them stood an estimated 7,000 Mexican policemen armed with guns and thick clubs. But the huge police presence couldn't stop violence breaking out in the stands as large groups of rival fans had infiltrated one another's sections.

Later, Roberto Cardona would claim that, as Honduras's most dangerous player, he was targeted for the entire game by El Salavador defenders and a neck-high tackle removed him from the equation late in the first half. Honduras later accused the referee and linesmen of crooked officiating and charged the entire Salvadorean team with cheating on the pitch, taking drugs, and attempting to steal their football boots. No matter how venomously the Hondurans protested, the facts were that in the dying minutes, Salvadorean striker Mauricio 'Pipo' Rodriguez blasted the winner to give his side a dramatic 3–2 victory. On the pitch at least, the war was over.

Less than six hours later, the first armed skirmishes took place on the border which separated the two countries, and an hour after that eight Salvadorean P-51 Mustangs, relics from World War II, bombed Toncontin Airport in Tegucigalpa. The first the outside world got to hear about it was when the Honduran President, via the only telex machine in the city, appealed for help from the USA via his ambassador in Washington.

That night a tropical storm blacked out Tegucigalpa. At dawn on the following day eight Honduran Corsairs bombed a fuel depot just outside San Salvador. Almost immediately the Salvadorean army launched a pre-emptive strike (the politicians would later claim they had intelligence that the Hondurans would invade later that day) and, using the same motorised vehicles which had taken the Honduran footballers to the border, got 75 miles outside Tegucigalpa before meeting armed resistance in the jungles and swamps.

Along an 800-mile frontier the respective armies began shooting and macheteing one another. In the six days of fighting, around 6,000 were killed and countless more injured or made homeless. Football stadia in both countries doubled up as makeshift prisons.

Pipo's intervention, like that of Gavrilo Princip's in Sarajevo in 1914, would forever see him saddled with the label of the man who sparked the war. Having previously kept his counsel about the whole affair, he told Spanish TV in 2009, "I think this was the most important sporting event of that generation and the fact that I scored the decisive goal elevated the match's importance throughout my life. People still think it was a goal which caused a war. This idea became more and more widespread and the importance of the goal appeared to grow as the stories became more and more embellished. But the goal clearly changed my life. It changed all of our lives."

There remain two distinct versions of just who started the Fútbol War, depending on the nationality of your informant. At the time there seemed no limitations upon the inventiveness and aggression with which the facts were reported and atrocities of all conceivable types seemed to grow more grotesque by the hour. Border skirmishes were reported as heavy fighting, while both sides routinely claimed great military victories in a seemingly unending stream of deliberate misinformation.

In Tegucigalpa, Manuel Molares recalled, "We felt utterly crushed by the defeat we'd suffered on the pitch, but I couldn't get my head around what so many people were saying. I met a soldier who asked me what it had been like to lose to a bunch of 'motherfucking whores.' How could we have failed to have beaten a side which the Honduran press reported had soiled themselves during the playing of the national anthems, contained at least six homosexuals and apparently turned up drunk to the match? He pulled out a .22-calibre pistol, fired shots into the air and told me he was going to find the Salvadorean players and shoot them in the balls.

"I asked him where he'd heard such complete and utter fabrication about the Salvadoreans. 'It came through from my commander,' he responded. 'Well, you tell him that he's told you a pack of bullshit,' I responded. The man paused, aimed his pistol at me and shouted, 'Are you sure you're not a Salvadorean pig? You seem to like defending their honour.' Then he sped off on his motorbike."

In San Salvador, Alberto Villalta and his team-mates pondered what would happen next. "We were treated like national heroes when we returned," he recalled, "but we hadn't qualified yet, and still had to get past Haiti in order to reach the Finals. It was very distracting. In theory, we had ten days to prepare for the match, yet others were acting like all the work had been completed now we'd beaten Honduras. As footballers, we found that immensely frustrating. In addition we discussed the fact that FIFA would be unlikely to allow us to play Haiti if we were at war. It was unsettling but we resolved that if we eventually did reach the Finals, it would be a fantastic achievement considering the cards appeared to be stacked against us."

In what proved to be another epic series of matches, Pipo scored a goal in the first game which El Salvador won 2–1 in Haiti, and broke his foot at the beginning of the second game, which his side lost 3–0 at home. With the nation sweating on his fitness, he spent several days with his foot in a cast, but after cortisone shots was deemed fit to play in the deciding play-off match. El Salvador triumphed 1–0 in the decisive game in Kingston, Jamaica and sealed their place in the Finals, but Pipo, forced to rest for three months after the match, was never quite the same player again. He suffered permanent damage to his foot and knee ("I placed huge strain on it when I played through the pain barrier") which would force his premature retirement in 1972.

But first there was the small matter of playing in Mexico. Holed up in the half-built Maria Barbra Motel, 10 miles from the Azteca Stadium, the Salvadoreans at least had time to draw breath and had agreed a more than satisfactory system of payments. They'd receive £300 a man for playing in the group matches and £100 a point for every one earned in Group 1.

Alberto Villalta recalls, "To a large degree we enjoyed ourselves and were able to get some room service and free drinks from the bar although we soon discovered that the waiters were having to run around to the hotel round the corner to collect them as not everything was operating in our hotel."

Coach Gregorio Bundio encouraged them to play a close passing style, but fitness and experience was against them from the start. 'Pipo' Rodriguez recalled, "We weren't as fit or well trained as we needed to be. In Europe, they were professionals who spent hours practising their skills. We felt this gulf when we played our matches."

The one advantage which El Salvador had over their opponents was their huge following in Mexico. An esti-mated 40,000 travelled to watch them, but despite their roars of encouragement Belgium, with goals from van Moer ('the Billy Bremner of Belgium') and Lambert, crushed them 3–0 in the Azteca in the opening match.

Next up came hosts Mexico, who'd recalled striker Enrique Borja, nephew of President Ordaz, after considerable pres-sure from the nation's top man. The Salvadoreans had the longest national anthem of all the teams in the tournament and, thinking that it had finished, the Mexican team, anxious to crack on with the game, ran off into their half before the referee summoned them back to wait for the end. Duly incensed, the Salvadoreans started well, as Rodriguez and Calderon clattered the post. With the scores level at 0–0 after 45 minutes, referee Mahmoud Kandil from the United Arab Emirates awarded the visitors a free kick inside their own half. Inexplicably, Perez instead took it for Mexico, Valdiva slotted the loose ball past Salvador keeper Magaña, and the referee allowed the goal to stand. The visitors protested and the crowd was in uproar with fights erupting between fans in the Azteca. With El Salvador psychologically crushed, the hosts finally ran out 4–0 winners.

With matters threatening to get out of hand once again, the Salvadorean team issued a mass apology for their behaviour. Pipo recalled, "Aggrieved as we were, we decided as a group that there had been enough fighting in the region recently so we stopped it before anything else started."

According to local legend, one Mexican fan who felt ashamed at the way his team had won the match, shouted "*Viva Mexico*" in a sarcastic voice, and was shot dead in a local bar.

El Salvador's final game was watched by just 15,000 fans in the Azteca as Russia cantered to a routine 2–0 victory. With the rain pouring down, rumbles of thunder could be heard in the distance. Given the echoes of gunfire which accompanied El Salvador's rocky path to the World Cup, this seemed an apt moment for the Central American state to bow out of the tournament.

Twelve years later both El Salvador, now ripped apart by a civil war, and Honduras qualified for the World Cup in Spain. Although an official peace treaty between the two nations had only been signed two years previously and sporadic gunfire continued around the border, relations had improved significantly over the years, so much so that Honduras (who'd long since qualified) even opted to play properly against Mexico in a qualifier to grab a draw which ultimately enabled El Salvador, now under the tutelage of coach Pipo Rodriguez, to reach the Finals. That was where the Salvadoreans' luck ended. Jet-lagged and exhausted after a 72-hour flight to Spain via Guatemala, the Dominican Republic, Madrid and Alicante, they were forced to beg and borrow training kit and balls from group rivals Hungary. Two days later, the Hungarians chalked up a record 10–1 victory in front of 23,000 fans at the Estadio de Nuevo in Elche.

Luis Ramirez 'El Pelé' Zapata had the distinction of scoring his side's only Finals goal to briefly claw the score back to 5–1, but even then there was an element of farce. Pipo recalls, "When Zapata scored the goal, he started cheering and celebrating and my players told him, 'Don't cheer so much because they'll get annoyed and score even more against us.' They did, racking up five more in 20 minutes. We were stigmatised by that defeat. Argentina only beat us 2–0 – Maradona had said he alone world score 10 against us – and we only lost by one goal to Belgium. We tightened up after the Hungary game and gave a good account of ourselves."

In 1970, the Salvadoreans had lost all three games in Mexico, and 12 years later the same thing happened in Spain. With a World Cup record of Played 6, Won 0, Scored 1, Conceded 13, they are statistically the tournament's worst performing side, along with the Dutch Antilles (who lost 6–0 to Hungary in 1938 in their solitary Finals match), Zaire in '74 (Played 3, Won 0, Lost 3, Scored 0, Conceded 14) and Cuba, thumped 8–0 by Sweden in '38 in their one Finals appearance.

Apart from Zapata, the only player to emerge with credit from the whole sorry affair was Jorge Alberto González ('El Mágico') who became a cult hero in the Spanish league with Cadiz and was selected for the World Cup XI, along with fellow strikers Zico and Paolo Rossi. When the other players returned home, several had their houses fire-bombed due to the disgrace of losing so heavily against Hungary and the entire squad had their free passes to league games revoked by their Football Association.

The civil war rumbled on for several more months (the team was allegedly split between those who supported the military government and others who backed the guerrillas) and Pipo, who admitted to being "psychologically exhausted" by the whole episode, opted to carve out a career in engineering, claiming that it was more lucrative than football. Honduras, on the other hand, earned plaudits by drawing with Northern Ireland and hosts Spain as they too were eliminated in the first round.

Although El Salvador have enjoyed upsetting Mexico on occasions during the last 28 years, they show no sign of reaching the Finals any time soon. Pipo looked back on his association with the national team with mixed feelings. "It's a part of life. Not all is good, not all is bad. The truth is that I have had the honour of scoring the important goal which beat Honduras back in 1969," he recalled. "I had the privilege of doing something great for El Salvador, but as a manager, I suffered the biggest defeat that El Salvador has ever had. These things are, shall we say, the logic of life, that you have to live with good and bad mixed together."

As if to illustrate Pipo's point, rivals Honduras qualified for the 2010 World Cup tournament against the backdrop of a military coup. "The situation at home spurred us on, and helped us unite," explained their jubilant coach, Reinaldo Reina. Proof indeed that football and politics is always likely to be a combustible, and occasionally irresistible, mix in Central America.

BATTLING DEMONS

On Sunday June 21st 1998, as Iran prepared to face the USA in a Group F World Cup match in Lyon, the rhetoric coming out of both countries suggested that something approaching footballing Armageddon was going to explode on the pitch. On the Fox Sports television channel the panel of journalists and media tipsters bandied around inflammatory phrases like "holy war," "the Mother of all battles," and "culture clash" with such monotonous regularity that veteran US striker Eric Wynalda, linked to the studio via an earpiece, threatened to break off communication if "this verbal warmongering continues." From Tehran, Ayatollah Ali Khamenei, the nation's spiritual leader, informed his team, "Tonight, I urge you to remember history, and defeat the enemy."

Other hard-line fundamentalists urged Iran to "slay the Great Satan", which they'd branded the USA ever since President Jimmy Carter broke off relations with Iran after militants stormed the US Embassy in Tehran at the start of the 1979 Islamic Revolution and held 52 Americans hostage for 444 days. The USA, always keen for allies in the Middle East, had previously supported the unelected Shah – the Iranian Emperor – who'd tried to modernise his country along Western lines and was ousted after the revolution. One of the former hostages, who admitted he despised 'soccer,' muttered an embarrassed "I suppose so, yes" when asked the leading question by a Fox panellist, "Inevitably, you'd rather your own nation defeated the one which held you captive for so long?" If politicians and the media were doing their utmost to fan the flames of conflict, the players and supporters at the Stade Gerland did their level best to ignore the hype.

French newspapers later reported that an Iranian extremist who had attempted to burn an effigy of US President Bill Clinton in the streets outside the ground had been restrained by fans from both sides and marched into the hands of the local gendarmes. Inside the stadium, rival supporters unfurled banners with messages including "Peace and Football Rule" and "Keep sport free of politics." Iranian players presented their counterparts with white flowers before the game as a gesture of peace and the Americans, in turn, gave them US pennants. The Iranians presented US skipper Thomas Dooley with a silver plate. Both sets of players posed together in an unusual joint photograph and hundreds of Iranian fans at the match wore T-shirts with a photograph of Massoud Rajavi, head of an Iraq-based group opposed to the Islamist regime.

Once the draw for France '98 had paired the two nations together, the Iranian government had had to weigh up the possible advantages of defeating the USA in front of the world, against the prospect of their exiled opponents airing their grievances on the most public stage of all. A group of quasi-Marxists – the People's Mujahideen – had a large presence at matches and sang anti-government songs.

Iran supporter and political activist Mehdi Minavand recalls, "There were many banners among the Iranian fans in the crowd which were raised depicting images of Massoud Rajavi and his wife, but stadium security had been alerted in advance to the fact that we would be unfurling these images, and they wrestled them away from us. (Author's note: There were clear echoes of a match in the Nou Camp in 1982, when the USSR took on Poland. Back home the Poles, in the form of the Trade Union Solidarity had been protesting against the Soviets, and in Barcelona, hundreds of Solidarnose flags were ripped away from demonstrating Polish fans by riot police, supposedly on the orders of Soviet TV. In his 2002 book *Terror on the Pitch! How Bin Laden targeted Beckham and the England Football Team*, Adam Robinson claimed Al Queda cells posed a huge terrorist threat during the '98 World Cup.) Before the tournament, the Iranian government had had long discussions with FIFA about the 'inappropriateness' of this Rajavi image, so the security was well primed. Some fans were even evicted from the ground for carrying them. But many of us still had the T-shirts and baseball caps on our heads depicting him. We were very pleased when we heard that foreign TV channels, with cameras looking directly at the crowd, started asking questions as to who this figure was. Many of us were well used to the fact that in Iran, football matches were one of the few places where one could attempt to express oneself freely."

To ensure that none of these images reached the population at home, Iranian television didn't show the real crowd on their coverage. Instead they plumped for a botched compromise and superimposed figures swathed in black coats and hats apparently protecting themselves against the biting cold of the French summer.

Tehran-born Mehdi Minavand regularly went to football matches in his native city with his parents and his sister during the 1970s. That was until the Ayatollah Khomeini, exiled for over 18 years, returned to Iran on a Boeing 747 in 1979 during the Islamic Revolution which ousted the Shah. Football clubs were disbanded and competition was discouraged because, according to a government directive, "Players have a tendency to behave aggressively when they play the sport. In the aftermath of games, supporters can also, under influences which aren't good for them, behave in an unbecoming manner."

The national team blundered on although, consigned virtually to the international wilderness after non-Asian sides largely refused to play them, their ranking slipped and they were unable to match the success of 1978 when they reached the World Cup Finals and drew with Scotland.

In 1987 the Ayatollah issued a new fatwa which prohib-
ited women (there was too much swearing in the crowd and
too much male flesh on show) from going to football matches.
In the days of the Shah an estimated 20 per cent of crowds
had been female, many of whom were prominent white-
collar professionals. After 1979 they were dismissed from
their jobs and could only watch football on television.

"My family were by no means supporters of the Shah and
there were many excesses of his regime – the way he treated
political opponents for instance – which appalled my
parents," explains Minavand. "But the passing of time clouds
one's memory and many of my generation came to associate him with a golden age of Iranian football. The sport
never died in my country after the revolution and women
never lost their interest in the sport. It was too important
to many of us for that. People actually forget that Ayatollah
Khomeini's son played football to a good standard and he
overruled fellow clerics and insisted that matches be shown
on television in the late '80s.

"The Islamic regime under the Ayatollah virtually eradi-
cated any semblance of Western pop music and movies, but
they could never kill off football. There were still local
leagues and of course children simply played on the streets.
Girls and young women joined in too and in my neighbourhood they would often remove the hijab from their
heads. It was the ultimate symbol that through football one
could rediscover one's identity and one's independence. The
authorities hated the sport, but they realised that banning
it would be dangerous, given the passion for it among so
many Iranians. Of course, it was an ongoing battle and you
would often have a visit from the basji – the religious para-
military – who would tell girls to put the hijab back on and
make notes of their names and addresses, but they weren't
as blinkered as official propaganda would suggest and occasionally they would even join in the games. For many
women, though, football was out of bounds."

By 1989, with the Ayatollah dying from prostate cancer,
his grip on Iran weakened and the government announced

that a semi-professional league would resume. But the Ayatollah's death effectively destroyed the national team's efforts to qualify for the 1990 World Cup. Due to the two-month-long official mourning period the Asian Football Confederation rearranged Iran's qualifiers and, forced to play three games in a week, the team failed to reach Italy.

Khomeinei's successor, Ayatollah Khamenei, took a greater interest in the sport and Iran approached the 1994 World Cup qualifiers with confidence, but Qatar defeated them at the first hurdle. Iran's manager was Ali Parvin, a hugely popular character who had been part of the Iranian squad which qualified for the 1978 World Cup. He was viewed as a dangerous figure by the authorities, who were keen to destroy the legacy of pre-Revolution football, and Parvin was known for making pro-Shah comments. Mehdi Minavand explains, "Parvin got fired after Iran lost to Qatar. They said it was because his team lost so meekly. But Parvin represented something incredibly dangerous to the religious elite, even though they appeared to have softened their stance. They wanted rid of anything which reminded them of the pre-Revolutionary football elite and especially any suggestion that Iran could be a secular football nation. Football was many people's real passion and the authorities loathed that. After Parvin got fired we would sing his name at matches. He was like an absent hero."

In 1997 the moderate Mohammad Khatami won the presidential election and personally visited the national team in a bid to cajole them into qualifying for the 1998 tournament. Although conservative religious forces continued to lambast the sport for diverting people's attention away from their religious and social duties, the team started to perform well and, due to pressure on the Iranian FA from Khatami, the Brazilian Valdeir Vieira was hired as team coach, the first foreign incumbent since the days of the Shah.

"The ramifications of Vieira's appointment made waves," recalls Mehdi Minivand. "Vieira wore a neck tie. Religious extremists disapproved. Neck ties had been worn by prosperous men under the Shah. Symbols like that matter in

Iran. Many wanted Vieira out. The thing was that Vieira now had many supporters within the game and with the team on the cusp of World Cup qualification no one in their right mind would dare to fire him – the consequences of such a foolhardy act didn't bear thinking about."

After blowing a chance to qualify in third place, Iran faced a two-legged play-off against Terry Venables's emerging Australia in November 1997, a side which contained rising stars including Harry Kewell and Mark Viduka. In front of around 120,000 supporters in Tehran's Azadi Stadium, Azizi levelled after Kewell had given the Socceroos, who'd preferred to train in Dubai before the match, an early lead. The game ended in a 1–1 draw. Conventional wisdom held that with the advantage of an away goal, Venables's side would comfortably win the return leg two weeks later, which would be played at the 100,000-seater Melbourne Cricket Ground. Five thousand Iranian expats were in attendance as Kewell and Aurelio Vidmar's goals either side of half-time gave Australia a 3–1 aggregate advantage.

Mehdi Minavand's sister, Atefeh Aghili, who watched in Tehran, recalls, "When Vidmar scored a second for Australia, I'm sure that many turned off their televisions. If they'd taken their chances Australia could have been 4–0 up, they were that superior. But then a madman invaded the pitch and cut the net with a knife. It took officials ten minutes to repair the damage and during that time the Iran players spent their time talking and regrouping. The Australians had nothing to do but sit and stew. It was a crucial disruption. I later heard that the man only invaded public events which coincided with the predictions of Nostradamus. I have no idea whether or not that is true. In the 77th minute, Bagheri pulled a goal back and in our neighbourhood of flats it was like an oxygen tank began breathing new life into all of us. Whereas before there was total, depressed silence, now there were cheers and shouts and yelps as the Australians were placed on the back foot."

The crowning moment arrived with just ten minutes left when Azizi slipped the ball to Mark Bosnich's left and scored

Iran's equaliser. Inside the Melbourne Cricket Ground the Iranian fans went wild at the final whistle and draped national flags over the players, as Venables's crestfallen team slumped to the turf. Iran had reached the World Cup Finals courtesy of the away-goals rule despite being outplayed for much of the tie. The Iranian Government wasn't prepared for what happened next at home.

Mehdi Minivand explains, "At the final whistle, all of us took to the streets. It was the only natural reaction. When something as joyful as that happens you want to share the feeling with other human beings. I'm told that in the country over 10 million took to the streets that night. It was the largest public gathering since the 1979 Revolution. That's how much reaching the Finals meant to us all. There was music blaring out from cars and from cafés. We all got outrageously drunk on spirits. We danced to Western music like Oasis and Blur. Friends of ours had smuggled in bootleg cassettes.

"Men and women mixed freely on the streets. My sister and her friends threw off the hijab in the road and danced on top of the cars. My father was furious with her for weeks afterwards! 'You'll never marry a good Iranian boy carrying on like that,' he told her. 'I don't want to Dad,' came her typically abrasive response. My mother thought it hilarious. The basiji arrived to try and restore order and told the girls to behave in a correct manner. They were ignored. Some of them gave up and joined in the dancing and the drinking.

"From the government's point of view it was a complete breakdown of order. Police were called to investigate a disturbance at the French embassy later that night. A 3,000-strong crowd had begun to throw flowers over the fence and chanted, 'See you in Paris.' In the streets, huge flags were unfurled and fans walked underneath them. It was a symbolic substitute for passing under a copy of the Koran, which is designed to place you under protection of our Holy Book. After I'd recovered from an awful hangover I wondered what would happen next. What had happened the previous evening showed there are things more powerful and spontaneous than the government could contain. It was a force of nature."

Mehdi Minivand didn't have long to wait for an answer. Playing for time in a bid to allow things to cool down on the streets, the government instructed the Iranian team to enjoy a short holiday in Dubai before making their way home. A monstrous celebration (men only of course) was planned at the Azadi, with the triumphant team scheduled to arrive in a military helicopter. Government officials, via TV and radio, implored their "sisters to stay away," and for the crowds to remain calm. Fans were instructed not to bring in newspapers and magazines, for fear of spontaneous bonfires around the ground. The pleas fell on deaf ears. Around 100,000 men squeezed into the stadium and 3,000 women, chanting for the team, gathered outside as riot police, armed with tear gas, hemmed them in.

In the crowd was Atefeh Aghili. She recalls, "From the moment we all gathered outside we knew that if we stuck together we could somehow force our way into the ground. When the sound of the helicopter throbbed around the streets, we started to push. The police, many of whom were just young boys, pushed back. It threatened to get nasty. We borrowed some songs from other civil rights movements. There was a chorus of 'We shall not be moved' and 'We shall overcome.' We sang, 'Aren't we part of this nation, too?' It was remarkable. The police didn't know what to do.

"Suddenly, over the megaphone, it was announced that, quietly and peacefully, we should make our way to the turnstiles, as we would be allowed in to the ground. It was staggering. This sea of policemen suddenly parted and in we filed. Of course, we sat in a separate section, but that night it felt that we had made our strike for womanhood. There were several hundred women behind us who had originally had their access denied to the ground. They barged through anyway. The eyes of the world were watching and the government couldn't risk a human tragedy. There were several stories that women, wearing baseball caps, trousers, baggy shirts, and with their breasts crushed down, had got into the ground with their husbands, brothers, and fathers, and denied the *fatwa*. I don't doubt that for a second."

Seven months later, at the World Cup Finals, the US dominated much of the long-awaited match against Iran, 500-1 outsiders for the World Cup. They hit the woodwork four times in the opening stages. Earlier in the day, Yugoslavia had drawn with Germany: the Yugoslavs already having beaten Iran 1–0 and with the USA having lost to Germany, defeat for either Iran or the USA in Lyon would send them home.

FIFA statistics revealed that the USA had 12 shots on goal, compared with three from Iran. But what counts are goals and in the 40th minute Hamid Estili scored after a lightning counter-attack and Mehrdi Mahdavikia killed the game off in the 84th minute after the US had laid siege to the Iranian goal for much of the second half. The estimated 8,000 Iranians in the crowd were jubilant. Brian McBride pulled one back, too little too late, in the 87th minute. US goalkeeper Kasey Keller explained, "It came down to us hitting the post too many times, and them getting one or two easy chances."

The reaction to the result from Iran's key figures spoke volumes about the political situation. Coach Jalal Talebi tried to play down the entire "grudge match" scenario, claiming, "It's a big victory for the Iranian nation, not because it was the United States, but because it was Iran's first World Cup win." President Mohammad Khatami's message was similarly congratulatory, but low-key, "Congratulations – this victory is a symbol of national unity." Ayatollah Ali Khamenei was rather more direct, his statement of congratulations to the team announcing, "Tonight, again, the strong and arrogant opponent felt the bitter taste of defeat at your hands. Be happy that you have made the Iranian nation happy."

Yet again, in Iran's main cities, millions took to the streets. Confectionary shops opened in the middle of the night to distribute free ice cream and sweets to the revellers. Tens of thousands of policemen stood and watched as, once more, the *hijabs* were discarded and both sexes mixed freely. "The most commonly used word that night," recalls Mehdi Minivand, was 'mubarak, mubarak' ('Congratulations, congratulations'). My cousin in Lebanon reported that in Beirut people fired guns in the air in celebration, as did the peoples of Cairo and in Ramallah, on the West Bank." Four days afterwards the Iranians lost 2–0 to Germany but they were still treated as heroes on their arrival back in Tehran.

Eighteen months later the Iranian team travelled for an international 'friendly' to California, which is home to one of the highest concentrations of Iranians outside Iran, and shared a diplomatic 1–1 draw in front of a 50,000 crowd at the Pasadena Rose Bowl. Although Washington and Tehran still had no diplomatic ties, the number of cultural and sporting exchanges had slowly begun to increase, evidence of the countries' thawing relations since Khatami's election in 1997. But there was still a degree of controversy surrounding the game. The Iranian authorities complained about the police searching the luggage of their team, while an Iranian extremist group called for beer advertisements to be removed from the stadium. Mehdi Minivand approached the new century with a profound sense of optimism. "We felt absolutely sure that through celebrating the joy of winning a football match in such large numbers on the streets, we would somehow hasten the modernisation of Iran. In victory, the shackles were loosened. We honestly felt football was so powerful a force that social change would inevitably follow, and quickly too. Such a view was wildly optimistic."

In 1999, a year after the Iranian national team had defeated the USA, the closure of moderate newspapers by the Khatami-controlled government prompted demonstrations on the streets of Iranian cities. Over a five-day period, students and political activists, many of whom had taken to the streets for football reasons a few months before, clashed with state forces. Although the protesters were finally driven back the government, fearful of reports of civil unrest, became increasingly hostile towards large public gatherings.

In late 2001, Iran defeated Iraq in a World Cup qualifier

and, predictably, the response to defeating the old enemy was similar to what had happened at the previous World Cup. Hundreds of thousands took to the streets in Tehran but instead of being met with smiles and handshakes, there were thousands of arrests and 20 people died in the ensuing panic as tear gas was dispersed by the police. An official government report later explained that many supporters had been chanting, "Zindibad azadi" ("Long live Freedom") and "We love America" after the win against Iraq. There were also reports that the victorious fans shouted the name of Reza Pahlavi – the exiled son of the late Shah. A solemn President Khatami went on television and called for the population to keep off the streets if Iran defeated Bahrain 10 days later, and thereby qualified for the World Cup.

The sheer ineptness of the team's 3–1 capitulation to the Bahrainis led to rumours that the religious elite had ordered the team to throw the match in order to prevent more spontaneous public gatherings. "When that story did the rounds," recalls Mehdi Minivand, "there was a huge amount of public disorder in our district. The joy of what had happened in 1998 was replaced by violence. Teenagers threw rocks and Molotov cocktails at the police and pictures of the Ayatollah Khamenei were burned. The basiji responded by using their batons. It was very unpleasant. Even if the conspiracy theories were untrue, the fact that so many believed them shows what a desperate state Iran was in. Khatami, once considered a reformist, was now bowing to pressure from the clerics." There were also allegations that an overzealous mullah kept the team awake to pray until late at night before the game.

"For many of us," explains Atefe Aghili, "it is embarrassing that when a major World Cup match comes into view, countries from this region are virtually labelled as basket cases when things become difficult. In 1982, when Kuwait reached the finals the referee, after originally allowing a goal by Giresse, eventually disallowed a French goal after the Kuwait team claimed they'd stopped when they heard a whistle from the crowd. The players protested to the officials and the President of the Kuwaiti FA, Price Fahid, strode onto the pitch and tried to instruct his team to walk off, before the referee reversed his decision. Since the ousting of Saddam in Iraq, all the stories came out that Uday used to control the team and torture them if they lost. It is a matter of some regret for many of us that the perception in the West is that Middle Eastern Nations are so combustible and unstable. It adds to a stereotype which already exists."

Iran's loss to Bahrain necessitated a play-off with the United Arab Emirates for the right to play Ireland in a final pair of matches which would decide who qualified for the World Cup. The Iranians put in an almost superhuman level of effort to defeat the UAE 1–0, after which the government ordered that a celebratory cake, made from over 12,000 eggs, be distributed to Tehran's populace in refrigerated trucks. The riots carried on regardless. The security was beefed up and a parachute regiment and army units were drafted in to counter attacks from masked men and hijab-free girls in several of Tehran's districts.

Mick McCarthy's Ireland finally edged out Iran in the play-off, winning 2–0 in Dublin and losing 1–0 in Tehran. There was no disgrace in that but for many of the Iranian women who'd greeted the '98 heroes upon their return there was widespread fury at the authorities' decision to allow 30 Irish women to attend the match in the Azadi, albeit under a strictly enforced dress code, whilst denying access to their own women. The official statement had claimed, "Irish women can't speak farsi, therefore they won't understand the cursing and foul-mouthed insults which will inevitably be generated throughout the match." Atefeh Aghili explains, "Reformist newspapers immediately seized upon the issue and pushed for change. To a degree, the media's pressure paid dividends, and in 2003 women were allowed in to watch Peykan FC – who played in Tehran's most well-heeled suburb – play a live game. The authorities chose the match because Peykan FC's fans swore and cursed the least of any supporters in the country. It didn't really address the issue at all."

Finally, in May 2005, Atefeh Aghili realised her dream and

with the white, green and red Iranian tricolour draped over her shoulders, she was allowed to watch her team labour to a 1–0 win over North Korea which nudged them slightly closer to World Cup qualification. Along with 20 other women, including Niloofar Ardalan, daughter of Iran's former international goalkeeper, she'd petitioned the Iranian Football Federation (IFF) to allow her to attend matches. Womens' attendance at football matches emerged as a key issue in the presidential campaign and one of the front runners, Akbar Hashemi Rafsanjani, a pillar of the political establishment who was trying to reinvent himself as the young people's champion, backed the lobbyists. The IFF caved in.

The womens' presence at the Azadi Stadium went largely unnoticed. Atefeh Aghili explains, "We were told to wear traditional headgear and long overcoats. We were instructed to sit hundreds of yards away from male supporters, in between two groups of Koreans. On no account, we were told, were we to speak or sing and draw attention to ourselves. Just in case we didn't understand the instructions we were circled by security guards who spent much of the game staring directly at us. It still represented progress though. The match marked the 16th anniversary of the death of the Ayatollah Khomeini. All around the ground, both inside and out, there were images of him on display. Before the match, five men delivered a *tavashih* – a recitation in Arabic of verses from the Koran. It could best be described as an austere night."

Since firebrand President Mahmoud Ahmadinejad came to power in 2005 Iran, described by George Bush as being at the hub of an 'Axis of Evil,' has been viewed as even more of an international pariah. The knock-on effects for football have been almost catastrophic. After coach Branko Ivankovi steered Iran to the World Cup Finals in 2006, Western politicians and human rights organizations, furious at Iran's continuing uranium enrichment programme and Ahmadinejad's calls for Israel to be "wiped off the map," demanded that Iran be thrown out of the tournament. Ex-Conservative deputy leader Michael Ancram said that

Iran's expulsion "would give a very, very clear signal to Iran that the international community will not accept what they are doing."

The ban never materialised, and the Iranian President regularly visited the national squad to impart his view that self-reliance and fierce independence would see both the football team, and the nation, through choppy waters. Those qualities weren't enough in Germany and Iran bowed out after losing to Mexico and Portugal and gaining a solitary point against Angola. Reports suggested that the Iran camp was divided between those loyal to and against the government.

Later that year, Iran was briefly suspended from FIFA because of alleged government meddling. The President of the IFF, Mohammed Dadkan, was sacked after fierce government criticism of the team's displays at the World Cup. His removal was orchestrated by a government-run physical education organisation. When Dadkan dared to protest, Ahmadinejad's brother Davoud, who headed a powerful inspectorate, intervened and ensured the dismissal was carried out. Dadkan later claimed to have been labelled a "Zionist collaborator" and an "alien." FIFA reached its decision after ruling that Dadkan's sacking broke rules on the independence of national associations from political interference. Iran was later reinstated after the IFF agreed to adhere to a FIFA 'road map' on reforming how football in Iran was run.

In June 2009 four Iranian stars were handed life bans from international football after they wore green wristbands during a World Cup qualifier against South Korea. The players' gesture, and the subsequent punishment, attracted worldwide comment after it was revealed that President Mahmoud Ahmadinejad had strongly objected to the players showing support for his defeated election rival, Mir-Hossein Mousavi, leader of the reformist Green Path of Hope movement.

In the days before that game against South Korea, hundreds of thousands took to the streets in protest at the alleged vote-rigging and corruption in the presidential election. The pro-government newspaper *Iran* revealed that the players who had made the protest, including the mercurial former

Bayern Munich star Ali Karimi, famed for his outspoken criticism of the IFF (he'd earlier claimed that Iranian football had regressed by a decade since the 2006 World Cup), had been "retired after their political gesture in Seoul." The four were banned from giving interviews afterwards and, according to media reports, when they arrived back in Tehran their passports were confiscated. Initially the team's chief administrative officer, Mansour Pourhiedari, had claimed the wristbands had been a religious tribute to a revered Shia figure, in the hope that it would deliver a vital victory. Ahmadinejad was unimpressed by the excuse.

The players' protest was linked by the press to the arrest of Mohsen Safaei Farahani, who headed the country's football governing body under former President Khatami. One pro-Ahmadinejad website accused Farahani, a member of the pro-reform group, of bribing the players to wear the green wristbands. Just to confuse matters further, German club VfL Bochum, where star striker Vahid Hashemian played, explained that the passpost story was a myth, and that the suggestion of an international ban was "utter fabrication." Coach Afshin Gotbi also insisted that the "national team door is always, always open to them" but the fact that none of the "gang of four" have figured in an Iran squad since suggests that there is more than a grain of truth in the story.

There may still be a ray of hope for the gang of four. In February 2010 a group of dissident lawyers from within the Green Path of Hope organisation lobbied FIFA with a view to getting the life ban repealed and other members of the organisation have vowed to carry placards depicting the banned players during future demonstrations. One of the spokesmen said, "As well as making no football sense to ban four of your best players, what has happened is a symbol of the denial of basic rights within Iran. We hope that the pressure we will apply will bear fruit, and enable them [the players] to wear the Iran shirt with pride once more." Although a keen follower of football, President Ahmadinejad is, perhaps unsurprisingly, said to be "unmoved" by the demonstration plans.

In Tehran, both Atefeh Aghili and her brother Mehdi Mini-vand grow frustrated at the lack of genuine reform in Iran. "On the day of a match at the Azadi," explains Atefeh, "you will still see groups of women protesting outside the ground, because despite the temporary reforms of 2003 we are still rarely allowed into matches – certainly not for the big internationals. I'm hopeful that one day we will be."

Her brother Mehdi adds, "All around us are images of the past. On the sides of buildings in Tehran there are pictures of the martyrs from the Iran–Iraq war. At the Azadi there are pictures of the Ayatollah Khomeini who did much to shape the Western vision of Iran. Protesters continue to collect and display images of the Shah. But we're missing the point here. There's a new urban generation to whom the Shah and the Ayatollah mean nothing. They demand change without harking back to the past and are unwilling to accept that things must remain the same. Some of those youngsters who took to the streets after our World Cup successes are now those who demand change. Their numbers grow, gradually. Many of our footballers now play abroad and are exposed to Western influences and have Western haircuts. It's probably David Beckham's fault. The clerics think so. In 2003, they blacked out images of him in Tehran advertising motor oil and razors. When Iran play abroad we see adverts and hear music on the TV that our government would rather we didn't see.

"The World Cup fascinates us because it gives us a glimpse of something supposedly beyond reach. I'd like to think that football is the vehicle for change in Iran. That's why the government tries to control it, and thinks it needs to control it. But it can't. Not in the long term. Football is too powerful a force, and it will eventually drive through reform in Iran."

9

PIRATES, ANIMALS AND THIEVES

In both the 1960s and the 1980s the blood feud between England and Argentina was characterised by flag-waving, jingoism and crude stereotyped newspaper headlines in London and Buenos Aires. And when the teams have locked horns at the World Cup, politics and football have often become dangerously entwined.

In football terms the mistrust dates back to England's isolationist days of the 1930s. England, Scotland, Wales and Ireland had withdrawn en masse from FIFA in 1928. FA Secretary Frederick Wall wrote that the news "had hit FIFA President Jules Rimet like a thunderbolt." By adopting their isolationist stance the Home Nations forfeited their right to qualify for the inaugural World Cup Finals in Uruguay.

One of the many reasons why the Home Nations withdrew was on account of FIFA's interference in the FA's policy on amateur footballers. FIFA acknowledged a definition of amateurism that, in the run up to the 1928 Amsterdam Olympics, allowed for 'broken time' payments to players to compensate for loss of earnings and other expenses, but the precise amount of remuneration was left to individual associations. The British labelled it 'shamateurism,' and did not reconcile with FIFA until after World War II. However, there were other reasons for the no-show at those early World Cups.

Speaking to me in 1996, former England and Arsenal defender George Male recalled a remarkable conversation he'd had with an FA official in the mid-1930s: "I told him that I believed it unfair and restrictive for us not to at least have a chance of playing in the World Cup Finals, and that we should rejoin FIFA. And then this pompous fool – in broad Geoff Boycott Yorkshire drawl – told me, 'Male, we'll learn nowt from playing spics, wogs and dagos.' I was shocked that he could say such a thing and I told him that it would be great for British football if we played the great teams from Argentina and Uruguay, who'd done so well in the 1930 World Cup. 'Think what we could learn from them,' I said to him. I was simply reflecting what Herbert Chapman often said to us, that you couldn't develop or improve your game unless you were exposed to different playing styles. The FA official's response was, 'We can't have you playing a bunch of South American darkies Male. You'd come back from swamp-land eating bananas and with a dose of the clap. Let them play between themselves.' I was left speechless. But this kind of insularity existed for years in the FA."

George Male believed that future England manager Alf Ramsey shared many of these prejudices: "Alf and I occasionally bumped into one another on coaching courses, and although he was fine on a certain level, to me he represented the kind of 'stiff upper-lipped' Britisher attitude which has given us a bad name, and which I held no truck with. I spoke to him once of his experience on a tour of Brazil with his club, Southampton, several years later. He loathed South Americans. All of them. 'Spitting, swearing in a language I didn't understand, diving, complaining, overemotional,' he ranted. In short, it was all the things which Alf found disgusting and alien to him. I put it to him that he couldn't tarnish all South American teams with the same brush. He just looked at me blankly. In '66, when I heard that he'd described the Argentina players as animals, I know he was referring to events on the pitch, but there was an awful lot of Alf's own prejudice mixed in there too. And it had been prevalent in the higher echelons of the English game for years."

I expected nothing else, of course, but just in case I was in any doubt, Alan Ball reminded me in advance that he would "never hear a bad word said of Alf Ramsey. I'd have run through brick walls for him, as would most of the '66 team." I travelled to Croydon in 2006 to interview the feisty, red-headed Ball who, at just 21, was the youngest member of Ramsey's World Cup team, to see him deliver one of his after dinner speeches, which he would invariably begin with the line, "It's nice to be squeaking to you." After regaling the audience with tales of his career at Everton, Arsenal and Southampton, the bulk of Ball's patter inevitably focused on the events of the summer of '66, as did the majority of the audience's questions.

What was interesting were Ball's opinions on the teams England faced in their most high-profile matches – Argentina, and firstly West Germany. On a boozy, blokey occasion such as this, I thought that there was every possibility that the anecdotes would take on a Stan Boardmanesque feel and drift towards the Luftwaffe, Hitler and the war, with occasional "Achtung" and "Fokkers" references thrown in for good measure. Not a bit of it. Ball was gushing about West Germany's sportsmanship, fighting spirit and never-say-die attitude in the final. Goalkeeper Sepp Meier was "unquestionably brilliant" (Author's Note: Hans Tilkawski was the German stopper in the '66 final) and Franz Beckenbauer "already showed signs that he would go on to become arguably the finest defensive player in the world." Ball also praised West Germany's comeback four years later in the heat of Mexico, when Helmut Schön's men fought back from 2–0 down to eventually win the match 3–2. "Many of us realised that in fact we were very similar to the Germans – kindred spirits if you will – as a race, and in terms of our ethics and our approach to football; we understood one another," Ball claimed. The audience murmured its approval.

He then moved onto the subject of Argentina. Exactly 40 years after the fateful quarter-final, which England won 1–0 courtesy of Geoff Hurst's goal, Ball's venom towards the South Americans remains unabated. "They were animals," he states. "Absolutely no question about it at all, they were the dirtiest, filthiest team I ever played against in my career and, remember, I played against Revie's Leeds year in, year out."

A member of the audience then asked Ball for his opinion of the tall, dominant Argentina captain, Antonio Rattin. "Alf warned us what kind of game it would be," came the response, "and in Rattin there was the personification of foul play. From the off he was spitting at the referee's feet, sneering at his decisions, leering in his face and the rest of the team would pull hair and dig nails in and spit at you too. He was what I can only describe as a dark, brooding, menacing presence. Honestly, what went on was disgraceful and Alf was right to call them animals afterwards." A day after the match, journalist Hugh McIlvanney had said of the whole affair, "Not so much a football match as an international incident."

After Ball had finished his speech and signed some copies of his autobiography, I met up with him backstage. We chatted amiably about his domestic career, but as soon as we breached the topic of England he grew more wary. "What's your angle?" he repeated several times. I put it to Ball that Ramsey's pre-match comment, "Gentlemen, you know what kind of a match you will have on your hands today," was tantamount to priming his players for a war of attrition before the match had even begun. "That's untrue," Ball countered, "because we knew of Rattin's reputation as being an aggressive, unsportsmanlike so and so – even in the tunnel he towered over his teammates and gave them orders – and like any great manager, Alf was simply firing us up for what he knew would be a battle and a half, which it was."

Did Ball think that Rattin was harshly treated by German referee Kreitlein? "In what sense?" "In the sense he was cautioned for an innocuous trip on Bobby Charlton and then given his marching orders for saying something to the referee in a language the official didn't understand. Kreitlein would later describe it as "violence of the tongue." "Well I played in the match and what you can't see is the spitting, the intimidation and the total lack of respect for the referee which they showed."

"According to the match statistics, England committed more fouls in the match than Argentina and the South Americans later complained that the referee was too lenient with tackling from behind, which is outlawed in Argentina. What's your opinion of that?" I asked.

"We were a hard team and we had players like Nobby [Stiles] and Jack [Charlton] who could take care of themselves, but they were at least up front about what they did. Nobby received a great deal of criticism about his tackle on the French player Simon a few days before, but it wasn't done slyly. It was under the nose of the referee. The Argentine players cheated. They were trying to get away with the things I mentioned to gain an advantage on the pitch."

Looking back at a re-run of the match, Bobby Moore's early blatant handball goes unpunished. There are a huge number of backpasses by England defenders, which Gordon Banks then gathers up in his arms. The pace is far slower than one would expect in the modern game but, nonetheless, some isolated incidents still have a jarring feel to them. The first bad challenge of the game is George Cohen's scything tackle on an Argentine midfielder, which would today be punished with an instant yellow card. The referee barely even glances at Cohen as he waves play on. In his after-dinner speech, Ball claimed the referee blew his whistle at least six times in the first ten minutes of the match. That is untrue – there is clear evidence of the England players attempting to rough up the Argentines, not vice versa.

Ball takes a blatant dive in his opponents' penalty box and, after Stiles attempts to decapitate an Argentine, a shower of spit is aimed in his direction. For much of the match, Argentina knock the ball around in neat passing triangles, compared with the England midfield's predominantly long-

Uruguay score the first ever goal in a World Cup Final in 1930 against the enemy from across the River Plate, Argentina, their victory prompting the stoning of the Uruguayan embassy in Buenos Aires.

The 1934 World Cup was a fascist love-in, which left Jules Rimet wondering who had organised the tournament – FIFA or Mussolini.

(top) The German team give the Nazi salute before their semi-final match against Sweden.

(above) Nothing could stop the Italians who won the trophy in front of Mussolini, who had taken the Swedish referee to dinner the night before.

(*top*) Italy won their second World Cup in 1938 in France, despite mass protests against Mussolini and fascism. Mussolini ordered the team to wear black in the semi-final in retaliation, the only time they have ever done so.

(*above*) Brazilian goalkeeper Barbosa lets Uruguayan stiker Ghigga's shot slip through his fingers to stun the host nation and win the 1950 World Cup. Brazil has never got over the defeat and Barbosa died a broken, unforgiven man.

(left) Paulo César Lima, the forgotten man of Brazil's 1970 World Cup winning squad. He reveals how the team underwent months of intensive preparations for the tournament, sponsored by the dictatorship of General Medici.

(below) Idi Amin took a personal interest in the Ugandan football team during the 1970s as they attempted to qualify for the World Cup, ordering his men to "break the teeth" of Tanzania players before a crucial match.

(*left*) President Mobutu of Zaire wanted the footballers of Zaire to represent the power of black Africa at the 1974 World Cup, but when they lost 9-0 to Yugoslavia he turned his wrath on the team.

(*below*) Ilunga Mwepu clears the ball for 'The Leopards' during the infamous Yugoslavia match, sporting the team shirt that Mobutu himself helped to design.

Fans in Haiti celebrate qualification for the World Cup in 1974 in the capital Port-au-Prince, the team had been greatly assisted by notorious dictator 'Baby Doc' Duvalier. Incredibly, Haiti took the lead against Italy in their first match (*above right*), but to the fury of Baby Doc one of their players failed a drugs test after the match. He was beaten up in the team's hotel foyer, sent home and imprisoned.

The two Germanys, West and East, meet in the famous Cold War clash at the 1974 World Cup. Three thousand carefully vetted East German supporters were allowed to travel to Hamburg for the match, accompanied by STASI guards who watched their every move and even accompanied them to the toilet.

(*top*) Argentina's home World Cup triumph united the nation, which is exactly what the country's military dictator General Videla had planned. Thousands of political opponents were 'disappeared' before the tournament and huge walls erected to block views of the slums from foreign visitors.

(*above*) The 1982 World Cup draw was a farce. The revolving cage full of plastic footballs with the team names inside jammed, the boys from a Madrid orphanage enlisted to help were told to 'get on with it' by a FIFA official on live TV and the Spanish national lottery was delayed for the first and only time in its history.

'You'll Never Take the Falklands!' – England fans in Bilbao for their opening match of the 1982 World Cup against France. With the Falklands War having ended just before it kicked off, the tournament was played with a backdrop of tension – Spain having abstained in the UN vote condemning Argentina's invasion of the islands.

When Andres Escobar was shot dead a few days after putting the ball into his own net against the USA at the 1994 World Cup (*centre*), his killer shouted 'own goal' each time he pulled the trigger.

(*above*) The players of Iran and the USA pose for a rare joint team photo to try and ease tensions before the 1998 World Cup meeting. When Iran qualified for the 1998 World Cup, Iranian women openly uncovered their heads and drank alcohol during the mass celebrations in Tehran.

(*left*) Before the 2002 World Cup qualifier between Egypt and Algeria, the Algerian team coach was attacked by stone-throwing youths. Khaled Lemmouchia, pictured here in an Algerian newspaper the following day, played the match with shards of glass still embedded in his head.

(*below*) Heightened security at a neutral venue in Sudan could not prevent rioting before and after the crucial play-off between the two countries which saw Algeria qualify for South Africa 2010.

ball approach. According to the England players' testimonies there was a great deal which the crowd and the referee didn't see. George Cohen spoke of "the pat on your shoulder that turns out to be a wrenching of your ear." Geoff Hurst spoke of never "having a moment's peace . . . not knowing quite why you are edgy." For Alan Ball, the greatest affront of all was the spitting. "In England," he told me, "you can headbutt, you can kick opponents in the nuts, but spitting is beneath contempt. All of us England players in the game were either spat at or spat on."

On 41 minutes Antonio Rattin, already booked for the challenge on Charlton, questions the booking of a team-mate. He is dismissed by the German referee Kreitlein for the "look on his face" and "violence of the tongue," even though he couldn't speak German and the referee no Spanish. Ordered off, Rattin took ten minutes to leave the field and as he finally departed he sat and sulked on the red carpet reserved for the Queen, allegedly aiming a middle finger in her direction.

On the final whistle, Alf Ramsey strode onto the pitch and stopped George Cohen from swapping shirts with González ("George, you are not swapping shirts with people like this") before making his "animals" comment.

After the match, one Argentine player urinated against a wall in the tunnel, FIFA official Harry Cavan's blazer was showered in spit, and a gaggle of Argentine players attempted to break down the England players' dressing room door, spoiling for a fight. Jack Charlton yelled out, "Let them in, I'll take them all on."

Ball claimed the "crowd booed and jeered the Argentines relentlessly during the match," but the truth was somewhat different. Simon Anstell, who was in the crowd, recalls, "This was the first time we'd seen Ramsey's 'Wingless Wonders' in action and at times they were frighteningly inept. It didn't exactly seem like a brave new world to me. In fairness to Alan Ball, as he says, much of the crowd couldn't see what the Argentines were up to off the ball. But we could see that the England midfield, with Charlton, Stiles, Peters and Ball, were limited in their approach. There was a lot of long-ball stuff, in comparison with the Argentines who, even when they were down to ten men, had a far better playing style about them and stroked it around beautifully. The crowd actually applauded the Argentines' play, even after Rattin was sent off. To be absolutely honest, most of us didn't understand why he'd been dismissed in the first place, and there was a great deal of confusion when he ambled off the pitch. We sang 'Why are we waiting?' but I distinctly remember that the only booing was due to England's over-physical, dull approach in the second half. Geoff Hurst's goal was a good goal – it had to be to beat what was a really well organised defence – but overall England's display against ten men in the second half was turgid. Apart from Alf Ramsey, perhaps, I doubt that anyone that day walked away from Wembley thinking that this team would win the World Cup."

There was some sympathy for Argentina amongst the English press. In the *News of the World*, Frank Butler considered that Kreitlein had been "too fussy, too dictatorial, and notebook happy." Danny Blanchflower claimed Argentina were "hard done by." The majority of the English press were loyal to Ramsey and the team. *The Times* headlined: "Destructive attitude of South Americans." But Brian Glanville later commented, "His own [Ramsey's] xenophobia was a kind of cloven hoof, which he could not help but show." and FIFA took a dim view of Ramsey's "animal" jibe, insisting: "Such remarks do not foster good international relations." Ramsey was subsequently fined for his comments.

Across the Atlantic, battle lines were already being drawn. In a rare moment of South American solidarity, Brazilian FA Chief João Havelange concocted an elaborate theory that the entire '66 tournament had been fixed against Brazil. He argued that in their matches seven of the nine officials were English "and they hadn't afforded Pelé sufficient protection," and that Argentina's "skill and perseverance would have overcome England had they not been reduced to ten men for more than half the match." "Duplicitous refereeing." he told the Brazilian press, and compliant FIFA officials – "England's quarter-final was switched at the last minute from Villa Park to Wembley to garner maximum home advantage" – proved that a plot was in place to further British political interests on the global stage by allowing England, West Germany and the USSR through to the semi-finals. Havelange claimed that Portugal were allowed to progress in order for England to regain a foothold in sub-Saharan Africa, the USSR to promote trade interests and West Germany, most importantly of all, were allowed through to the final so that Britain's passage into the EEC would be smoothed, allowing them to act as a counter-weight to Charles de Gaulle's France. Preposterous though the entire scenario was, Havelange's theory was widely believed in Argentina.

The day after the defeat against England the Argentine players flew back to Buenos Aires and were afforded a heroes' welcome at the airport. Rattin was treated like a national hero, wrapped in an Argentine flag and surrounded by female admirers "who kissed him ecstatically on both cheeks," according to the Reuters news agency, and the hysterical mob carried a giant plastic globe symbolising the fact that Argentina were "moral winners of the World Cup." One newspaper printed a picture of the official mascot, World Cup Willie, dressed in pirate regalia to reflect their opinion of the English.

Juan Peroto lived in Buenos Aires and went to the airport. "As a nation, it was felt we'd been cheated out of it by the English," he told me. "There was particular needle because Argentina had once been under the control of the British Empire and there was a feeling that the old colonialists were still trying to suppress us by foul means. We believed that England had hacked their way to victory. Stiles was hated because of his tendency to tackle from behind, which simply wasn't the done thing in Argentina. But Ramsey in particular came in for criticism. How dare he call us animals? was the line many took on him. It was his Little Englander approach which irked us so much. He was virtually calling us savages and lesser beings. He reminded many Argentines of the type of English industrialists who once got rich at our expense. Ramsey was a throwback to colonial times, the type of figure who'd milked our grandfathers so he could grow fat on the profits."

President Ongania told the returning team, "Your brilliant performance, your courage and your fighting spirit have earned you the joyful welcome which awaits you from the people and government of the nation." The Argentine press was apoplectic about events in England. La Razon barked, "Wembley Scandal" and Cronica opined, "The famous lion has cut its mane and lifted its mask. Footballistically speaking, it's a poor fish. Spiritually, it's still the pirate that despoiled the Caribbean and robbed us of Las Malvinas." In Buenos Aires, Juan Peroto recalls "sporadic chants of 'Las Malvinas Son Argentinos' ('The Falklands Are Argentine') and 'Muerte a los Ingleses' ('Death to the English'), and Ambassador Sir Michael Cresswell was placed under armed guard inside the British Embassy for several days. The blood feud, and the war of words, intensified.

Having managed to offend the entire continent in 1966, the Latin American press got its own back on Ramsey four years later in Mexico. Argentina may not have qualified for the 1970 World Cup but lingering resentment existed in the region anyway. Colombian journalists gleefully printed stories of captain Bobby Moore's arrest over false accusations of theft in a jeweller's shop in Bogotá shortly after the team arrived in South America. Jeff Dawson's excellent book Back Home: England at the 1970 World Cup confirms that in the immediate aftermath of the tournament, Foreign Office intervention was needed to ensure that diplomatic relations between England and Columbia weren't severed. Ramsey claimed Mexican journalists had deliberately encouraged youths to play music and honk their car horns outside the Guadalajara Hilton all night before the match against Brazil (Alan Ball recalled Ramsey "swearing and cursing, telling us all that South Americans were bloody nutters") thus depriving his team of their pre-match sleep.

The fact that England took their own food to Mexico in a bid to stop the players suffering from stomach bugs – Ramsey arranged a sponsorship deal with Findus – further infuriated the locals. One Mexican newspaper headline led, "If you are going to throw fruit at the England team, remember to wash it first."

When the food arrived on the dockside by boat, incensed Mexican officials insisted on burning the vast bulk of the produce on the dockside, much to the delight of the press, and leaving the England players to survive on fish fingers (which were classed under a different category of food-stuffs) for the bulk of their stay. "The Champions Are Dead" and "England Go Home" were just two of the headlines printed by Mexican papers after Ramsey's team lost to West Germany in Leon.

Alan Ball grimaced at the memory of the 1970 World Cup. "It wasn't Alf's cup of tea at all," he admitted. "All that heat, the noise, the colour, the dancing, stomach bugs and the pressure. It just wasn't Alf's scene. It wasn't his turf and he wasn't in control like he was in '66. When Gordon [Banks] went down with the bug before the Germany game, Alf was furious, saying, 'This would never have happened at home.' Alf just wasn't diplomatic enough to get through it all. Of course we backed him to the hilt, as he did with us, but I did used to cringe a bit when he would sweep past Latin American journalists and say nothing, or give them short shrift. Bobby Moore said to me, 'They've got to fill their newspapers with something and if Alf won't talk to them, they'll just make up stories anyway.' And so it proved."

By the time of the 1982 World Cup, some 16 years after England had beaten Argentina at Wembley, both nations were mired in economic crisis. By March, inflation in Argentina was running at 600 per cent and the unemployment rate and the number of strikes in major cities skyrocketed. Nonetheless, the military junta, now led by General Leopoldo Galtieri, pressed on with its policy of persecuting and torturing opponents, but awareness of the regime's crimes was spreading and the numbers protesting outside the Presidential Palace each week increased. Juan Peroto recalls, "There was real pressure on the government and Galtieri decided that the best course of action was to reclaim *Las Malvinas*. It was a hugely popular move and the expectation was that we would win because of our proximity to the islands and the fact that they were poorly defended by the British."

Defender Luis Galván, a squad member in 1982 explains: "We all knew that Argentina was on its knees both spiritually and economically, and it was tough for both ourselves and many of our families. To a man the squad believed that *Las Malvinas* were ours and, coupled with that, we believed we could retain our title in Spain. There was a surge of nationalism although deep down most of us realised that winning football matches and reclaiming some islands wouldn't solve our problems. Galtieri visited the training camp in February, embraced Mario [Kempes] and Diego [Maradona] and told us that by winning the World Cup again and reclaiming Las Malvinas, Argentina could be great once more. About six weeks later, our navy set sail to retake the islands."

England's entire qualification campaign for the 1982 World Cup had been fraught. A defeat away in Basle against Switzerland had led to calls from an increasingly savage press for manager Ron Greenwood to resign. "If we can't find 11 players good enough to beat the Swiss," claimed Brian Clough, "then it's time we packed our bags and went home to our memories of 1966 and all that."

After the match English fans had gone on the rampage in Basle, prompting calls from FA Chairman Bert Millichip to "bring back the birch" and confiscate the passports of those supporters who were "dressed in an offensive manner." But it was the 2–1 loss to Norway in Oslo in September 1981 which, in journalist Mike Langley's words "really brought home how far England's standing in football and as a world power had fallen. *The Observer* would later vote Norwegian TV's Bjørge Lillelien's stream of consciousness at the end of the match ("Lord Nelson! Lord Beaverbrook! Sir Winston Churchill! Sir Anthony Eden! Clement Attlee! Henry Cooper! Lady Diana! Maggie Thatcher, can you hear me? Maggie Thatcher, your boys took one hell of a beating! Your boys took one hell of a beating!") the greatest piece of sports commentary ever.

Former *Sunday People* writer Mike Langley says, "In one sense it was a piece of weird and wonderful commentary, but in another, what he was saying brought home our post-imperial decline. Lillelien was telling us to gather all our national heroes and all our delusions of grandeur and shove them in the dustbin, because as a power on the football pitch and on the world stage generally, we were finished. When the England team loses on the big stage our insecurities as a nation rise to the surface. The fans rioting abroad, to many people, highlighted the decline in standards in Britain. I remember talking to the Argentine manager Menotti who told me, 'While the rest of Europe has advanced tremendously in the past ten years, English soccer has declined.' It was unpleasant. There was an air of impending doom, but England had luck on their side. Hungary dropped points in the group and Paul Mariner's goal against them at Wembley in November 1981 put us into the Finals for the first time in 12 years."

Argentina launched a full invasion of the Falklands on 2nd April, with Galtieri claiming, "I'll destroy the last bastion of British imperialism." Days later, Thatcher dispatched the Task Force amidst concerns about whether the British Navy had sufficient firepower to win the war after budgetary cuts. Mike Langley recalled Menotti likening the Falklands conflict to "two fat, flabby old boxers who'd seen better days, but wanted one last shot at glory to help them forget they were in terminal decline."

The conflict quickly became inextricably bound up with the forthcoming World Cup. On 3rd April, *The Sun* headline boomed, "It's War" and in the same publication, John Akass wrote, "It is an intoxicating feeling. There must be at least a couple of generations who don't know what this is like."

Akass was talking specifically about war, but at a push, he could have been referring to anyone under the age of 17 who had no recollection of Alf Ramsey's team participating in the heat of the 1970 World Cup.

At a friendly match between Argentina and the USSR at the Monumental in Buenos Aires, home fans unfurled a giant banner urging the British to leave the Falklands and chanted, "He who does not jump is an Englishman."

Spurs midfielder Osvaldo Ardiles, booed throughout Tottenham's Easter games, flew back to Argentina and laid low at his family's Cordoban ranch. He would complete a loan move to Paris Saint-Germain after the tournament. Fourth Division Stockport County announced that they would abandon a strip of blue and white stripes modelled on Argentina's shirts. "It hardly seems appropriate, given the current circumstances," said their chairman.

World Cup hosts Spain abstained in a United Nations vote which saw all members, bar Panama, deem Argentina the aggressors in the conflict. The tabloids printed stories of British expats in Spain being shunned by their neighbours and outside English bars, flags were torn down and burnt. According to Sir Neil MacFarlane, Sports Minister under Thatcher, The Sun's headline "World Cup Crisis" put "unnecessary fears into the British fans that a World Cup withdrawal, in protest at Spain's abstention and amidst security fears, was imminent." Jimmy Greaves advocated a second Home Nations tournament in which all gate receipts would be handed to servicemen's families. At this juncture, Thatcher's intervention became crucial. In early June, she stated in the House of Commons her "belief that a good showing by the England team in Spain will prove an excellent fillip for the servicemen in the Falklands." Behind the scenes, MacFarlane now admits "the situation was utterly chaotic."

MacFarlane claims Thatcher wanted England, as well as Scotland and Northern Ireland, to play on because of a wish to "see the England team prove itself on the world stage," whereas Labour leader Michael Foot reckoned it was a "throwback to the days of the Roman emperors, who used wars and sports as a way of diverting the public's gaze away from difficult domestic issues." A MORI poll had suggested that with the decline of manufacturing cities and regions in the Midlands and the North of England, urban tension in major cities and increasing unemployment, Thatcher was the least popular of any post-war British Prime Minister and she would become even more unpopular if she withdrew the Home Nations from the World Cup.

For the first time, MacFarlane reveals his version of events: "Margaret Thatcher had an emergency meeting with the Queen shortly before the tournament. Both were of the opinion that the Home Nations should go to Spain. Yet both Margaret and myself were mindful that the phones and telex machines in the Foreign Office were going mad with rumour at the time about a possible withdrawal. The FA and the Foreign Office discussed the situation fully, but there was no solution to the 'doomsday scenario' of meeting Argentina in a later round. It would have been played behind closed doors, or even scrapped. We just hoped the situation never arose."

The tabloids fanned the flames. On 12th May, eight days after the *General Belgrano* was torpedoed, *The Sun* screamed "Wallop" and "Gotcha" and the *Daily Mirror* predicted, "World Cup pull-out looming." Twenty thousand copies of a government advice booklet for travelling English fans were pulped.

Bert Millichip had a turbulent relationship with Margaret Thatcher. He told me, "She didn't especially like football and I didn't much care for her politics. She was happy to meet the players. She liked Kevin Keegan, but she fretted over the reputation of the fans and the image they presented of England to the rest of Europe."

Millichip claimed they met shortly before the tournament and that Thatcher "talked about the Task Force and referred to how World War II had sealed Winston Churchill's reputation as a war leader. A political animal like Thatcher was well aware that if Britain prevailed in the Falklands, and the Home Nations did well in the World Cup, it would boost her own popularity at a time when she was struggling in the opinion polls."

When Thatcher's memoirs were released in the early 1990s, the link between the war and the World Cup wasn't explored at all, but Millichip recalled her "fixing me with one of her looks and telling me that, come what may, the Home Nations would be going to the World Cup." Brian Clough would later describe her as "football's mortal enemy" but Thatcher's forcefulness in 1982 proved decisive, even if her reasons for doing so remain clouded in doubt.

When the Argentina squad arrived in Spain they discovered the grim truth: their government had lied to them about the Falklands War. Galván recalls, "In Spain we read a different version of the news from the one we heard at home. We'd been lied to by Galtieri. It was difficult, because in our squad was Jorge Valdano, who lived in Spain. He'd warned us to expect a shock when we read the Spanish newspapers. He'd been accused of being 'un-Argentine' because he knew that actually we were losing the war and was simply telling the truth. Immediately the morale in the squad collapsed and our performances were well below what we were capable of."

The England team, with injured captain Kevin Keegan urging his team to "make the troops in the Falklands proud," arrived in Bilbao (labelled 'the Middlesbrough of Spain' because of its heavy industry) immediately settled into their surroundings and cruised through the group matches against France, Czechoslovakia and Kuwait with a 100 per cent record. The players I spoke to for this book were completely apolitical in their responses. Kenny Sansom encourges me to remember that "English players aren't interested in politics, as a rule," and recalls the stifling heat, Bryan Robson's quick goal against France and Ron Greenwood ordering his players to go out and get drunk after they made it through the group stages.

England fan Simon Anstell recalls travelling to Bilbao with "some trepidation. But because this was Basque country, and Basques were anti–Spain, the reception we received was cordial. We heard chants of '*Malvinas Son Ingleses*'

['The Falklands Are English'] and there were hybrid England/Basque flags as well. Some fans even carried the *Ikurrina*, the Basque flag. But of course, there was always an edge. After England beat France in the first game, more supporters came across from home and my main memory of many of them is the number of bulldog tattoos, the sunburn, the swigging of cheap lager, the Union Jack T-shirts, the bellies and the chants of '*Malvinas, Malvinas, Inglaterra.*' I wouldn't say that it was a raving endorsement for England or Englishmen. Many of the locals looked on with bemusement, but it was always threatening to spill over. One night a group of England fans, sunburnt to a crisp and drunk, turned up to a disco with a donkey in tow, chanting songs about the Falklands. Apparently the doorman was so dumbstruck he let them in. They could get away with this in Bilbao – but not in the rest of Spain."

In Madrid, during the second round of matches, the problems began. At the opening ceremony on 13th June the Spanish crowd had booed the English flag relentlessly. Bert Millichip had walked out in disgust. The Argentine forces' surrender the day after the opening ceremony meant that when English fans arrived in the Spanish capital a fortnight later, the atmosphere was like a powder keg.

Anstell recalls, "We'd heard that a fellow by the name of Mike Buckley had been stabbed by a baying mob of right-wing Spanish fans [the *Fuerza Nueva* – National Front] screaming '*Gibraltar, español*' and '*Muerte a los Ingleses*' ('Death to the English') and the atmosphere in the city's bars wasn't good at all, especially when the supporters who'd come from Bilbao waved Basque flags in the faces of the Spanish. There were lots of England fans chanting 'One Maggie Thatcher' and 'You'll never take the Falklands.' The chant I remember most vividly was when we annexed a Madrid bar and the chant went up 'We're on the march with Maggie's army.' There was a sense among many of the younger fans I spoke with that with the Falklands War and the World Cup coinciding, this was a chance for Britain to stand up and be great again – to prove itself."

England were eliminated after goalless draws against West Germany and Spain and during the match against the Spanish, fans complained that the police were heavy-handed with them, arrested several on the [apparently] mistaken assumption that they were inciting the crowd with chants of 'Malvinas, Malvinas.' In Madrid's Barbara de Braganza quarter, police swept in and tore down any England flags displayed on hotel balconies.

The events that summer had vastly different consequences for the two leaders. Galtieri was removed from power and democracy restored to Argentina. The Argentine army's internal investigation recommended Galtieri be stripped of all rank and face a firing squad for human-rights violations against fellow Argentines, but instead he was sentenced to 12 years in prison. "It's ironic to think that if we had succeeded at the '82 World Cup we might have bought Galtieri more time to carry on with what he was doing at home. Perhaps then it is a good thing that we performed relatively poorly," explains Galván. Thatcher, her popularity (partly) restored, remained as Prime Minister for another eight years.

In Mexico four years later, with Argentina set to meet England in the quarter-final, the Argentine players, in public at least, urged fans and the press to "forget about politics." Privately, it was a different matter. By all accounts, Maradona urged his teammates to put the English in their place. The tabloid Cronica announced, "We're coming to get you, pirates," and The Sun reported that a 500-strong 'death squad' called the Barras Bravas would turn the quarter-final into a "football Falklands." During the previous match against Paraguay, England supporters had sung, "Bring on the Argies – we want another war." Nearly 8,000 riot police were on standby. Simon Anstell recalls: "We were funnelled through an X-ray machine on the way in. There were police everywhere. In the event, there was no trouble."

On the pitch, though, the 'Hand of God' fuelled the fires of enmity between the two nations. Kenny Sansom recalls,

"Maradona's second goal was probably the best goal any of us had ever seen, but the first goal was blatant cheating. Of course, if it had been an England player we wouldn't have gone up to the referee and said 'Don't allow it,' but we were cheated out of it by Argentina. You could tell by the way he ran, with his half glance at the referee to see if he'd allowed it, that he knew what he'd done. I later heard that he encouraged his teammates to come and hug him so the whole thing didn't look so dodgy. I'm not saying we'd have won the game if the goal had been disallowed, but I felt strongly we'd been burgled. The game had been stolen away from us. We'd been deceived." Maradona later confirmed, "I think I preferred the one with my hand . . . it was a bit like stealing the wallet of the English."

Argentina striker Jorge Valdano later referred to the goal as a form of *viveza* ('tricking'). "*Viveza* is deeply rooted in the average Argentine, and when you get away with it you celebrate: you are the smartest to others. In other countries it is regarded as a form of deception, crime. In Argentina, it is celebrated."

Luis Galván, who'd retired by the '86 World Cup, explains: "For many in Argentina there was a huge feeling of satisfaction that we'd pick-pocketed the English. It was tit-for-tat. They'd arranged our defeat in '66 at Wembley and stolen *Las Malvinas*. We'd returned the compliment."

Alan Ball recalls meeting Alf Ramsey at a function in London some weeks after England's defeat against Argentina in 1986: "They haven't changed, have they Alan?" he was ranting. "That was the worst example of cheating I've ever seen on a football pitch. Bloody Argentina."

Former Argentina midfielder Diego Simeone later admitted to simulating injury to get David Beckham sent off during their 1998 World Cup second-round clash, after the England midfielder flicked a boot out against his leg after Simeone had clattered into Beckham's back. If this incident had occurred at any point during the previous 30 years, Simeone's play-acting would doubtless have been held up as an example of South American feral cunning. But instead, the English press turned on Beckham himself and despite his two-page apology in the Mirror (whose headline after the match had been "10 Heroic Lions, One Stupid Boy"), he remained, in the press's eyes, the villain, not Simeone. It wasn't the only case of role reversal played out in the media.

In Argentina La Nacion spoke in almost reverential tones of the "great swipes made by the wounded lion of England." referring to England's brave performance before losing in the inevitable penalty shoot-out, and other newspapers suggested Beckham's sending off had been harsh. As David Downing points out in England v Argentina: World Cups and Other Small Wars, "In earlier years, Beckham's petulant flick would have been seen as something intrinsically foreign, the sort of thing one might expect from a Latin, but never from an Englishman." Jimmy Greaves's assessment in The Sun was that, "with the huge influx of continentals into our game, we're now so used to players doing what Simeone did, that it no longer shocks us."

In 2005, when the two met in an international friendly, The Times reported, "by the unpleasant standards of previous confrontations, the skirmish between England and Argentina edged towards the saccharine, although the concept is deeply relative. The latest encounter featured punches on the terraces, songs about the Falkland Islands, jibes regarding players' sexuality and general churlishness that, believe it or not, represents a significant thaw in diplomatic relations."

But with oil-drilling licences now up for tender in the South Atlantic, and billions of dollars at stake, not to mention the combustible Diego Maradona in charge of Argentina, the rivalry between the two nations still has the potential to spill over, particularly with the World Cup on the horizon.

10

ALL THAT GLITTERS

In September 1970, two months after steering his Brazil side to the summit of world football, coach Mario Zagallo flew to London and saw Arsenal draw with Chelsea in a violent, corrosive encounter at Stamford Bridge. When a journalist asked him what he made of it all, Zagallo responded, "It's no wonder that England doesn't produce any Pelés." A stroll down Ipanema or Copacabana beaches in Rio, on the other hand, proves exactly why Brazil has won more World Cups than any other nation. For hundreds of yards, with the Atlantic waves lapping over the white sand and the players' feet, teenage boys and girls gather in groups of four and five at the water's edge and play a seriously advanced version of 'head tennis'. With heels, shoulders, knees and heads, they flick the ball effortlessly to one another. Only very rarely does it fall to earth or drop into the ocean. From a distance, the view is no less remarkable, as dozens of footballs bob up and down rhythmically in a clear blue sky.

On other parts of the beaches, high-speed five-a-side matches, with the emphasis on dribbling, back-heeling and one-touch passing, are in full swing. Gesticulating grandly towards the impromptu kickabouts, the azure blue sea, the beach and the sun-worshipping, well-heeled Ipanema women, former left-winger Paulo César Lima aka 'Caju', the anti-hero and 12th man of the Brazil team of 1970, grins at me and says, "This, my friend, is Brrrraaaaaazzzzzzziiiiiilllllll!"

In the years after Brazil won the World Cup, European camera crews, anxious to beam a nugget of Rio glamour back home, would invariably seek out this Ipanema icon, who seemed to have taken up permanent residence on the white sands with his friend Jairzinho. It was the beach football-loving Caju, famed for frolicking in the surf in his swimsuit with an assortment of beach lovelies, and for his imported garish Italian designer suits, who came to encapsulate the romantic ideal that all Brazilian footballers of that era lived their lives on the sand and in the sea. In the early '70s, Caju and Jairzinho would cruise along the roads next to the beaches in the former's custom-made orange Fiat Spider, lapping up the attention from Rio's beachgoers.

In Brazil, the exploits of the class of 1970 aren't mentioned as frequently as outsiders might assume. Most of the people I met in Rio were keener to discuss the shattering defeat to Uruguay in 1950, corruption in football, or the decline of the domestic game. In *Futebol: A Brazilian Way of Life*, Alex Bellos pointed out that there is only one book that has been devoted to the famous team of 1970 – Garry Jenkins's *The Beautiful Team: In Search of Pelé and the 1970 Brazilians* – and that it has never been translated into Portuguese. Remarkably, eight years after its publication, the situation is unchanged, although several books have investigated the connection between football and politics at the time. A former teacher I am introduced to in Brazil even claims that the victory in 1970 "was an affront to freedom and democracy," because of the heavy involvement of the ruling military junta, led by General Medici.

The vision of Brazil's golden shirts, shining against an electric-green playing surface, pouring into viewers' living new rooms brought football's vibrant new Technicolor age to life around the world. But there is a dark underbelly to Brazil's success in 1970, and with the exception of Tostão, who was vehemently opposed to the government of that era, few have ever spoken about it. In his autobiography,

Pelé mentions briefly that he met the increasingly autocratic General Medici at the time of the World Cup, but doesn't provide detail on his involvement with the team before, during and after their victory. At the same time that Brazil were lifting the trophy in Mexico, the President was enacting laws imposing censorship on the national press and ruthlessly crushing urban guerrillas and leftist extremists who dared to question his authority. "It's true that things went on in Brazil which didn't reflect well on the country," shrugs Caju. But without Medici's involvement, it is questionable whether we would ever have won the World Cup at all."

By the late 1960s, the military junta which came to power shortly after Brazil's qualification for the 1970 World Cup was desperate for international recognition, as it sought to accelerate the country's modernisation programme. A fanatical Flamengo fan who was well aware of the global publicity which a World Cup victory would bring, Medici poured millions of dollars into ensuring that the Brazil squad was the best prepared of any of the finalists. The *Jornal do Brazil* would later exult, "Brazil's victory with the ball compares with the conquest of the moon by the Americans."

A number of football writers have also drawn links between Neil Armstrong's first step on the moon and Carlos Alberto's late strike against Italy in the final; both were iconic moments in the telecultural age's formative era and the moon landing and Brazil's victory were arguably the ultimate scientific and sporting achievements of the 20th century. The sky seemed to be the limit, but in real terms, the space race of the 1960s, into which both the USA and the USSR poured unfathomably large resources, provided an unexpected spin-off benefit for Brazil.

In the build-up to the World Cup Captain Claudio Coutinho, a retired army captain and military physical-training expert, was despatched to NASA in Florida, to study the training programmes which the Apollo astronauts had been put through. Coutinho returned with a fitness regime based on the Americans' Cooper Test, in which a player's physical condition could be monitored and measured with extreme accuracy. Even as far back as 1958 the Brazilian football federation [CBD] President João Havelange and his Vice President Paulo Machado de Carvalho had drawn up a 40-day training plan which involved doctors, dieticians, neurologists, cardiologists and ophthalmic surgeons which became known as *concentracao*. It threw up some fascinating results. Measured for 'intelligence and psychological balance,' Pelé and Garrincha, the eventual stars of the tournament, had originally been dubbed "too infantile" to participate. Captain Coutinho's 1970 programme, technically an extension of *concentracao*, appeared to be from another planet.

Caju recalls, "We all went to Mexico with custom-made boots, and our shirts were made specifically to keep us cooler in the heat. Our shirts previously had old-style green collars, but they got drenched in sweat, so we changed to shirts with round necks. Our diet was closely controlled and we received information about vitamins and proteins which was way above anything which came for years afterwards. We were seriously physically fit. If your performance levels dropped, you were taken to one side. The players began to develop an almost telepathic understanding because we were practising all the time. The senior players, specifically Pelé, Gerson, and Carlos Alberto, had a great deal of sway in the camp. They told the coaching staff that in 1966 they felt that the European sides had embarrassed them with their physical fitness and that, frankly, we weren't there for a holiday in 1970. That message was repeated again and again. When I played in Europe, people often said that we got straight off the beach to play, because we appeared so relaxed and in control on the pitch. They didn't have a clue."

The intensity of Brazil's training camp, with its security guards, spotlights and guard dogs, was too much to bear for some of the younger stars, and cost them their shot at immortality. "It was like a military operation. We were shut away at Guanajuanto from May onwards, and it was hard," recalls Caju. "Two weeks before we flew to Mexico our sleep patterns were changed to accommodate what was coming.

Even our food was prepared with Mexican oils and vegetables. Guys like myself, Marco Antonio [defender] and Edu [winger] were young. Marco Antonio eventually lost his place in defence to Clodoaldo. One night Marco Antonio, Edu and I decided to go out but we were caught at the back gate by a security guard and he told Admiral Jeronimo Batsos, a real disciplinarian at the camp whom Medici insisted join the group, and who us kids feared. Marco Antonio was reprimanded for what he did and ended up getting one run-out against Peru. Edu never played at all after the qualifying rounds."

President Medici's direct intervention finally saw Pelé's place in the squad confirmed, after Brazil's pre-tournament coach João Saldanha questioned his general fitness and the extent of his short-sightedness. Caju recalls, "For a while the talk was that Pelé might not make the final squad at all. Such a prospect was unthinkable, but I believe that if Saldanha had remained in charge, and Medici hadn't got involved, Pelé might possibly have missed out." Medici also oversaw the elevation to the 1970 squad of arguably Brazil's most flamboyant ever striker, Dadá Maravilha ('the Wonder'). An unused substitute in 1970 Dadá Maravilha, at first glance, appears to be a peripheral figure in Brazilian international football history. But General Medici's admiration for the striker altered the course of Brazil's fortunes.

In his pomp, Dadá Maravilha added a raft of alternative suffixes to his preferred forename, including Peito-de-Aço ('Steel Chest'), Jacaré ('Alligator') and Beija-Flor ('Hummingbird'). Ever the master of self-publicity he used three straplines. "Only three things hang in the air: a hummingbird, a helicopter and Dadá Maravilha." More infamously, there was, "Better than me, there is only Pelé; the rest don't come close" and, "I believe in God, but I trust in Dadá." Originally a construction worker who played amateur football, he first came to the attention of the national press when, as a youngster with Atlético Mineiro his coach informed the team, which was trailing by three goals at half-time, "Now our situation is really problematic." The cocky striker piped up: "If the situation is problematic, I have the 'solutionatic'. Goals." My translator in Rio assured me that in Portuguese the phrase sounds equally as daft, but in the second half he scored four times and the legend of Dadá Maravilha, who still has a tendency to speak about himself in the third person, was born.

These days, the burly former striker describes himself as "a free spirit with several business and media interests" and his beaming smile and relaxed nature suggests that he continues to live life to the full. "I always believed that football was there to be enjoyed. Much of what I said was tongue in cheek and I'd say these outrageous things to brighten the lives of the fans. But on the pitch I was a serious competitor and I scored plenty of goals."

As the 1970 World Cup approached, media pundits lobbied for Dadá's inclusion in the squad and, with his blinding speed, prolific strike rate and high-profile persona, General Medici pulled a few strings behind the scenes and arranged his transfer from Mineiro to his own team, Flamengo. At a time when Medici was, via media outlets, spinning one-liners to the nation – in the year before the 1970 World Cup, he ensured that the phrase "*Ninguem segura mais este pais*" ("Nothing can stop this nation now") was prominent on billboards and TV stations across Brazil – he spotted a kindred spirit in the larger-than-life, self-confident Dadá Maravilha, who by now had even begun to name his goals. Modest as ever, Dadá explains: "He wanted Brazil as a nation and as a football team to show its self-confidence, its playfulness, its skill, its art and its beauty. I think he saw a great deal of that in me." In late 1969 Dadá had complained to the press about full backs holding onto his shirt to prevent him from scoring and a week later appeared on the playing field with an old and discoloured shirt for a game. When a TV reporter asked him why his top was so ragged-looking, the response was, "I asked my mother to wash it ten times, and now if someone holds my shirt, it will tear apart and I will score." Medici then took things several steps further and started to lobby coach João Saldanha (nicknamed João sem Medo, 'Fearless Joe') to include his pet player in the full national squad.

A former TV commentator and journalist, Saldanha had been a surprise appointment as national coach in the late 1960s. With his haggard features and 50-a-day nicotine habit he quickly gained a reputation as a hothead. He'd demanded complete freedom over team selection but when Medici was selected as leader of the right-wing junta in October 1969 an immovable force met an immovable object. Using his propaganda body AERP, Medici's face became instantly recognizable around Brazil. Second only to Pelé's, in fact. Medici quickly clashed with the outspoken Saldanha, a communist back in his youth. After a visit to Europe, Saldanha decided that he needed to bulk up his defence in order to counter "the brutal play and lenient referees" which his team would encounter in Mexico and drafted into the squad the tough-tackling Marco Antonio and Baldocchi. Caju recalls, "Medici was rumoured to disapprove of Saldanha's drafting in of big defenders. He wanted the image of Brazil's players to be one of beauty, not brute force." Saldanha also refused to allow the players to attend a dinner arranged by Medici at the Presidential Palace as it would have altered the training schedule.

Worse than that, it seems, he didn't rate Dadá Maravilha. "I don't choose the President's ministry and he can't choose my front line," replied Saldanha after a journalist reminded him that the striker was the President's favourite. Caju recalls, "Saldanha was a great coach, and a deep thinker, but he was always blowing his top. If he wasn't threatening to punch journalists who criticised his tactics he was arguing with other managers." A week after this quote, Saldanha was dismissed, on account of his "fragile mental state." Nothing more was said about Pelé's eyes or fitness and Dadá Maravilha, under the more malleable new coach Mario Zagallo, was in the squad.

Forty years later, a half-embarrassed Dadá shrugs and grins at the memory of what happened. "I was a pawn in the whole thing. The President wanted me in; Saldanha didn't and he was sacked and replaced by another guy. Such is life. I was just a footballer and what the military wanted at that time, they got. And Zagallo made his point too. Having accommodated me he then chose not to play me. It was a large fuss about nothing, in hindsight."

Of the Brazil squad from that era, it's Caju who is considered the most outspoken, the most edgy, and in his idiosyncratic way, the most influential. My fixer Carlos and I met him in one of the bars dotted along Ipanema promenade. An hour late, he informs us that this is positively prompt for a "*Carioca* who prefers to sleep during the day." I'd been warned that he could be obstinate and elusive and that he hates the English. In 1997, he was the subject of a documentary directed by Joao Moreira Salles, in the third part of the *Futebol* television series. Salles and his team tracked Caju for a week in an attempt to discover what an ex-footballer does with his time. Scraping a living off the rent from the five properties he owns in Rio, he regularly gave the crew the slip. His hectic nightlife made him a hard man to pin down. Most of his week was taken up by looking at sports cars which he could no longer afford, visiting his lawyer, blagging a game of football here and there in the Lagoa area (I got the impression that little has changed) and attempting to convince FIFA to allow him to participate in the forthcoming World Cup draw for France '98.

These days, his financial situation is tricky to gauge, although he has popped up recently on Brazilian chat shows sporting a long white goatie beard. At first, Caju fixes me with the sort of hawkish, suspicious stare once reserved for opposition defenders, but after enjoying some coconut milk, he is bonhomie personified, and constantly reminds me that Rio beaches are the best in the world. I don't need too much convincing. He admits he was fortunate after his late-night indiscretion at the training camp: "I'd played under Mario Zagallo before in club football and he knew what I could bring to the team. I knew I was never an automatic choice though and that's how things turned out. I know that I could have effectively been cold-shouldered, like Edu or Marco Antonio."

Firstly, he carries out his obligatory hatchet job on Alf Ramsey's England. "Ramsey constantly appeared to be eating a lime or a lemon all the time. Then there were the England players, in those pristine white kits, looking us up and down like we were shit. It motivated me, it made me think, 'Fuck you.'" The watching millions may remember Bobby Moore and Pelé's comradely embrace at the end of the match, Banks's heroics in goal from Pelé, or Jairzinho's winner, but not Caju. He's still hung up about the sweatband issue. "Out came England," he sneered, "wearing one white sweatband each. It was bullshit. Who did they think they were?" If I still wasn't aware of Caju's contempt for the England team and their solitary sweatband fetish he oscillates his left arm and, using the fingers from his right hand to circle his wrist, says, "Bull . . . shit," very slowly in English. He lightens up somewhat. "Both sides played very well. Bobby Moore was outstanding against Jairzinho, and [Francis] Lee put his foot in. I was scared when Astle came on because our defence could be fragile against big, physical strikers. England slowed down and played a continental game, due to the heat. Some of their guys with fair skins were frying out there. We deliberately came out late for the second half and left them baking under the sun for ten minutes. It was above 100 degrees out there but that was down to FIFA pandering to the demands of European TV and playing games at noon."

Against Romania in their final group game, Caju sparkled and he, along with Tostão and Pelé, dominated the tempo of the match for long periods. Late on he hit the crossbar with a rasping drive and he set up Jairzinho's goal. "I started to feel like a first-teamer," he recalls.

But with Gerson fit once more for the knockout stages, Caju once again became Brazil's 12th man. He was substitute against Peru in the quarter-final and, with bad memories of the *Maracanazo* still haunting several of his teammates – "Their fathers had told them stories of the loss in 1950 since they were babies," explains Caju – Brazil laboured against Uruguay in their semi-final. With the scores tied up at 1–1 he prepared to come on as a late substitute when the unthinkable happened. "Clodoaldo, who usually fainted whenever he got near goal, scored. We won the game. My chance was gone."

He did at least play a cameo role in the final, when he snatched the match ball out of Italian player Domenghini's hands after the final whistle. The ball was intended for a local church but eventually ended up in the hands of a Rio businessman whom Caju "sort of" knows.

Caju laughs uproariously at the memory of Dadá Maravilha. "He was a great goalscorer," he recalls. "But the entire system would have had to have been changed to fit him in. He was only interested in scoring goals. You needed more against sophisticated, brick-wall defences. He was too much of a risk." In fact he did have a small, but vital, role to play after the final. When Brazil's victorious players completed their lap of honour at the end of the match, the lid of the Jules Rimet trophy fell onto the turf. A Mexican boy scooped it up and made off with it. Quick as a flash Dadá Maravilha pursued him into the crowd and wrested it back from him.

Ironically, when Dadá Maravilha's move to Flamengo failed to work out, President Medici engineered Caju's move to the club to support the flamboyant striker. Caju's spell there was more successful than Dadá's.

Although Dadá made only the occasional national team appearance, he continued to prosper in club football where he scored goals at an alarming rate and, according to legend, masturbated before games in order to "feel light like the wind." After he retired he announced that he was "poised to become coach of the millennium" when he took over the reins at Nacional of Amazon and pioneered the revolutionary "convex floating midfield trio." Such tactics were lost on the team, and pretty much everyone else, and he was fired after two months.

At around the same time, he claimed to have seen UFOs and his marriage and finances collapsed. After his last, bizarre public utterance, "My sex power has increased, I have no doubts; seeing a UFO is an aphrodisiac," he disappeared for almost a decade before returning to eke out a living as an outspoken pundit.

Both players recall partying to the full upon Brazil's return home in 1970. Yet the celebrations weren't to everyone's taste. In the build up to the World Cup, President Medici had ordered the execution of Marxist guerrillas Carlos Marighela and Carlos Lamarca. The designer of Brazil's iconic kit back in the 1950s Aldyr Schlee, by then a university professor, also suffered regular harassment from the military regime. The persecution of those who opposed him was hardly a national secret. The victory provided Medici with the perfect media opportunity. According to popular legend, he draped himself in a national flag and ran out to play football in the square outside his palace after the final whistle went in Mexico City. After throwing open the doors of his Presidential Palace for the first time since the take over, he told the nation on TV, "I identify the success of our national team with intelligence and bravery, perseverance and serenity in our technical ability, in physical preparation, and moral being." The team was flown directly from Mexico City to capital Brasilia for the victory procession through the streets, lined with an estimated 500,000 people.

One astonished observer was David Voares, who had come under investigation from the military during the late 1960s. An avowed communist, his staunch opposition to Medici's government saw him removed from his teaching job on the outskirts of Brasilia and incarcerated for several months. Voares still speaks of some of his friends who were murdered by the Medici regime. He remained a passionate football fan and supported the team in Mexico, despite the hardships at home. What happened next horrified him. "Like many others, I went to the capital to welcome the team back, but I couldn't believe what I saw. They were riding high on giant red *bombeiros* (fire engines), flanked by tanks and troop carriers. I know that people needed to see them, but soldiers lined the route, with their guns pointing at the crowds. 'Is this a celebration of football or a show of military power?' I shouted to my friend. I wasn't the only one to be shocked by the sheer number of troops there. It was a statement of intent by Medici and I thought it sullied the achievements of the team. When kids tried to shake the hands of the players the troops cocked guns at them and told them to stay back. In the weeks that followed there was a radio jingle which you heard all the time, *Pa Fente Brasil* ('Forward Brazil'). People forgot that it was originally a football chant for the national team now the government had adopted it. Pelé's face was everywhere alongside Medici's. The team's triumph became Medici's triumph, and that was wrong. There are many in Brazil who, whenever they think of the 1970 triumph, automatically think of Medici's regime. To the outside world it was the greatest World Cup ever, and to some extent they are right. But I don't think of Pelé when people mention 1970, I think of Medici."

Playmaker Tostão told Garry Jenkins that he regrets not boycotting the reception with the President, as "I was very angry with the situation at home." After retiring from the national team shortly afterwards he had to endure listening to the Government inspired "*Marcha do Tostão*" which Medici used to capitalise on the public's pride in the triumph.

Alongside Pelé, Caju became arguably Brazil's most high-profile black player after 1970, even though his outspoken nature, reluctance to follow Zagallo's instructions and chase back ("I liked a more free role") and tendency to get into fights both on and off the pitch saw him drop in and out of the national team. It was his social life which made him internationally famous. At Ipanema he socialised with stars from the world of Brazilian TV and cinema and broke down racial barriers with a string of blonde girlfriends. When he moved to Marseilles for a brief spell he partied with French music impresario Eddie Barclay and other members of the Nice jet set. After he returned to Rio he dabbled in the fashion industry and had numerous business interests. His finances were built on shifting, sinking sands. "I got divorced and I only earned real money when I signed for Marseilles," he claims.

These days his teammate from 1970, Marco Antonio, also seems to be a permanent fixture on the masters circuit around Rio, where the post-match socialising is as important as the match itself. Marco Antonio eventually carved out a decent enough career for himself but mention his and Caju's name around Rio and people tend to grin ruefully, in much the same way English fans of a certain vintage shrug when Stan Bowles or Alan Hudson's names crop up in conversation. Caju claims to be ". . . cool about what people say. I'm in good company. Guys like Eder in 1982 and Josimar in 1986 played one tournament only, shone, and burnt out. Some great players like Weah and Giggs never played in one. I was at the party twice. I'm proud of what I achieved."

Having missed out on glory in 1970 salvation, such as it was, arrived four years later, when Zagallo handed him a starting place for every one of Brazil's matches at the World Cup in Germany. With retirements and injuries, though, things weren't quite the same. Caju recalls, "There had been some disquiet about all the politics in Brazil. Tostão's early retirement had partly been down to what was going on in Brazil. We found it hard in Europe and ran into a Dutch team who were at the top of their game." Brazil wore unfamiliar blue in their crunch games against Argentina (Caju helped set up both goals for Rivellino and Jairzinho in a 2–1 win over the old enemy) and their 2–0 loss to the Netherlands, which eliminated them. Defender Luís Pereira's late psychotic lunge at Neeskens, which saw him sent off, was a gesture as far removed as one could get from the glory of 1970. Rumour also had it that General Medici was none too impressed by Caju's and Jairzinho's afro hairstyles.

In a sense, the fortunes of the national team reflected those of the nation. In the immediate aftermath of 1970, economic growth rates went up and Brazil began to export more manufactured goods. By 1973 the oil crisis had destroyed the economic miracle, the Jules Rimet trophy (which Brazil kept after their third World Cup success) had been stolen from a shop where it was on display – it was never seen again – the squad had disintegrated and Medici had become a desperate man.

After the World Cup triumph, Medici spent much of his time trying (and for the most part failing) to make his mark in world politics. Official documents released in 2008 revealed that, along with Richard Nixon, he'd plotted to overthrow Cuba's communist regime led by Fidel Castro. The plot failed. In 1973 he backed Nixon and the CIA in overthrowing Chile's democratically elected Marxist President Salvador Allende. His replacement, the right-wing, autocratic General Augusto Pinochet, was from precisely the same mould as Brazil's President.

Medici spent the months leading up to the 1974 World Cup trying to persuade Pelé to rejoin the national squad; 40 million TV viewers saw Elza Soares lead the singing of *Come Back Pelé* and CBD President João Havelange wrote a grovelling letter to the player encouraging him to "remember [his] devotion, as a citizen and three times World Champion, to the inner yearnings that beat in the heart of Brazil." Pelé later claimed in his autobiography to have turned down Medici personally.

A month after Brazil failed to retain their crown in Germany, Medici handed over the presidential reins to Ernesto Geisel, who immediately set about establishing *détente* with the Chinese, and (gradually) democratising the country. David Voarez recalls: "The football team got worse, but life in Brazil got better. I think that's a reasonable price to pay. Others disagree."

In 1970, *Jornal do Brazil* suggested the national team's triumph would "create a blueprint for others to follow." In some ways it did, but not quite in the way most Brazilians had hoped. The conditions in Mexico were unique and the extreme heat, which reduced some games to virtual walking pace, played right into the Brazilians' hands. The Netherlands' Total

Footballers took over Brazil's mantle four years later to a degree, but they were a slightly different breed. Caju explains: "Physically, they were far more robust than us. They knew how to play the system. In 1978 they even roughed up Argentina on their own patch in the early stages of the final! But remember, they didn't actually win it."

The 1970 World Cup was a false dawn; the end of any lingering innocence and the beginning of a brash, exploitative new era. Over the next decade a wave of military coups across the region and elsewhere would give unscrupulous generals the chance to exploit football for their own ends. Chile's Pinochet used the national stadium in Santiago to murder around 3,000 political opponents and Bolivia's General Garcia Meza appointed himself patron of the country's leading club. The Duvaliers saw the benefits of a prosperous national team in impoverished Haiti, and Mobutu likewise in Zaire. Most infamously, Mario Kempes's face was used to the full by the Argentine junta in '78, much like Pelé's had been eight years before by Medici in Brazil. The class of 1970 are still referred to as 'the Beautiful Team.' The motives of those despots who followed Medici's example and exploited their national teams in the years that followed were far less appealing.

11

DAS DEUTSCHE DUELL

"Some of the team reckoned they would return home as heroes after we defeated West Germany 1–0 in 1974 in the first group stage," recalls former German Democratic Republic (GDR) goalkeeper Wolfgang Blockwitz, "but the reaction at home was mixed. Many East Germans were actually hostile to our victory, or plain indifferent. In my local area, some party members tried to use our victory for political gain." Nothing is ever straightforward when it comes to penetrating the tangled web of intrigue which surrounds the bizarre history of East German football and the 1974 World Cup clash between the two Germanys has spawned a myriad of myths. Although both sides progressed to the second round, and West Germany eventually won the World Cup, the game soon became referred to as 'Football's Cold War'; in Germany it simply became known as 'Das Deutsche Duell.'

One of the most enduring rumours surrounding the match is that prior to the game in Hamburg, the East German team underwent rigorous political and ethical training at their camp whilst the West Germans, captained by Franz Beckenbauer, were so relaxed they were almost comatose. In fact it was Beckenbauer's men who were holed up in their rural training camp under tight security, in response to the violence at the 1972 Munich Olympics and increasing Red Army activism. As helicopter gunships whirred overhead the camaraderie within Helmut Schön's squad deteriorated rapidly. Former defender Berti Vogts recalls, "Many of the team would willingly have packed the whole thing in and gone home, such was the unmitigated pressure on us. We slept three to a room, there were policemen everywhere, and there was one telephone per corridor. It was hardly luxurious or glamorous. It was more like a boot camp."

At the same time, GDR coach Georg Buschner urged his men "to forget the insane babble about the match and concentrate on the football." It was difficult for his players to do that, especially with a spot of (obligatory) Stasi attention and tempting endorsements pushed their way, but ultimately the GDR players were a good deal more relaxed than their opponents prior to the game. Matches between the neighbours had thrown up unexpected results in the past but the circumstances surrounding Jurgen Sparwasser's winner for the underdogs in '74 – then and now – serves to illustrate how football both united and divided East Germans as the Cold War rumbled on.

A dozen yards beyond Berlin's Checkpoint Charlie Museum – photographs on the outside walls show stills of John F Kennedy's "Ich bin ein Berliner" speech at the Brandenburg Gate in 1961 and Ronald Reagan's plea to Mikhail Gorbachev to "tear down this wall" in 1986 – lie a raft of gift shops which pay bizarre homage to the 41-year history of East Germany. For a few euros visitors can indulge themselves in a spot of Ostalgia (nostalgia for East German life) and get their hands on some themed merchandise, including navy blue GDR tracksuits and models of Trabants, the bone-juddering two-door car with a fibreglass body and a 600cc engine which was immortalised by U2's *Achtung Baby* album cover in 1991. There are even DVD copies of *Goodbye Lenin*, cinema's most famous nod towards Ostalgia, in which the mother emerging from her coma yearns for East German pickles and Communist-controlled TV.

East Germany is, in some ways, cool again. At least the more kitsch and palatable side is. But the Ostalgia ends when it comes to football, and apart from the tracksuits there isn't so much as a trace of the GDR's fleeting moment of World Cup fame. It seems bizarre, given that the GDR never qualified for a major tournament again, that more isn't made of events in Hamburg in 1974.

Under coach Georg Buschner the East Germans had defeated Cruyff's Holland, Beckenbauer's West Germany and Platini's France in friendly matches. Indeed, they were nicknamed the 'World Champions of Friendlies.' But it was never quite enough. In 1964, they had just missed out on World Cup qualification after losing to Hungary (a last minute GDR winner was suspiciously ruled out and the referee subsequently banned by FIFA) and they were pipped at the post three times for European Championship qualification. In Tor!:The Story of German Football, Ulrich Hesse Lichtenberger comments, "In short, whenever there was a qualification competition, you could bet the GDR would end up one point short."

Interviewing East German stars from 1974 comes with a stern warning: "Steer clear of questions on politics and the Stasi. Stick to the football." It's tricky not to stray. Even the blandest of enquiries scares off several members of the team. "It's over with – there's no point in revisiting the past," and "I was never interested in the adulation of the crowd. I was never a celebrity; there's nothing else to talk about here," are two of the more negative responses. A couple of members of the '74 side are more accommodating and are candid about the circumstances surrounding the clash with West Germany and the complex legacy which has resulted.

The softly spoken and thoughtful Wolfgang Blockwitz was the most willing to discuss how East Germany's moment in the sun is tied in with its cultural and historical legacy. "Most people tend to look for historical absolutes," he explained. "People seem to think you will find two kinds of responses; either loyal East Germans who were delighted that we won because they thought it was a victory for communism over capitalism, or countrymen who despised us because they hated all we stood for and didn't want anything to do with a divided Germany. Well, that's very simplistic. Most of us in the squad had our own views on the politics but we didn't discuss it because it wasn't really the done thing in Eastern Germany in those days. We wanted to win because we respected our coach and because we were the underdogs. It had nothing to do with politics, and it wasn't as if we hated the West Germans. Some people also assume that it was the first time both Germanys had met competitively. It may have been the first official clash, but we'd met in Olympic matches previously."

Strictly speaking, the 1974 match was the sixth encounter between the two sides, and the previous contests had been laced with a fierce sense of Cold War intensity. The most infamous clashes took place in the summer of 1959 in a double-header which became known as the Geisterspiele (ghost matches), due to the lack of spectators at the games. For the 1960 Rome Olympics, the GDR had proposed a two-legged qualifier between West and East, with the winners going on to represent Germany at the Games. In what GDR coach Heinz Krugel described as "a disgrace to football and an insult to the sportsmen on both sides," it was decided that the qualifiers would be held behind closed doors. The first leg took place in East Berlin's gigantic Walter Ubricht Stadion in front of 40 armed policemen and a few journalists and underdogs West Germany surprisingly won 2–0. Anecdotes surrounding the match are sparse but revealing. GDR midfielder Roland Ducke described the atmosphere as "horrendous – we weren't allowed to speak to our opponents" and West Germany's Matthias Mauritz claimed he was called "a Nazi and a fascist" by his opponents.

A week later the second leg was even more strained. Journalists, informed the clash would take place in "the Duisburg area," were only driven to the Rheinstadion in Düsseldorf shortly before the kick-off and there weren't even any ball boys present. West German TV commentator Gunter Wolf-bauer was told by his bosses to refer to teams by the names of their respective football associations – DFB and DFV, as the Federal Republic didn't recognise the East German state. Wolfbauer was told the commentary would be cut if he dared to utter "GDR," as the West Germans recorded a 4–1 aggregate win.

In 1963, over 50,000 witnessed the GDR thrash the West 5–1 on aggregate and at the 1972 Olympics in Munich the East Germans once again beat their Western counterparts, this time 3–2 in front of 80,000 at the Olympiastadion, with a late goal from Eberhard Vogel on their way to claiming a bronze medal. Instead of acknowledging the strengths of the GDR side, which would claim Olympic gold in 1976 in Montreal, huge swathes of the West German football fraternity, including former coach Sepp Herberger, claimed the matches counted for little as his amateur sides – plucked mainly from the lower leagues – had effectively been playing professionals (officially labelled 'state amateurs') who'd abused their status.

The Hamburg-based *Abendblatt* newspaper ran headlines about what might happen if the two nations' full inter-national sides should ever meet and whispers were already circulating about the alleged misuse of drugs by athletes behind the Iron Curtain. East Germany coach Georg Buschner, granted full access to Western media reports, seized on an ideal opportunity to cajole his side as the 1974 World Cup drew closer. "Buscher was an outstanding moti-vator," recalls Blockwitz. "He would feed us Western stories about the drug smears, and the assumptions that we were Eastern bloc automatons. He fed those stories from the Olympic matches to us as well. 'Can you believe what those journalists are writing about you?' he'd ask. When we learnt that we were to be in West Germany's group, he smiled at us – this was rare – and said, 'Now we'll see what happens.'"

From the outset, the chances of speaking to Buschner, long since retired and living near Jena, appeared remote.

Notoriously suspicious of journalists, his mantra had always been, "These days, only one per cent of what is said or written on football is about the game. The other 99 per cent isn't even worth talking about." In 2002, Buschner was still active at a grassroots level in Jena, a town in former East Germany, and, after I nudged the local soccer school for a response, they finally produced his telephone number, evidently with Buschner's permision. I left the initial contact to Rob, my translator, who confirmed that Buschner was willing to meet us at his house. "Tell your friend not to get above himself," Rob was warned, "and as soon as I feel he's pushing things too far, I shall tell him to leave. You'll both have one hour with me."

Given Buschner's record as a fearsome disciplinarian, I never doubted that he'd carry out his threat if he saw fit. "Don't ask him about long hair, flares or Mercedes," warns former midfielder Martin Hoffmann with a chuckle, "or you will be out of his front door quickly." Wisely or unwisely, I decided to avoid sticking to Herr Hoffman's advice. After arriving at Buschner's neat house in a suburb and knocking on the door several times, Rob and I wait outside for several minutes before a slightly flustered and cranky former GDR boss opens the door. "Apologies, I've been asleep," he explained. A stickler for punctuality and self-discipline, Buschner was, for a few minutes at least, on the back foot and therefore possibly more accommodating than normal. With his grey hair swept back, Buschner's legendary piercing gaze was in evidence. "It's mind games, he's seeing if you're strong enough to hold his look," I was later told. He made for fascinating, if edgy company, who delivered his answers in a brisk and clear fashion.

"What ingredients made that East German side more successful than those which came before or after?" I asked him.

"A team ethic is the most important factor. Everything needed to be sacrificed for the benefit of the team. That needed to be coupled with a sense of discipline both on and off the pitch. The balance was right in '74."

"Did your role extend beyond purely coaching in '74?"

"There was a great deal of conversation between myself and party officials about how the World Cup was viewed at home. But I never told the players of this. I told them simply to play their game and focus on the football. I was a shock absorber, in that sense."

"Some of the players have suggested that the Party was extremely active with the players around the time of the match. Is that true?"

"Ask them. I can't speak for others."

"It's been suggested that if more emphasis had been placed on the individual those East German sides could have achieved more in the '70s and early '80s." (Cue venomous look.)

"That question disappoints me. I was getting to quite like you. You're almost going down the lazy 'Eastern bloc robots' route. I'd remind you that England in '66 were labelled 'Ramsey's robots' in some quarters. You pick the best team, not necessarily the best players. However, because I do quite like you, I'll admit that you are correct in one sense. There was a degree of political pressure to ensure that the individual did not garner all of the attention. But it was never as rigorous as many would suppose."

After negotiating their way past Hungary and Czechoslovakia in qualification, the media spotlight intensified on the close-knit group of players, drawn solely from Oberliga outfits including Carl Zeiss Jena, Dynamo Dresden and Dynamo Berlin, and various carrots were dangled in front of their noses. Martin Hoffmann recalled, "Many of us were contacted by car companies to see if we were interested in an upgrade. In those days, only the privileged few drove bigger cars in East Germany and, being young, I wanted to drive something a bit bigger than a Trabant. Buschner put a stop to that. 'Don't get above yourself. You'll look like an idiot,' he told us. Later he told me that he preferred me to drive the Trabant because it was slower and safer." Buschner confirmed at our meeting: "Driving a bigger car in East Germany immediately opened you up to suspicion and jealousy. I was protecting the players. They were just youngsters who didn't know better."

Wolfgang Blockwitz was approached by a tailor who cut suits for leading Party officials, and he suggested to the team that they also get suited and booted. "'Absolutely not,' Buschner told us. 'I'm not having you all running around like a bunch of pretty boys.' He also hated long hair, especially if it was styled. 'You look like girls,' he'd bark. 'It will get in your eyes when you play.' Later he admitted that there was little he could do about us growing our hair, short of cutting it himself." Twenty-five years later, even Buschner chuckled at the memory of threatening to take a pair of scissors to each and every member of the squad. "It's a generational thing, I suppose. I heard that Bill Nicholson banned the photographer from taking the Tottenham players' picture until they had shorter hair and I felt the same. I let it go in the end though – but I never liked it. And then some of them turned up in stack-heel boots. What on earth was that all about?"

Most, if not all, members of the squad, also received visits shortly before the World Cup from Party officials. Buschner confirms he had "regular meetings with officials surrounding the logistics and the importance to the nation of World Cup qualification." Blockwitz was more candid. "I received a knock on the door one night about nine-ish. I believe that the entire squad was spoken to by the Party, but you'd have to ask them. Three men in suits asked me if they might 'have a conversation.' I had little choice but to let them in. It was reasonably relaxed but the message was very clear, nonetheless. I was told that, along with my teammates, I needed to conduct myself as a model citizen. Should we prove successful and stay in accommodation outside the East there should be no wild celebrations, no fraternising with Western footballers, journalists or women. 'We'll be keeping an eye on you,' they said." Blockwitz laughed and shrugged at the memory of his brush with the Stasi. "That's how it was, I suppose."

Although Germany had been divided since the early 1950s, it was only at the Munich '72 Olympics that the GDR had competed as a sovereign state for the first time, finishing third in the medal table behind the Soviet Union and the USA. In *German Football: History, Culture and Society*, Tomlinson and Young point out that the GDR was a "rather artificial nation" which lacked fundamental features of national identity, including "a historic territory or homeland, common myths and historical memories, a common mass public culture and common legal rights and duties for all members." In short, the East German government needed sport as an identificational factor more than most other countries.

"It's true," confirmed Buschner, "that East Germany had an identity problem in many senses. Sport tends to be a good way to bind a country and to give its people a common focus. Look what happened with Ireland under Jack Charlton in 1990. The problem with football – on the international stage – for the government was that there were too many variables. You can train a sprinter or a long jumper relentlessly behind closed doors for years and concentrate huge amounts of resources on them. If they don't make it you can always withdraw them and no harm is done. Team sports are different. On that level, the authorities couldn't guarantee the national football team's success and that irked them."

Nonetheless, with East Germany safely qualified, the government had to work out a way to use events to their best advantage and, shortly before the tournaments began, events over the border – involving footballers and politicians – played directly into their hands. In April, West German Chancellor Willie Brandt was forced to resign after it was revealed that one of his advisers, Gunter Guillaime, was an East German spy, working under the firm guidance of Markus Wolf. The fact that Guillaime had remained undetected for several years was a major coup for the East. It wasn't the only reason for Brandt's departure. Dogged by rumours of infidelity and heavy drinking, East German newspaper *Der Biltung* soon ran stories about the "terminal decline of the decadent West."

West Germany's footballers, at war over bonuses, hardly helped matters either. Five days before their first match at the 1974 World Cup Finals the squad, having learned that the

Dutch and the Italians had been promised around £16,000 a man if they won the tournament (the German football federation had decided that just £4,900 was in order for manager Helmut Schön's team) threatened to strike if the amount wasn't raised by the German Football Federation. Thanks to feverish negotiations with the top brass by Franz Beckenbauer the amount was raised to around £11,000 a man, but Schön, who warned his men that "people will spit on you in the street if they find out," threatened to send the entire squad packing and play a second string.

FIFA's new President João Havelange had vowed to ensure a "bigger and more Technicolor tournament," and one of the spin-offs was that commercial considerations became prevalent for competing players. The Scots and the Dutch also argued with their Football Associations over possible bonuses during the tournament. "'Look at those West Germans, ripping themselves apart over money,' a Party official pointed out to me," recalled Buschner. "'They'll destroy themselves, won't they?' There is a grain of truth in there. If a football team is more concerned with boot deals and shirt sponsorships and cars, their mind isn't fully on the task, is it? For me, commercialism in football really began at that World Cup, as power shifted from the authorities and the coaches to the players."

Another story which was widely reported in the West, specifically by German tabloid Bild Zeitung, was that the night before Holland played Brazil, there had been a "naked party" in the Dutch players' hotel, involving four players and two German girls. Although the newspaper claimed to have photographs to support the story, none were ever published. Nonetheless, party officials in the East subsequently informed Buschner of the episode after the tournament. "It might have been that the Dutch weren't completely focused on the World Cup," he admits. "Such distractions were evidence of the temptations which were around at that time for big name players."

"But surely not in the case of the East German side?"

"Absolutely not."

West Germany laboured against Chile in their opening group match, winning 1–0 thanks to Paul Breitner's long-range effort, as the Berlin crowd howled in derision at the hosts' cautious approach. Matters hardly improved against the Australians: Beckenbauer and the team were slow-handclapped during the 3–0 win as the crowd once again despaired at the worrying number of misplaced passes. Afterwards the West German skipper, in a fit of pique, even refused to shake hands with Australia captain Peter Wilson. Buschner's men eased through their first two matches, seeing off Australia and drawing with Chile. Yet the East's matches had failed to ignite public interest and less than 20,000 attended their opening clashes. As the all-German clash drew nearer, Martin Hoffmann recalls the increasing media attention afforded to the showdown. "Where I lived in the East," he recalled, "I could get Western television and it was all the news appeared to be focusing on for several days."

The media was especially interested in the face-off between Schön and Buschner. Dresden-born, Schön had fled the East after crossing swords with future East German Chancellor Erich Honecker and sports official Manfred Ewald – who gained notoriety for arranging mass doping within the GDR's sporting system. Appalled at the government's increased involvement in football, Schön and his family fled East Berlin, before becoming established in the West. "Of course, our newspapers disguised this history," recalled Buschner, "and spoke of an ideological clash. It was nonsense. Helmut and I had huge respect for one another and I know it pained him to have left Dresden in the first place. We were purely football men, who wanted no part of an ideological clash but we nonetheless found ourselves in the midst of a storm."

The West German players, who were bussed from Malente to Berlin, passed through the East briefly, and were puzzled by the reaction they saw. Berti Vogts recalls, "Many people watched us travel through – in fact some of the streets were lined with people. Many of those we saw – especially older people – gave us the thumbs up and waved flags – not the GDR flag but West German flags. It was bizarre and unlike anything we'd encountered before. Helmut Schön explained it all to us though – it proved that many citizens in the GDR didn't wish to live there and they resented the fact that they could no longer watch their favourite Bundesliga sides due to the divide."

The game in Hamburg on 22nd June, in keeping with the rest of the tournament, began in rather a kitsch and folksy way. Although boot moguls like Adi and Horst Dassler were waiting in the wings with deals for leading players, the emergence of both sets of players onto the pitch was accompanied by folk dancing, performed by girls especially selected from Bavaria. Helmut Schön had originally suggested that this would retain the Germanic feel to a tournament which was becoming increasingly commercial. Then there were klaxons – the unofficial musical accompaniment for the 1974 World Cup. "The sound was absolutely deafening," recalled Martin Hoffmann, "and there was no way in which you could hear yourself think out there. Coming from a country in which communal activities like crowd singing was actively discouraged, it was quite a culture shock. From the outset, most people seemed to be of the opinion that we would lose 5–0 at the very least."

But West Germany's attacking lynchpins, Muller and Grabowski, were smothered by an East German defensive blanket. Buschner recalled, "We had to accept that, player for player, they were superior to us, but that we could hit them on the breakaway when the time came. We were very effective on the counter-attack." In the first half Gerd Müller slammed the ball against the post after he'd swivelled and turned. ("He was a physical freak," recalled Buschner. "That long torso and ridiculously powerful legs meant he could turn quicker than any striker in the game.") Bonhof's follow-up shot then whistled inches over the bar. The match appeared to be petering out into goalless draw before the (almost) unthinkable happened. In the 77th minute, after latching onto a Hamman through-ball, GDR midfielder Jürgen Sparwasser controlled the ball, held off the challenge of Horst Hottges and Berti Vogts before driving the ball past Sepp Maier. Vogts recalls, "For a second I thought Jürgen had skewed it wide, but then Sepp and Horst and I all looked at each other in disbelief. It wasn't a good feeling."

At first the crowd went silent, save for a tiny knot of 2,000 travelling East German supporters shoe-horned into a corner of the Volkspark Stadium in Hamburg, and then the vast majority of spectators began to jeer and whistle the West German team. Dieter Lehmann was one of those supporters who had been deemed 'suitable to travel' by the authorities in the East. "There was a ballot amongst Party members and, as you can imagine, the thought of travelling across the border excited many of us. The tests which decided whether we could travel were really stringent. They were based upon our previous work for the Party and obviously your record had to be pristine or you couldn't go. The round trip was unbelievable. I was picked up in Dresden by a bus which had its own toilets, and food was provided on the coach so we had no opportunity to get off until we reached Hamburg. It was the same coming back. No hotel, no celebration, nothing. At the match we were all issued with a GDR flag distributed by a Party official, told to sing the national anthem enthusiastically when the team lined up and, if we needed to go the toilet in the ground, the people on the end of our rows would accompany us. 'Remember, we'll always be watching and listening to you,' we were warned. There were Stasi everywhere in our section – we joked afterwards that we could tell who they were because they spent more time watching the crowd than the game – but all of us really cheered when Sparwasser scored. On reflection, it was like a military operation, or an outing for kids in a primary school, and the authorities couldn't risk the embarrassment of any defections. But you have to remember that being granted permission to travel to the West in those days was a huge privilege for us."

One of the most enduring myths surrounding the game was that West Germany deliberately threw the match, in order to avoid progressing through to the harder looking second-round group containing Holland, Argentina and World Champions Brazil. Buschner reacted angrily to the suggestion. "That's nonsense. Helmut was devastated by the result and the squad almost went into meltdown afterwards." Schön's players later confirmed that they'd sat up drinking and smoking until dawn, almost unable to comprehend the shame of losing the match. From that point onwards the sensitive Schön relied increasingly upon Beckenbauer to control his fractious squad but Buschner still retained his iron grip upon his team. "He allowed us to have some beers after the game and said well done but pointed out that within four days we'd be facing Brazil in Hanover so there was no time for distractions," recalled Wolfgang Blockwitz. Away from the cameras, both sides swapped shirts, although Buschner's men had been warned against it beforehand

The East Germans were nudged out of Group A in the second round by Brazil (1–0) and Holland (2–0) before saving face against Argentina with a 1–1 draw. Wolfgang Blockwitz recalls, "The team was wide-eyed with excitement about playing Brazil, but they couldn't believe how they were fighting and arguing amongst themselves. The only one who really impressed them was Rivellino, who scored an unbelievable free kick after Jairzinho ducked out of the wall and created a gap through which he blasted the ball." Buschner was hugely impressed by Johann Cruyff, "who sliced and weaved through us at will. Ultimately, we couldn't live with their individualism. There is no shame in that." Meanwhile, Schön's men gathered themselves and grew stronger, easing past Sweden, Yugoslavia, and Poland in Group C, and reaching the final, where they beat Holland 2–1. Thirty years after the tournament, Martin Hoffmann recalled, "The irony is that our victory over them simply spurred on West Germany, forced them to collect themselves, and they ended up as winners anyway. We were still seen as 'Little Germany.' Even in victory, nothing is straightforward."

After arriving back in East Germany, Sparwasser and his teammates received a mixed reception. "It was rumoured that I received financial benefits, a new car and a smart, rent-free apartment," he recalled, "but that is totally untrue. All of us received the *Verdienter Meister des Sports* (Meritorious Champion of Sport) and that was about all. Some of my neighbours in the East, who clearly had their own thoughts on political matters, shunned me – others congratulated me for bringing honour to the nation. That's how it was for many of the others, I believe." In 1988, a year before the Berlin Wall fell, Sparwasser defected to the West. Teammates are guarded about their comments. East German captain Bernd Bransch said, "I was surprised that he defected, as he had a good job and a good life in Magdeburg, but I cannot pass judgement and I accept he made his decision for himself and his family."

In 2006 the surviving members of the team were person-ally invited by World Cup Organising Committee Head Franz Beckenbauer to attend matches of their choice and a week before the tournament began both sets of players gathered in Munich and recreated the match.

"We were all proud to see young Germans celebrating in Berlin and the major cities during the tournament – proud to have fun under the one flag. For so long the country was split and flag waving in Germany, with all the conno-tations of war, was often considered unacceptable," explains Martin Hoffmann. "There is now a feeling that one can be a nationalist in a positive way. Whereas the 1974 World Cup was dominated by talk of a divided Germany, now things have improved in that respect. There is a positive feeling."

Twenty-one years after the collapse of communism, the former Eastern part of Germany is grappling with high unemployment and crime. The East's economic problems are mirrored by the collapse of once famous Oberliga clubs like Magdeburg, Dynamo Dresden and Carl Zeiss Jena, who have suffered multiple relegations. "We've been bled dry," explains Wolfram Löwe. "As there are so few sponsors in the East, the best players head West and we have no chance." "The absolutes we once took for granted have gone with the fall of communism," explained Buschner, "and it is true that some yearn for those certainties which once existed. We now live in a very uncertain world."

Two things are certain, however. Firstly, when Georg Buschner succumbed to prostate cancer in 2007, the outpouring of sympathy and affection for their former manager from the boys of 1974 was heartfelt and genuine. "He was a superb man manager who worked in very difficult circumstances, and deflected all the pressure away from his team," explained Hoffmann. Secondly, his former charges could scarcely wait to upgrade their cars from the rickety Trabants which Buschner insisted they drove, to Mercedes, Astras and Volkswagens. "Whenever I see those Trabby safaris which tourists can take in Berlin, I always chuckle and think of Buschner," admits Wolfram Löwe. "A friend told me a while back that although he (my friend) hated everything East Germany stood for, even he cheered when Jurgen scored that night. It was because when he used to go on holiday to Hungary, West Germans in their big Mercedes and their Jaguars would sneer at his little Trabant. For once, little East Germany had made him feel proud. And also, we had the better national anthem."

Maybe a degree of Ostalgia has crept into football after all.

12

SUNSHINE AND SHADOW IN BOGOTA

In September 1993 the Colombian football team, or *'Cafeteros'* ('Coffee Growers'), shining brightly in their golden tops and blue shorts, received the customary hostile welcome from 80,000 home supporters at the Estadio Monumental in Buenos Aires. A confetti storm, a shower of insults, boos, coins and catcalls – all were designed to throw the hungry visitors off the scent. For the opening ten minutes Gabriel Batistuta and Claudio Caniggia attacked at will, and Argentina seemed destined to gain the win required to confirm their qualification for the 1994 World Cup Finals in the USA. TV cameras focused on the injured Diego Maradona, sat in the stands behind the wire fence, wearing his Argentina top and conducting a spot of community singing. As one, the home supporters boomed *"Argentinos, Argentinos"* with their side pressing for the opening goal. But it never arrived. If the 1978 World Cup final was, from Argentina's point of view, the Monumental's greatest afternoon, the events of this night, 15 years later, would become its nadir. This was to be Colombia's night, their moment in the sun, before the *Cafeteros*, somehow inevitably, were cast permanently in shadow.

Forty-one minutes into the match Carlos Valderrama controlled the ball, looked up and nudged it through for a surging Freddy Rincón. At a gallop he rounded disbelieving Argentinean goalkeeper, Sergio Goycochea, and slammed the ball into the gaping net. "When I scored," explains Rincón, "it took a couple of seconds for me to realise that I'd done the damage, because the whole arena went totally silent. It's very odd and it was actually quite disorientating, because as a footballer, you rely on sound to judge what is happening around you. Then I heard the shouts and screams of my teammates and I was able to celebrate." After the break, as Argentina poured forward in search of an equaliser, the hosts left huge gaps in midfield which Colombia exploited to the full. "It was a night you can only dream of," explained Rincón. "Valderrama and Asprilla were unstoppable." The crowning denouement was Asprilla's stunning lob over Goycochea to make it 4–0. At that point the humiliated home crowd abandoned booing their own side and started to cheer Colombia's every move.

In the dying seconds Antonio Valencia made it 5–0. Rincón recalls, "We wanted that night to go on forever. For a while, anything seemed possible." Given the colour of their shirts, their skin, and their raucous celebrations, the *Cafeteros* were reminiscent of Brazil in their prime. The only saving grace for Argentina was that it wasn't the old enemy who'd demolished them at home; now an exhilarating third power had well and truly emerged in South America. When the Colombian team flew back to Bogotá they were greeted by an ecstatic President César Gaviria who awarded every member of the side the Boyacá Cross – the highest honour a Colombian civilian can receive. Homecomings to the capital wouldn't always be so sweet.

The Argentine press, clamouring for Maradona's return to the side after the 'Monumental Massacre,' lambasted their team. *El Grafico* ran the headline "Shameful" across an all-black front cover. A seething Goycochea, clenching his fist menacingly at his tormentor, the outspoken commentator José Sanfilippo, was taken to task on Argentine TV and coach Alfio Basile described the defeat as "a crime against nature." The Colombians, their qualification for the 1994 Finals now guaranteed after four wins and two draws, including a 2–1 home win against Argentina three weeks earlier, partied.

Colombia's coach, the former dentist Francisco 'Pacho' Maturana, said, "That result was excellent because we showed the world that Colombia can rise to the big occasion." There were spontaneous celebrations on the streets of the country's main cities, including Cali, Bogotá and Medellin but, in a nation becoming increasingly overrun by drug cartels and organised crime and which accounted for 10 per cent of the world's homicides, 150 people were shot dead that night across Colombia. Bogotá resident Denis Silva recalls, "I went onto the streets. It was a heady mixture of lawlessness, breathlessness, drunkenness and celebration – you could sense it almost spiralling out of control already. In the streets, guys were firing their guns into the air in celebration, in front of families out enjoying themselves. Bang, bang across the whole city, all night and into the early hours. People were letting them off everywhere. I asked one fellow, 'Hey man, why do you need to do that?' – I was pointing to his pistol. 'Can't we put them [the guns] away tonight?' He replied, 'This is Colombia. We fire guns when we are happy, and when we are sad.' For me that explained a great deal about what came afterwards. Guns are just a way of life here."

In Medellin, South America's most lawless city at the time, two people were killed that evening by 'friendly fire.' After the Colombian side sobered up, reality began to slowly sink in. Hernán Gómez, Maturana's Assistant, told Pacho that the team was in for it now. "They [the media] were going to start saying that we were the best team in the world. That 5–0 scoreline worried me because there was no sense of perspective in the country." Freddy Rincón recalls: "The sense of giddiness eventually made me uneasy. When all is said and done, it was just one game in the qualifying tournament. That was all. Some went on like we'd won the World Cup." A sober dissection of the match revealed that Colombia keeper Óscar Córdoba, brought in to replace the wildly inconsistent René Higuita, had made a series of miraculous saves from Batistuta and Caniggia and that the desperate Argentine team, without Maradona, their talisman, had afforded Colombia acres of space in midfield; a luxury unlikely to be awarded to the *Cafeteros* in the Finals. Nagging doubts remained about the one paced Valderrama, and the team's tendency to channel everything through 'El Pibe' ('the Kid'). Amidst the gunfire and alcohol, such fears were banished to the back of Colombian minds.

The Colombian press described the victory in Argentina as a "parricide." A disbelieving Diego Maradona, who'd stated before the match, "We must keep things as they have been historically; Argentina on top, Colombia below," suggested the outcome had "clearly gone against the grain." Fifty years before, as Argentine football tore itself apart over the knotty issue of professionalism, over 50 professionals had fled to Colombia. By the late 1940s, a whole host of South American stars had flocked to the promised land and played for the likes of Cali, Medellin and Millionarios in Bogotá. With eight Argentines in their team, including Alfredo di Stéfano, Millionarios were known as 'Ballet Azul' ('the Ballet in Blue') and between 1949 and 1953 won four titles. Leading players trousered an enormous $500 a month, compared with the restrictive maximum wage in operation in Buenos Aires. Football in Colombia began to sparkle, until the likes of di Stéfano decided to move to Europe instead and Brazilian and Argentine leagues also introduced professionalism to stem the tide of departures. Yet the Colombian national team flopped badly on the world stage and domestic strife was never far from the surface. Fifty thousand people died in 1950 as the government crushed communist rebels and the domestic league shrank back into its shell as General Gustavo Rojas Pinilla launched a coup d'état, murders and the omnipotent drug cartels became ubiquitous in Colombian life.

Apart from the 1962 World Cup, where they were eliminated in the first round, the *Cafeteros* failed to qualify until they reached Italia '90.

Originally, Colombia had been awarded the rights to host the 1986 World Cup, but with the cocaine trade increasing exponentially, leading clubs were at the mercy of narcotics traffickers, desperate to launder their ill-gotten gains, and the government handed its right to host the tournament back to FIFA after a spate of disasters in the '80s. In 1983 the Minister of Justice, Rodrigo Lara Bonilla had been assassinated six months after declaring, "The Mafia has taken over Colombian football." The following year Hernán Botero Moreno, a key figure in the Medellin cartel and the President of Atlético Nacional, had been extradited to the USA after being accused of drug trafficking and money laundering. The Colombian First Division had closed down for a week in solidarity and over the next few years, along with 200 judges and 1,200 policemen, football officials had been targeted by vengeful cartels. Investigative journalists Jaime Ortiz Alvear and Carlos Arturo Mejia, who had dared to ask one searching question too many about football ownership, were also gunned down.

As the national team prepared to fly to Italia '90, the country's most senior referee, Jesus Diaz, selected to officiate at the tournament, explained to Joáo Havelange, "My wife and children have begged me to give up refereeing. When it's a matter of life and death you have to consider the feelings of others. I can't keep on tormenting my family." The Colombian Football Federation (CFF) announced, "The law of the bullet is killing our sport. We cannot allow a competition to continue that is dominated by psychological coercion and physical threats." The gunfire rumbled on regardless.

In the Colombian city of Santa Marta, there stands a seven-foot high statue of Carlos Valderrama. The architect has done a good job sculpting El Pibe's defining feature, his electrified afro, but some foreign visitors don't really grasp what all the fuss is about. His spells in Europe with Real Valladolid and Montpellier were low-key and, as he wound down his career in Major League Soccer in the USA, what little pace he possessed ebbed away. But in his homeland, Valderrama remains an icon, the first of the 'Golden Generation' to emerge in the late '80s under coach Maturana. Freddy Rincón explains, "For Colombia, Carlos was able to impose his style of play on the game. When he was on form, he could control everything around him. That's the sign of a great player. Everyone remembers the hair, and it's true that he was the first to bring a kind of tropical and flamboyant image to the Colombian game. As a captain he was fantastic. There was a great deal going on around our games at times – lots of whispers and some unsavoury characters on the scene – but Carlos would always tell everyone before and after the match, 'Todo bien' ['Everything is cool'] and he brought a dignity and calm to the job. We needed him, and he was good at dealing with people from all walks of life. He was a working-class man. Many of the team from the '90s came from tough backgrounds, and some associated with the wrong crowd, but Carlos lived life in the correct manner.

Colombia's other emerging talent, by the late '80s, was Albeiro Usuriaga. There's no statue of him in his homeland, just a raft of people who shrug and shake their heads whenever his name is mentioned. A tall, quick-footed attacker, nicknamed 'El Palomo' ('the Pigeon'), he was tipped for greatness by Pelé when he exploded on the international scene. "Usuriaga will rapidly become the talk of South America, and then world football within five years," predicted the great Brazilian striker. In 2004, I met El Palomo in an upmarket Medellin wine bar, with Frank Sinatra crooning gently in the background. Usuriaga was visiting friends for "a party weekend," as he described it. Now ostracised from the game, the dreadlocked striker had lost none of his fire and passion for football, or his star quality. Our conversation was regularly interrupted by well wishers (many were young women clad in spray-on clothes, who handed him their phone numbers), to which Usuriaga responded with a shrug and a smirk. Although friendly and unfailingly polite, his gaze regularly drifted into the distance and he admitted to having "a few things going on" at the time. Although he didn't elaborate, I could hazard a guess as to what those things might be.

A maverick talent from the wrong side of the tracks, Usuriaga spent much of his career drinking in the last-chance saloon. After testing positive for cocaine in 1988 he was found in possession of stolen goods two years later. On one famous occasion he evaded police in a car chase for three hours. When they did eventually bring his stolen Mercedes to a screeching halt they let him off with a derisory fine. After all, he was Usuriaga. He'd been behind some of the greatest moments in the Colombian game. His goal in the 1990 play-off against Israel secured the *Cafeteros'* qualification for Italia '90, and he spearheaded Atlético Nacional of Medellin to victory in the 1989 Copa Libertadores, the only time a Colombian side has won the trophy.

Maturana, however, decided against including him in the squad for the 1990 World Cup, stating, "You never know what's going on inside his head." A few weeks later, he elaborated. "It was a long and difficult reflection. On the one hand there was his individual worth, his capacity to come up with something of the cuff. On the other hand there was the paucity of his contribution to team play. In our minds the second factor was foremost." Fourteen years later, El Palomo was remarkably calm about the whole affair. "At the time I hated Maturana with a passion, but now I understand more where he was coming from. He was trying to build a team, a unit, and although there was plenty of scope for flair within it he wouldn't tolerate disobedience. After we beat Israel I partied for a long time, mixed with people who weren't necessarily good for me and put stuff in my body which wasn't great for an athlete. I know that I've often been described as a prototype Asprilla, but tell me, what South American player doesn't like to party?"

So the *Cafeteros* travelled to Italy without their mercurial star. Freddy Rincón recalls, "Manturana was trying to build a team with all the necessary components. He wanted us to play a short passing game based on players' individual skills but he recognised that different qualities made a team. In midfield you had tough tacklers like Alvarez and Gabriel Gomez and then up-front you had guys like myself and Valencia, who came from the Cali region and added the attacking flair. It saddened me that we didn't take Usuriaga to the World Cup in 1990. I think that he'd have made as big an impression as Gascoigne did, but he missed out. I sympathised with him up to a point, because in the end it came about from his lifestyle. Lots of players in Colombia can't distance themselves from guys they grew up with."

During the tournament Colombia's performances lurched from the sublime to the ridiculous. Rincón scored a superb injury-time equaliser against eventual winners Germany, after a series of cushioned passes with Valderrama, which took his country into the knock-out phase. The richness of their counter-attacking – the ball travelled from the Colombian penalty box to the back of the German net within six breathless seconds – and the ecstatic celebrations, provided a tantalising glimpse of the *Cafeteros*' raw potential. Yet the eccentric René Higuita's penchant for acting as the team's unofficial sweeper spelt their doom in the last 16 when he was robbed by Roger Milla in injury time and the Cameroon veteran scored to secure his country's 2–1 win. "We were shouting, 'No, no, don't do that René,' explains Rincón. "But that was his nature. You couldn't change him, and we were knocked out of the tournament." 'El Loco' ('the Madman') was unrepentant, claiming, "To imply that we lost because of me is just wrong"; the Colombian press blamed him nonetheless.

A dangerous pattern was developing. Colombia became infamous for their flaky combination of electrifying attacking and fragile defending. The media was becoming increasingly adept at launching witch-hunts against players it viewed as underperforming. As larger-than-life characters like Higuita and Asprilla rose to prominence and attracted infamy for their extracurricular activities, the Colombian league became increasingly attractive to villains from the cocaine cartels who viewed their star players as commodities to be sold to wealthy European clubs. It was in their interests for the national team to prosper in World Cups in order that their assets could appreciate in value. One young star, Atlético Nacional's classy defender Andrés Escobar, had already attracted the attentions of AC Milan scouts and was due to move from the Medellin club to Europe after the 1994 World Cup. "It was in everyone's interests to do well," explains Rincón. "There was so much riding on that tournament for all sorts of unscrupulous figures. And they weren't guys whom who you wanted to annoy."

To cap it, none other than Pelé, hardly the most accurate of tipsters, was touting Colombia as potential winners of the 1994 World Cup to be held in the USA. Bogotá daily El Tiempo reported that astrologers foresaw great things for the national team. Colombian beer giant Bavaria, which owned several leading media outlets across the country, also began to sponsor the team. There wasn't a journalist around who hadn't heard stories of the huge bets which drug cartels were supposedly placing on Colombia to do well. Grainy footage exists of the team's final press conference before they flew to the USA. Valderrama and Escobar, rapidly gaining a reputation as an articulate, media-literate member of the team, occasionally shot each other furtive glances, betraying their nerves. "We were a bit edgy, I'd agree, but then we knew that this could be our moment," explains Rincon. Albeiro Usuriaga, still in regular contact with several members of the team, was more direct: "They were absolutely shitting themselves."

Defeat against Romania in their first match severely dented Colombia's hopes of progressing through to the knockout stages of the 1994 World Cup. For the opening period of the game their crisp passing threatened to slice the opposition apart, but as soon as Raducioiu rounded off a classic counter-attack for the opposition and Hagi's cross-cum-shot looped over the stranded Córdoba the Cafeteros were sunk and eventually lost 3–1.

"After that the pressure to beat the USA in the second

match was unbearable," explains Rincón. Both Valderrama and Asprilla hit the woodwork before the nadir was reached. As the USA's John Harkes crossed the ball for teammate Ernie Stewart, a stretching Escobar diverted the ball past a stunned Óscar Córdoba into his own net. For a couple of seconds Escobar lay prostrate on the lush turf, staring skywards. Colombia lost 2–1. Though they rallied to beat Switzerland 2–0 four days later, with the luck finally going their way, it was too little, too late. Their World Cup was already over: now the recriminations were about to begin.

It soon emerged that on the day of the USA match, Maturana and midfielder Gabriel Jaime Gomez had received telephone death threats informing them their Medellin homes would be torched if Gomez played against the USA. Gomez was replaced by Gaviria and didn't play in the match.

Along with several of his teammates, Rincón has always refused to blame the death threats for Colombia's capitulation. "It ran far deeper than that. We lacked pace and width and in the first two games we tried to play our way through solid, brick-wall defences. By the third game against Switzerland we'd started to adapt but it was too late by then. We missed some chances in the first two games and Óscar [Córdoba] was also unhappy with his positioning against Romania. I'd also say that there wasn't the experience within the camp to be successful. Look at Brazil and Argentina. There is a culture of World Cup success there. We never had that." After all the hype, Colombia were the first team to be eliminated from the 1994 World Cup, and at home the press sharpened their knives. "Humiliated by the United States," ran the predictable La Prensa headline. Several of the team opted to take holidays in Las Vegas or Disneyland, rather than go home and face the music. Going against the wishes of his family, Andrés Escobar took the more difficult option and flew back to Bogotá. So did Faustino Asprilla, who recalled Escobar telling him, and other members of the squad, "I know that you like to party, but stay at home for a while and stay out of trouble."

As the joint national team coaches – Maturana and Gomez

– prepared for the press conference from hell, Escobar and Asprilla talked of 'the Mafiosi' which awaited them in their homeland. They weren't referring to gangsters but the Colombian journalists. At Bogotá's El Dorado airport, Gomez made the ultimate faux pas. Leaning across to Maturana he whispered, "Look around this room. Soon I will take some of these sons of bitches with me." Gomez was unaware that his microphone was already switched on. The press vented their fury, viciously lambasting Valderrama and Asprilla in the newspapers over the forthcoming days for their perceived laziness. The only member of the team to emerge with any credit from the tournament was Escobar. In his newspaper column, he wrote, "Don't let the defeat affect our respect for the spirit of the game. See you later, because life goes on." At the press conference, some journalists applauded him as he walked into the room. "At least you have the guts to face us," said a writer from one of the Bogota dailies. The clearly embarrassed Escobar squirmed his way through the conference as assorted hacks circled around the national coaches like vultures around fresh carrion. In a bitterly ironic parting shot, Escobar commented, "I'm now going to look forward to the next World Cup Finals." He never spoke publicly again.

In the ten days that followed, most of the players disregarded Escobar's instructions and ventured out onto the streets. Lozano and Alvarez were roughed up in Cali, and Córdoba claimed to have received verbal abuse and physical threats wherever he went. On Friday 1st July Escobar ignored his own advice and, with three friends, shared a few bottles of Colombian firewater (*aguardiente*) at the Padua disco in Medellin. In the early hours of the following morning the group ran into notorious local gangsters the Gallon brothers who began to taunt him about the own goal he'd scored against the USA. The normally passive Escobar eventually rose to the bait and was shot dead by the Gallon brothers' chauffeur, Humberto Munoz in the parking lot outside. Munoz, allegedly screamed "Own goal" each time he fired one of six shots into the defender's chest. Escobar was left to bleed to death inside his car. Forty others were shot dead in Medellin that night. The following day, influential Colombian journalist Enrique Santos Calderón wrote in El Tiempo, "For the first time in my life I am ashamed of being Colombian."

Ten years ago, in an effort to draw a line under the most infamous event in Colombian football history, Padua disco's owners renamed the bar Club Guarna. The picture of Escobar which still hung on the wall when I visited in 2004 meant that the establishment retained its air of ghoulishness. The barman saw me peer at the photograph and look around uneasily. With an air of resignation, he commented, "You are a journalist. We get lots of them in here from Europe and America. So many of them want to come to the place where Andrés Escobar had his last drink."

Thanks to the tenacity and unparalleled networking skills of my fixer Celso Edmundes, I met up with Juan Carlos Metiche, a policeman who had worked in this often edgy urban sprawl for the best part of 20 years. He commented, "This place used to be full of pimps, hookers and drug dealers. It makes you wonder why Escobar came here in the first place. Nowadays rich Medellin University students dance here to Kylie Minogue."

Metiche was anxious to lay to rest some of the more fanciful theories which swirled around in the aftermath of Escobar's murder. One story claimed the Gallon brothers had staked $800,000 each on Colombia to win the World Cup and this was their chance to exact revenge on Escobar. "That's totally untrue," claims Metiche. "It's misleading because the Gallons were known as the 'Medellin Mafia,' but they didn't have a massive network in Colombia at all. The city's police went through their accounts and transactions very carefully in the weeks after the shooting and there is no evidence to suggest that they wagered anything on the tournament. In 1994 we estimated that there were 400 hired assassins in Medellin – guys who'd willingly shoot anyone if you paid them. It would have been very easy for the Gallons to have hired a sicario [assassin] and had Escobar shot that way. They would have then avoided any connection with his murder. The truth is that the murder was down to a parking lot bust-up which went very badly wrong. But people won't accept that."

When he wasn't on duty in Medellin, Metiche was also a regular at Atlético Nacional matches, and Escobar's murder affected him deeply. "He was a courteous and polite footballer who did his job with very little fuss. At Christmas time, along with his girlfriend Pamela, he used to drive through the poorer parts of town and hand out presents to the children. Escobar could easily have gone to university if he hadn't played football. He was a genuine role model. Thousands turned up at his funeral but none of the Colombia players were allowed to attend because of security fears. Luckily, his spirit lives on. What upsets many of us is that although players like Andrés [Escobar] and [Carlos] Valderrama represent the positive side to Colombian football, it's guys like Higuita and Asprilla, by nature of their lifestyles, who get the headlines throughout the world. Those conspiracy theories – that Escobar had been the victim of a hit by a cartel – made it even worse."

Signed by Newcastle from Italian club Parma for £6 million in January 1996, Faustino Asprilla arrived at St James' Park, preceded by the news that he was strongly connected to the Colombian 'business community'. He'd already left his wife for a porn star and despite "shedding many tears for Andrés Escobar and his senseless, senseless death" admitted that he carried a large hand gun for "security reasons" and once took it into training at Parma as a prank. "This is normal for leading Colombian players," admits Asprilla's former international team mate Rincón. Throughout his spell at Newcastle, Asprilla came across as aloof and distant, claiming to be unable to speak a word of English. Unlike many of his Newcastle teammates, he was regularly seen socialising in Tyneside nightclubs, invariably clad in shades and a black leather trench coat. These days, 'El Pulpo' ('the Octopus') occasionally pops up in men's magazines across the world, and holds court on his former hell-raising days.

Asprilla's misdemeanours pale in comparison with those of René Higuita. Famed for his scorpion-kick save from

England's Jamie Redknapp at Wembley in 1995, he was great friends with international cocaine dealer Pablo Escobar. During the early 1990s, Escobar was sentenced to three years in prison and, after striking a deal with the authorities, he was allowed to build La Catedral prison on his acres of land in Medellin. He was the only prisoner. As well as containing luxury jacuzzis and swimming pools, the complex also had a football pitch. It was there that Higuita featured in games involving Pablo Escobar's associates. The relationship with Escobar wasn't simply a sporting one. In 1991, Escobar was responsible for kidnapping the daughter of Carlos Molina, a rival cocaine baron. Higuita helped secure her release by delivering a ransom of US$300,000 to his friend. Afterwards Higuita spent seven months in prison on charges of profiting from a kidnapping. The charges against him were later dropped but Higuita's chances of playing in the fateful 1994 World Cup were over. Although still playing into his early 40s, he remains tarnished by his double suspension for testing positive for cocaine in 2002 and 2004. After being voted 'Colombia's Ugliest Icon,' Higuita appeared on TV show 'Cambio Extremo' ('Extreme Change') and underwent £30,000 worth of plastic surgery, comprising a nose job, silicon chin implant, a skin peel and "aggressive liposuction." "Bodily I am perfect," he stated afterwards. Although he wasn't available for a face-to-face interview for this book, he sent me a message via his people telling me, "God has blessed my career" and that he "is a loyal friend who has no regrets about his past associations."

"Drugs, porn stars, kidnappings, guns," Metiche laments. "That is how the outside world views Colombian football, even though many of these events happened over a decade ago. Let's be honest, if Higuita or Asprilla had been shot dead back in 1994 no one would have been surprised, given the company they kept. The shocking thing was that Andrés Escobar was always horrified by corruption in the national leagues. Why do the innocent always suffer?"

Outside Atlético games, T-shirts, badges and banners bearing Andrés Escobar's image continue to sell in large numbers and fans' chants at home games still pay homage to their fallen idol. "Even those who never saw him play sing his name," explained Metiche, "because what happened to him hurt so many people and the pain still lingers. For five years afterwards the club retired the number 2 shirt. His brother Santiago had nothing to do with football for several years afterwards, but now he's coaching again and it's good that the Escobar family are back involved in football."

Andrés lies at the Campos de Paz cemetery on the outskirts of town. "The city is in a far better shape than it was," explained Metiche. "The number of homicides has been reduced since 2000 after a government crackdown on gangs and tourists come to see Fernando Botero's artwork and the 'Festival de Flores' ['the Festival of Flowers']. We also have a metro system and a flourishing university. But inevitably, many people will always associate Medellin with Andrés Escobar."

Escobar once commented, "In football, unlike bullfighting, there is no death. In football, no one dies, no one gets killed. It's more about the fun of it, about enjoying." The mere mention of his murder still provokes strong feelings in his native city. Humberto Munoz, who was supposed to serve 43 years in prison for the murder was freed in 2005 due to good conduct. The Gallon brothers spent a matter of days behind bars and were released after paying a fine. "As a country, we have never got to grips with the issue of justice," laments Metiche. Numerous books have been penned on the subject and arguably the most influential is Gonzalo Medina's 'Una Gambeta a la Muerte' ('A Challenge of the Death') which delves into the cultural impact of Escobar's murder. Medina writes, "Escobar is an Antioquian, a descendant of Spanish immigrants. And we Antioquians consider ourselves to be the pioneers of the Colombian nation. Andrés Escobar was and still is an example of traditional Antioquian values and virtues. But the other famous Escobar, drugs boss Pablo [no relation], is the symbol of the other Antioquia: people aiming at ruthless self-enrichment and the use of violence to achieve their goals. We are a people of enormous contrasts. The bad world oppresses the good, and we were forced to face that. Fortunately, things have changed for the good in the last few years. What happened to Andrés Escobar would not happen as easily nowadays."

In recent years, with the national team failing to qualify for the World Cup since 1998, it might appear on the surface that Colombian football is cleaning up its act. This is partly due to a shrinking talent pool of players and the fact that after Escobar's assassination Colombian football lost its swagger and its smile. The drug lords, aware that there is less money to be made in domestic football, are hibernating, but could easily emerge once more if the national team wakes from its slumber. Two weeks after taking my leave of Medellin in 2004, Juan Carlos Metiche sent me a disturbing message, confirming that Albeiro Usuriaga had been assassinated. Rincón was stunned, but not surprised, and frankly nor was I. Gunned down outside a Cali nightclub at the age of 37, his murder sent the rumour mill into overdrive once again. El Palomo and Escobar may have been total opposites, but the theories behind their murders are almost identical. Were betting syndicates with long memories taking revenge on Usuriaga? Had he insulted a local drug baron? Andrés Escobar's murder remains the most high-profile killing in Colombian football's murky history, but Usuriaga's death proved that the story could be updated at any point. In 2006, international striker Elson Becerra, best known perhaps for his attempts to revive the stricken Cameroonian striker Marc-Vivien Foe during a Confederations Cup match in 2003, was slain in a Cartagena nightclub after a row with a gang on the previous day.

13

NORTH AND SOUTH

As the nervous Italian players trooped onto the pitch at the Daejeon World Cup Stadium in South Korea on 18th June 2002, even experienced campaigners like Paolo Maldini and Francesco Totti, veterans of Milan and Rome derbies, were shocked at the level of intensity which greeted them. Veteran boss Giovanni Trappatoni was overheard comparing the din with a Beatles concert in the 1960s, and *La Gazzetta Dello Sport* later spoke of "a crimson tide of passion." The choreography was also something to behold. Along one side of the ground, supporters held up shining red and white plastic cards, spelling out messages of impending doom for Il Trap's men. One read, "Welcome to the Azzuri's tomb." Another warned, "Again 1966!" A huge level of respect, to the surprise of many foreign visitors considering the modern relationship between the two nations, existed in the South for North Korea's shock 1–0 defeat of the Italians at the World Cup in England 36 years previously.

Four and a half million of the country's 48 million people packed into Seoul's 240 squares, parks and stadia to watch the match on big screens. Before transmission began, the message 'Remember 1966' was emblazoned across the big screens. And when Jung-Hwan Ahn soared above Paolo Maldini to head the South's winner in the dying moments of the last 16 clash, the reaction from their opponents was disturbingly reminiscent to that of 36 years before.

In '66, the Italian players returned to Genoa Airport in disgrace and were pelted with rotten tomatoes by a baying mob. Coach Edmondo Fabbri, who quickly became known as "a man named Korea," sought solace in concocting a bizarre string of conspiracy theories. His accusations, made public in *Stadio* magazine in August 1966, caused a scandal. Signed players' statements claimed that they'd been negatively doped. Giacinto Facchetti claimed a series of injections administered by the team doctor had made him feel "a sense of insecurity and fear." Some Italian writers claimed that Fabbri had written the statements and the players had signed what they were given without reading it. As soon as the letters hit the press the majority of players retracted their comments. Facchetti claimed, "I didn't want to make that statement in the first place" and three others said, "nothing strange or untoward had happened at all." Years later, after his sacking and ban from the game for eleven months, Fabbri reiterated his claim, "Some people wanted Italy to lose and, unfortunately, they helped us lose."

The defeat is part of cinematic history in Italy. In Mario Tullio Giordano's six-hour political soap opera *La Meglio Gioventu* (The Best of Youth), three Italian youngsters taunt locals in a seaside town with chants of 'Korea, Korea.' It would prove to be a recurring mantra aimed at underperforming stars by fans during the 1966/67 league season. In succeeding World Cups, the Italian press warned of the impending threat of tomatoes and "another Korea."

Despite scraping into the last 16 in 2002, the Italian team, press and manager were furious that during the group stages four Italian goals had been wrongly disallowed for offside. Il Trap began to lash out during games, kicking over water bottles, screaming at the fourth officials and punching the perspex screen behind his dugout. Against South Korea, Vieri missed an open goal, and Ecuadorian referee Byron Moreno ruled out another good-looking Italian strike, before sending off Totti for diving. After the match the Italian players trashed their dressing room. Perugia President Luciano Gaucci vowed that Korean goalscorer Ahn would never play for his team again, claiming, "I have no intention of paying a salary to someone who has ruined Italian football." Gaucci stuck to his promise. The following day, *Gazzetta dello Sport* editor Pietro Calabrese claimed, "We were knocked out in order to level out some old problems between us and the bosses of FIFA and UEFA. Shame on them, shame on the World Cup."

The majority of Italian ire was reserved for the Ecuadorian referee, Moreno. Entire websites were dedicated to Moreno abuse and in the Italian press a false story did the rounds that he'd bought a brand new red Chevrolet after the World Cup. The 2002 tournament was the latest in an ever-growing line of 'football thefts.' "Twice a Korean team has now stolen the trophy from us. In that sense, Korea is a single entity," concluded *La Gazzetta dello Sport*.

Koreans have a unique perspective on the achievements of their teams, too. In 1966, the North reached the quarter-finals and in 2002, South Korea was eliminated by Germany in the semi-finals. "If the two Koreas were united," claims '66 hero Pak Doo-Ik, we would win the World Cup."

Conventional wisdom suggests that, divided by the de-militarized zone since 1953, North Korea, the world's last true bastion of communism, and South Korea, openly sparring with Japan for economic supremacy in the region and brazen about its market potential, are polar opposites in every sense. Daniel Gordon, whose 2002 film *The Game of Their Lives* helped shed light on life in North Korea, the planet's most hermitic nation, says this is a simplistic viewpoint, especially when it comes to football. "The general feeling in both nations is that any World Cup success for either nation is simply a *Korean* achievement. It doesn't come down to whether the South or the North achieved it. It's a *Korean* success."

On closer analysis, there are some uncanny similarities between both sides' experiences in '66 and 2002, despite the obvious ideological and economic differences between the two nations. The governments in Seoul and Pyongyang realised that a World Cup adventure represented an ideal political opportunity to showpiece their respective nations, and both sets of players, albeit in vastly different ways, were fêted as heroes after the tournaments.

In *Going Oriental: Football After World Cup 2002*, David Winner explains that South Korea's unexpected success in reaching the semi-finals, along with the emergence of the USA, Japan, Turkey and Senegal (who defeated former colonial masters and World Cup holders France in their opening match) as genuine powers, was akin to a kind of football chaos theory, in which a new order threatened the old guard. Back in '66, Portugal coach Otto Gloria, after witnessing his side battle back from 3–0 down to defeat the North Koreans 5–3 at Everton's Goodison Park, in what was arguably the match of the tournament, claimed, "What North Korea have done illuminates world football. It is thrilling to think that some-where on the planet is a team which could leap from the shadows and surprise everybody." As Winner also points out, via the musings of chaos populist Manus J Donahue III, the fact that the '66 and 2002 Finals were contested between established nations shows how the old order quickly re-establishes its superiority. Defeat against the Koreans didn't spell the death knell of Italian football either. The *azzuri* would win the European Championships in 1968, and reached the World Cup Final in 1970. Four years after Il Trap's low point, Italy won the 2006 World Cup.

Of course there were massive differences between the World Cup experiences of North and South in 1966 and 2002. In 2002, Seoul exploded to the sound of celebration after the Italy match. "There were parties everywhere. You couldn't see anything but red and white," recalls George Thompson, who travelled to the Far East for the tournament. "There were red and white fireworks, Roman candles; there were congas down the streets, and trumpets and drums blasted out all night. You couldn't move for red and white flags with Guus Hiddink's face on them. Afterwards, satellite channels showed the South Korean President, Kim Dae-jung, dancing in his presidential palace, and one channel just showed endless repeats of the goals against Italy." By contrast, few North Koreans ever saw Pak Doo-Ik's 1966 goal on the solitary state TV channel, which still only broadcasts for five hours a day. Even for the 2010 World Cup, state-run television will not broadcast North Korea's games and will only screen highlights if the team wins. Michael Breen, author of *Kim Jong-il; North Korea's Dear Leader*, says, "They will get footage from South Korea and it will be heavily edited to suit the regime. Only the ruling elite with access to satellite channels will be able to watch games involving other countries. Once North Korea get knocked out, I would be amazed if there were any mention of the World Cup at all."

Korean football has had a turbulent history. It was effectively halted by both World War 2 and the Korean War. The onus on reconstruction after years of conflict in the 1940s made organised matches difficult, if not impossible. After the nation split in two in 1948, the respective leaders began to realise that World Cup qualification could prove valuable to them.

The South Koreans qualified for the 1954 World Cup, but only arrived 10 hours before their first match against Hungary. They lost 9–0 and, unsurprisingly, were later eliminated. It would be another 32 years before they reached another Finals. Under Park Chung-hee, dictator between 1961 and 1979, the nation was transformed from one of the poorest countries in the world into an affluent one. South Koreans worked extremely hard to turn their economy around and after Chun Doo-hwan took over in 1979, football began receiving financial backing from state-controlled industry. Following the success of the Seoul Olympics in 1988, leading politicians realised that hosting a World Cup could prove the most influential of all sporting events to South Korea.

In January 2002, President Kim Dae-jung explained, "If the event is organized successfully, the image of Korea will be improved and we can expect an enormous economic impact of up to US$14 billion and the creation of 350,000 new jobs. By showing off the IT industry of Korea we will invite investment and tourists from overseas." All this came at a time when, according to a poll, 40 per cent of overseas observers had 'division' as their first association with the country. Official slogans for the World Cup included 'Welcome the World' and 'Dynamic Korea,' as a clear statement of intent for banishing any talk of division or hostility.

Mindful of the terrorist attacks on New York in the previous year, security was incredibly tight throughout the entire tournament. Anti-aircraft guns were installed inside the stadium at Seoul to prevent a terrorist attack during the opening game between champions France and Senegal. The Government insisted on a six-mile no-fly zone around stadiums hosting matches. Submarines and warships patrolled the coast to thwart the chance of maritime attacks.

The methods used to try to get Koreans to present a more 'civilized' society to Western tourists during the World Cup horrified some South Koreans. Political activist Che Bumhohn explains, "The government's civic improvement campaigns were an affront to Korean culture. Basically they were divided up into ten points and the most offensive was urging us Koreans to smile more. Apparently, Westerners are non-plussed by our 'expressionless faces,' and this was deemed unacceptable as we prepared to greet Europeans en masse. Vendors and restaurants were also pressurised to stop selling roasted dog as, once again, foreign visitors found the whole thing unpalatable. Vendors found themselves closed down if they wouldn't sell burgers to cater for visitors. The pojangmachas (informal bars in alleyways) were shut by these ubiquitous health-and-safety officers as they weren't considered regimented or aesthetically pleasing enough for Western Europeans. Having English and German friends as I do, I don't think they would have objected too strongly. Even our toilets were considered unacceptable. There was a 'Clean Toilet, Clean Korea' campaign which urged Koreans to adopt the traditional European-style single-file queuing system. For me, much of what happened in 2002 wasn't a Korean experience at all: it was simply a capitalist sell-out."

Also bubbling under the surface was the rivalry between the co-hosts – South Korea and Japan. FIFA's decision to allow co-hosting of the tournament for the first time was controversial as historically both nations had despised one another. Japan's brutal colonisation of South Korea in the first part of the last century included the banning of the Korean language and cultures, and forcing men to work for slave wages and women into prostitution to serve the Japanese army. By 2002 both nations were locked in a bitter rivalry over developing the most advanced mobile phone system. For the World Cup Japan would spend more than $5 billion renovating stadia and adding roads and bridges. South Korea spent around $2.5 billion on its stadia and the new international airport that opened near Seoul in 2001. Shortly before the tournament, populist Japanese conservative Shintar Ishihara provoked demonstrations on the streets of Seoul by claiming, "We liberated South Korea, we didn't crush it at all." Ishihara also publicly defended the actions of the Japanese in Asia during World War II which led to further demonstrations in Seoul. Che Bum-hohn explains, "There was a petition signed by around 250,000 Koreans imploring our politicians to publicly condemn these comments by the Japanese, and to urge FIFA to do likewise. But the petition fell on deaf ears and the general feeling was that Korea was now getting a reputation for bleating on about World War II when actually we should move on and forget about it. Many of my countrymen, and I include myself in this, chose not to do so."

Just before the World Cup draw in December 2001, Korean magazine *Shin Dong-A* ran a prediction of the Korean team's results as chosen by 11 football experts. Only four predicted that Korea would progress to the second round. The overwhelming fear of the KFA and Korean people was that their team might be the first host nation not to make it into the second round. After all, they'd never actually won a match in the World Cup at all. More importantly, the spectre of being outdone by co-hosts Japan became, according to

Newsweek Korea, a national obsession. Highly experienced international coach Guus Hiddink was appointed and soon convinced the Korean authorities to close down the K-League for most of the year to allow him uninhibited access to his squad. To add to the already impressive levels of fitness and stamina amongst his players, Hiddink demanded that the players cover more efficiently for one another, which would help build a more cohesive unit. Driven onwards by relentless support from the crowds during the tournament, Hiddink's men would harry more technically gifted opponents like Figo, Totti and Morientes, exhausted by the physical and mental demands of European seasons, until they wilted under the pressure.

Song Chong-Gug, who scored against Turkey in the third-place play-off, recalls, "Korean football was traditionally dominated by family ties, academic backgrounds and age. That was true at every level of the game, from the playing side to the administrative side. When I arrived on the international scene and we had international gatherings, older players would eat their meals before the younger ones. We were expected to carry their bags and clear up after them. When Guus Hiddink came in he argued that this was wrong and immediately set about changing things and introducing a more meritocratic way of operating. Now we all ate together and trained together and us younger players were instructed to, when appropriate, give orders out to older players. Things were now based on performance, not seniority. Not everyone liked this change."

"In a way, Guus Hiddink pointed out Korea's weakest points," explains University of Hawaii history professor Choe Yong-Ho, "and he couldn't have made a successful team under the old Korean leadership style. To a degree though, this had the effect of polarising the nation. The older generation didn't always approve of Hiddink's methods, and they found the younger players' new gelled haircuts and the lack of deference to the team's elders disconcerting. The Hiddink revolution was greeted with unease by

many in South Korea, even when the team began to outper-
form expectations."

In the months leading up to the 2002 World Cup, officials from both sides of Korea's Demilitarized Zone, the
Cold War's final frontier, spoke of the possibility of staging
some of the matches in Pyongyang. South Korean leader
Kim Dae-jung explained, "We are keen to promote this
World Cup as a Korean achievement and if Pyongyang
were to host some of the matches the world would see
that the two states are at least willing to engage in a positive dialogue." South Korea's offer was firmly rejected by
the regime in the North. As the tournament progressed,
South Korean guards at the 38th Parallel would blast out
commentaries of their team's matches across the border
in an effort to teach the North Koreans a "social and
cultural lesson."

The number of supporters on the streets in South Korea
dramatically increased as the 2002 World Cup progressed.
According to the newspaper *Dong-a-Ilbo*, the four and a half
million with daubed red faces and replica kits who watched
the Italy game in the squares swelled to six million for the
quarter-final against Spain and an astonishing seven million
for the match against Germany in the semi-final. On 29th
June, the day of the third place play-off, a North Korean
gunboat attacked a South Korean patrol boat in the yellow
sea, killing five South Korean sailors. Ironically, a fax had
been sent from the North Korean FA to the South Korean FA
congratulating them for reaching the semi-final a week
before. Pyongyang later described the gunboat attack as
"regrettable" but many in the South believed it was Kim
Jong-il's way of attempting to dampen the patriotic fervour
in the South.

After the World Cup the *Dong-a-Ilbo* also reported that the
Korea National Tourism Corporation had worked out how
host cities could use their profile to boost the number of
visitors to their respective cities. The 'Post-World Cup Policy'
helped establish six new professional clubs, increased investment in youth football, and utilised the World Cup stadia

by turning them into huge discount shops and giant leisure complexes. "The real champions are the Korean people," concluded *Newsweek Japan*. A government survey suggested that 42 per cent of Koreans now felt friendlier towards Japan than previously. After the tournament, arguments in Korea about Hiddink's impact – not just in football, but also in politics, economy and education – raged for months. Writing in the *Newsmaker*, Professor Herschell L Grossman said, "The performance of the South Korean team in the 2002 World Cup has demonstrated to every Korean in a way that is easily seen that meritocracy yields better results than cronyism . . . Hiddink has expedited change and his success has made it look revolutionary. It remains to be seen how fast, in what ways and with what effects South Korean society will continue to change. The Western model of a meritocratic society is not easy to emulate."

In the eight years which have followed the 2002 World Cup, the South Korean economy has continued to grow. In 2009 it was estimated as being the world's eighth largest exporter of goods, Asia's largest, and Korean companies like Samsung continue to pursue multi-billion dollar contracts in the West. South Korea's citizens have more access to broadband than any other country in the world.

"Unquestionably," argued President Lee Myung-bak last year, "the 2002 World Cup showed South Korea in an entirely new light, and just as the Red Devils [the fans] cheered the football team onto a new plateau, our workforce has done likewise with the economy in the intervening years."

Yet some continue to question the changes in the South since the World Cup. Although crowds in the K-League are higher than eight years ago, market forces dictate that a large number of Korean stars ply their trade in Japan or Europe. Many of the World Cup stadia are white elephants.

Che Bum-hohn argues, "In some ways, there is a more divided society since 2002 and the World Cup definitely speeded up this process. Korean traditionalists argue that what Westerners called 'cronyism' was actually evidence of respect, social solidarity, and responsibility, which they believed were positive features of Korean society. A good percentage of the population reject individualism and meritocracy, because they believe that traditional tenets of Korean society are now being eroded. Not everyone wants to adhere to Western ideals. During the World Cup, I knew of many activists who, in the 1980s, had been beaten by riot police and had streaming eyes after being tear-gassed, as they campaigned for a democratic South Korea. During the World Cup, many couldn't bring themselves to go to those squares in cities – now places of celebration – because of the bad memories of what happened with the riot police. Too much of what has happened in the past is being forgotten. Society will be cleansed of what is important, if we are not careful. To me and many others, the World Cup represented the emergence of a non-political generation who are primarily individualistic. That doesn't rest easily with me, and many others in my country."

When it was announced that the 2002 World Cup was to be staged in Asia, Western journalists, their curiosity piqued, began to ask more searching questions about the fate of the North Korean team who'd famously beaten Italy and reached the quarter-finals back in 1966. In the ensuing years, they'd effectively vanished. After four years of intensive negotiations, Daniel Gordon and his British film crew was finally granted access to the surviving members of the team, and made his film The Game of Their Lives. The players' stories were both illuminating and occasionally bewildering.

Throughout 1966 the Cold War warmed up considerably. Much to Moscow's displeasure, two American Gemini spacecraft became the first to rendezvous up above, although the Soviet Union later drew level in the space race as Luna X orbited the moon. An H-bomb fell off a B52 bomber and it took three weeks for US reconnaissance to locate it on the Atlantic seabed. In Vietnam, US bombers attacked the Demilitarized Zone between North and South. And the fact that a team from Communist North Korea would be participating in the eighth World Cup in England only added to the Cold War intrigue. With only one place reserved for the whole of Africa, Asia and Oceania, there was a mass boycott of nations from these regions in protest, leaving only North Korea and Australia to compete for the remaining place.

As the two nations were still technically at war, a neutral venue was found for the two legged play-off, and the authorities settled upon Phnom Penh in Cambodia for both matches. The Australian team, made up mainly of British expats, were a gifted group of individuals, but were destroyed (9–2 over two legs) by the fast, organised Koreans. Australian player Geoff Sleight, who along with his teammates watched the North Koreans train before the first match, said, "To us they looked like they were out of the army. They looked regimented and they did as they were told. On the other hand, we felt we were liberated and free-thinking. We felt our way was best." The Koreans correctly surmised that their rivals lacked pace and cohesion.

Unbeknown to the Australians, the North Koreans had been touring the Soviet Union and Eastern Europe in the months leading up to the qualifier. Coach Myong Rye-hyun recalled, "We were mentally determined, physically fit, and full of energy. Our great leader [Kim Il-sung] stressed that to be an excellent footballer you must run fast and kick accurately." Kim emphasised that, like the country itself, the football team must adhere to the principles of the Chollima movement (speed and hard work). The Korean War had left the North flattened and Kim had emphasised that only hard work and discipline would rebuild the nation.

"As players, we followed this idea of Chollima," explains Myong Rye-hyun. "In Korea, people would say to us, 'You do well on the football pitch, and we will take care of the economy.'" The team even adopted the Chollima theme in their team song, "Carrying the nation's honour on our shoulders, We are the glorious Chollima football team, We can beat anyone, even the strongest team, We will show others who we are, that's right, Fight and win, Let's raise our national flag to the sky in celebration."

A couple of months before the team flew to England, Kim summoned the team to him. He told the players, "European and South American teams dominate world football. As the representatives of Asia and Africa, as coloured people, I urge you to win one or two matches."

Behind the scenes, the North Koreans' participation in the World Cup was shrouded in doubt, because the British government didn't recognize North Korea. In an official memo to the Home Secretary, one Foreign Office official wrote, "The North Koreans have thoughtlessly beaten the Australians, and given us a headache." Fearing that allowing the team in might set a dangerous precedent for other countries where sovereignty was questioned (East Germany being the prime example), the Foreign Office considered refusing to issue the North Koreans with work permits. With Sports Minister Denis Howell heavily involved in negotiations, it was agreed that no anthems would be played at any matches throughout the tournament, apart from before the final and the opening game. However, the Football Association was anxious to promote the World Cup as a festival of nations, and North Korean flags, with their red star, flew in England alongside those of the 15 other participants. So as not to offend the South Koreans, British authorities ordered that the team would be referred to as North Korea, never the People's Democratic Republic of Korea.

Based in Middlesbrough for the opening round of group matches, and rated as 1,000–1 outsiders by bookmakers, the North Koreans quickly adapted to their new surroundings. As a Boro fan who'd seen his team relegated to the Third Division during the 1965/66 season, Denis Barry, along with thousands of others, felt a deep sense of curiosity when the Chollima football team rolled into town. "It was a real honour for Ayresome Park to stage World Cup football," he explains. "The ground was renovated for the tournament, and we had a great chance to show off our playing surface. The feeling was that it did the town and the club great credit. Looking back, there was a great deal in common between Middlesbrough and the North Koreans. We were out on a geographical limb and were underdogs in most senses of the word. We soon discovered that the Koreans were fine ball players and the Middlesbrough crowd has always been appreciative of good ball players." Holed up in the Saint George Airport Hotel, the North Koreans' training pitch was situated next to the petrochemical plant. It was hardly glamorous, but then as Denis Barry points out, "It wouldn't have been such a compelling or unusual story if they'd played their matches, say, in London. They would probably have been swallowed up by the entire experience."

"Not tough enough. Clever Koreans outpowered," ran the *Daily Express* headline after the Soviet Union thumped them 3–0 in their opening match. Against a backdrop of Brylcream, Marlboro Light, and Newcastle Brown advertisement hoardings, Myong Rye-hyun's team (whose average height was five foot five) simply couldn't withstand the Russians' combative approach and seemed set for an early exit from the tournament. But having seen the Koreans bounced around the pitch, the Ayresome Park crowd had begun to get behind them. Goalkeeper Ri Chan-myong pulled off a succession of miraculous saves and the Korean midfield ran hard and fast at the Soviet defence, much to the crowd's pleasure, but they were unable to convert their chances into goals. In their second game, against Chile, they trailed 1–0 with just five minutes remaining. The crowd, now treating the Koreans as if they were the home side, grew more raucous as time passed. With just five minutes remaining, Pak Seung-jin rifled home a coruscating half-volley from the edge of the box. "They haven't cheered like this in Middlesbrough for years," claimed BBC commentator Frank Bough. Afterwards, with local dignitaries pouring into the Korean dressing room, local boys, anxious for autographs, swarmed around the players like bees around a honey pot.

As North Korea prepared to face Italy in the decisive group match on 19th July, Kim Il-sung's instructions rang clearly in the players' ears. "If I hadn't succeeded in carrying out my role within the team," explained goalkeeper Ri Chan-myong, "I would have failed in the tasks set by the Great Leader." The Koreans drew heavily on the state philosophy of 'Juche,' which sets out that everyone is responsible for one's own destiny. Rich, young and glamorous, the Italians were expected to cruise into the quarter-finals; at home, the Italian media claimed that anything less would be a national disgrace.

But after captain Giacomo Bulgarelli was forced off late in the first half after a clash with a Korean (there were no substitutes in those days), the Italians began to feel the strain and on 41 minutes Pak Doo-Ik blasted the ball past Albertosi. Despite several excellent second-half chances, Italy were out and in the public scandal which followed all bar Albertosi, Facchetti, Rivera and Mazzola were axed, permanently. Several of the Ayresome Park crowd invaded the pitch to embrace the victorious Koreans. Denis Barry recalls, "There was such a strong bond between us and that team. It was an unforgettable day, and a massive event for the whole community."

The North Koreans took on Portugal in the quarter-finals at Goodison Park. Spooked by the presence of religious iconography at Loyola Hall near Liverpool, the Catholic retreat previously booked for the Italian team, and forced to sleep in single rooms the staunchly atheist team, who'd always roomed in pairs, struggled to adapt to the alien conditions, much less sleep well. An estimated 3,000 supporters, many of whom proudly waved the North Korean flag, made the two-hour homage from Middlesbrough to Liverpool to see their adopted team take on the might of Eusebio and Torres. Denis Barry recalls, "A group of us decided to travel across to the match, and we'd made a banner which said 'Pak Doo-Ik, Crown Prince of the Orient.' It was a lovely, exciting day out, on a beautiful summer day, and back then it was relatively easy to gain access to World Cup games. It wasn't the commercial event that it is now. We couldn't believe what we were seeing. Korea went 3–0 up within 20 minutes. The crowd was in a state of disbelief, and were chanting, 'Easy, easy.' But then the footballing part of your brain took over, and you knew it couldn't last."

Reality came in the form of Eusebio, whose combination of speed and power had accounted for Brazil in the group stages. The Mozambique-born striker scored four goals as his side eventually ran out 5–3 winners. After his first goal he picked up the ball from inside the net, ran quickly back to the centre circle, and placed the ball firmly on the spot. It was a statement of intent if ever there was one, and the North Koreans, now facing arguably the best player in the world, had no answer. "More experienced sides would have sat on their lead," explained *The Guardian*'s David Lacey, "but the North Koreans lacked the experience to make the Portugese do the work. They lost their discipline."

When the team flew back to Pyongyang, they received a heroes' reception and apologised to the nation for, in the end, bowing out so meekly. One headline in a national newspaper claimed, "Pak Sung-jin plays like magic, and the goalkeeper plays like a spiritual god." It was arguably the last time that North Korea was viewed in a positive light across the globe. Since then, the tales have all been about repressive dictatorship, membership of George Bush's 'Axis of Evil,' and reportedly widespread famines inside what has been described as the 'Jurassic Park of Communism.' The North Korean players disappeared under the radar. According to rumour, their hero status in North Korea went with it, and the demigods of '66 would find themselves restricted by more earthly concerns.

Shortly before Daniel Gordon and his team entered North Korea to film their documentary, Kang Chol-hwan – a former political prisoner and the first person to escape from the North Korean gulags and tell the story of his imprisonment – made a startling revelation in his book *The Aquariums of Pyongyang: Ten Years in the North Korean Gulag*. Written in collaboration with French writer Pierre Rigoulout, he alleges that during his incarceration, he met North Korea's top scorer in '66, Pak Seung-jin. In the book he insists Pak, sentenced for 12 years, earned himself the nickname 'Cockroach' because he survived a three-month stint in the sweatbox (a small shack with no openings) by devouring centipedes or cockroaches to boost his energy levels. He'd been sent there for stealing nails from the camp's construction materials shop, and subsequently punched the guard who tried to apprehend him.

The book claims that, along with many of his teammates, Pak Seung-jin had celebrated North Korea's victory against the Italians by embarking, "on a wild drinking binge and, by the end of the night, was seen carrying on in public with some girls. In Pyongyang, the national team's barroom antics were judged bourgeois, reactionary, corrupted by imperialism and bad ideas."

Daniel Gordon interviewed Pierre Rigoulot for the film, although the conversation didn't make it into the final cut. Gordon explains, "There was too much 'he said, they said' about it all. It didn't quite sound right," and he remains sceptical as to the validity of the claims.

"We asked the local pub owner in Liverpool whether he'd served them alcohol. He confirmed that the Koreans drank water and soft drinks all night, although there may be some truth in the suggestion that their entourage, including dieticians and trainers, did drink beer. We later discovered photographic evidence that at the time Pak Seung-jin was supposed to be in the gulag, he was playing football in India. One of the first questions we asked the team was whether any of them had been jailed after the World Cup. To a man, they categorically denied the claims.

"When the team speak about Kim Il-sung in the film, they were visibly upset when they spoke of his death in 1994. It was he who would have ordered their incarceration. I never got the impression they were crying crocodile tears. It's possible that the team was purged in the late-60s – in terms of many established players being dropped from the side. It's even possible that the author of the book, Kang Chol-hwan, met another Pak Seung-jin. I'd also suggest that the North Korean government wouldn't have allowed us to speak with the team if they really had been jailed, much less allow them to travel to England as a group all those years later. But that is the nature of things in the region. The regime never confirms or denies anything."

In South Korea, Che Bum-hohn has also heard of the stories surrounding the class of '66, and has seen *The Game of Their Lives*. "The rumours were that they were jailed because the team was almost becoming as popular as Kim Il-sung, which would be unthinkable in an autocracy. There was also a tale that Pak Seung-jin was singled out because he followed up Pak Doo-Ik's shot against Italy and kicked it back into the net after Pak scored. Apparently, the regime thought it too individualistic an act. It's amazing what sticks isn't it? Then a story did the rounds in 1994 that after North Korea failed to qualify for the World Cup, Kim Jong-il made the entire team and its coaches work in a chicken-plucking factory for six months afterwards as a punishment. It's now part of World Cup mythology, but there was never any proof that it happened."

For the first time in World Cup history, both Korean teams will be present at the 2010 tournament. In recent years, a series of 'friendlies' have been played between the two nations, which for diplomatic reasons have tended to end in draws. There has even been talk of the two countries groping their way towards unification. Yet even these friendly matches are laden with political intrigue. South Korean war veterans have protested outside the stadiums during games, angry that the matches endorse a new unification flag (the South Korean government have refused to allow the North Korean flag to be flown, as this would violate the country's National Security Law.) They also object to the fact that both governments agree not to play their national anthems before the games and instead prefer the traditional Korean folk song *Arirang*. And of course, the games are never shown live in the North. Only victories are screened later on North Korean TV.

When the two sides met in a World Cup qualifier in Seoul in April 2009, South Korea scored the winner with just three minutes left, prompting claims from their opponents that their football team's water had been poisoned. A statement carried by North Korea's official news agency KCNA on Sunday called the alleged act "a product of [South Korean President] Lee Myung-bak government's moves for confrontation with the DPRK [North Korea]." The statement also accused the match's Omani referee of bias, adding, "The match thus turned into a theatre of plot breeding and swindling."

"North Korea decided on everything, including accommodation, and we were never involved in the process," came the official response from Seoul. All of this came at a time of heightened tensions on the Korean peninsula surrounding the North's launching of a long-range rocket, which triggered the UN Security Council to call an emergency meeting. Their home qualifier against the South in October 2009 was moved to Shanghai because the North's authorities refused to allow the playing of the South's national anthem on home soil.

Comparatively little is known of the North Korean team which has finally emerged from the shadows and will take the field in South Africa. Taewoon Park, from South Korea's *Sports Seoul* newspaper, suggests their rise is mainly as a result of military-style training. With clear echoes of '66, he explains, "Their teamwork is really good and their stamina is probably the best in the world. Half of the current national team squad plays for 4.25 Sports Group which is the army team, and so they have been playing together since they were 15."

Intriguingly, the partial opening of the Bamboo Curtain has also made a positive impact on the national team. Star striker Jong Tae-Se, nicknamed 'the People's Rooney,' plies his trade in Japan. Others have moved to Russia and Switzerland, and are now exposed to a higher standard of football. With the North Korean economy in dire straits, Kim Jong-il may be forced to accept more foreign aid and as a result, crank open his borders a little more. His football team is unlikely to eclipse the achievements of the class of 1966 however, and despite rumours to the contrary, the prospect of a unified Korean team at future World Cups is as remote as ever.

14

THE VOODOO GANGSTERS

Arriving in any new country is often a case of sensory overload. You emerge from the blandness of your aircraft into an explosion of sights, sounds and unfamiliar smells, and – in the case of Haitian capital Port-au-Prince – a wave of tropical heat which wraps around your face like a warm, damp towel. It's impossible not to feel wired and nervous as, after a two-hour flight from Miami, the plane, bound for Toussaint Louverture International Airport, descends towards Hispaniola, the Caribbean island which Haiti shares with its wealthier neighbour, the Dominican Republic. Declared the region's poorest country by the United Nations a year before the devastating earthquake of 2010, British travellers had been warned to visit only "if strictly necessary."

On the face of it my edgy Caribbean adventure wasn't necessary – strictly speaking anyway. However, after months of frantic and often fruitless transatlantic telephoning and emailing, several of the surviving members of Haiti's 1974 World Cup squad – I'm reliably informed – are ready to tell their remarkable story for the first time. The team's star striker, Manno Sanon, had unburdened himself to me on the telephone two years before his death in 2008 and I had email contact with several other players and officials in the months before my visit. But Sanon always insisted, "You get yourself over here, my friend; otherwise you won't understand the impact which our qualification for the Finals in Germany had on Haiti."

A few months before deciding to follow Sanon's instructions, my would-be fixer Jean Samou, a local bank clerk whom I'm put in touch with via Manno Sanon, warns me, "Don't come here if you're squeamish, or if you think you're coming for a Caribbean holiday." After meeting me at the airport he takes one look at me, snorts derisively and informs me, "You'll stand out like a sore thumb and get yourself kidnapped if you're not careful." Although he's half joking, Trailfinders warned any client bound for Haiti in the previous week to be on their guard against "sudden, violent uprisings, and illegal road blocks."

Even the passport checker gets in on the act. "Why are you here buddy?" he asks. "You a James Bond fan? We've had a few of them from the USA and Europe here recently." Port-au-Prince, despite being hit by outbreaks of typhoid and dysentery, had benefited economically since 2008 from Daniel Craig's visit to the city's decaying docks in The Quantum of Solace. When I inform him of the purpose of my visit – to interview those connected with Haiti's 1974 World Cup adventure, he shoots me a quizzical look. "You looking for voodoo and the Duvaliers," he chuckles, "or music and sunshine? You'll get both if you do your research properly." During my brief stay the passport checker's words prove uncannily accurate.

According to a recent UNICEF report, the Haitian economy has remained almost stagnant for a decade. The vast majority of the population scrabble a living in agriculture or move to the capital to work in the plethora of struggling small businesses. The average wage is around US$500 a year. Already hanging by the thinnest of threads, the 2010 earthquake abruptly destroyed many of the city's fragile, hastily constructed buildings, and snuffed out tens of thousand of lives and jobs with it. But it wasn't always like that. Back in the 1950s, Europe's literati, including the likes of Noël Coward, travelled to Haiti for inspiration, and were captivated by the tropical climate, rich history and stunning coastal views, along with the colonial gingerbread houses which are perched perilously close to Port-au-Prince's shanty towns. The tourist trade took a huge battering due to decades of political turbulence, and the tourists who disembarked from the huge cruise ships which docked in Port-au-Prince had a ghoulish fascination for the herds of swine which foraged amongst the refuse left around the beaches when the tide went out. The US$19 per night hotel I stayed in the middle of town (most tourists prefer to stay in the upwardly mobile Petionville region in the hills above the capital, with designer shops and boutiques, but Manno Sanon told me I'd be a fraud if I did) was classic high schlock – all brown wallpaper and deep orange carpets. And no air conditioning. The owner explains, "This place was a fashionable establishment 30 years ago. But like everything else around here we're in a timewarp. Architecture, music, football . . . most people hark back to what happened 30 years ago. And don't drink the water, by the way, else you'll spend most of your time here on the toilet."

Fittingly for a nation dogged by natural disasters, political upheaval, economic boom and (mainly) bust and a series of despotic rulers (the Duvaliers – François and his son Jean-Claude are the most infamous), Haiti's 15 minutes of sporting fame at the 1974 World Cup represents much more than a purely sporting adventure. Stories of black magic, partial deification of Haiti's star players, music and secret police involvement are intertwined with the whole story.

Although football had been played in Haiti for years, it was François 'Papa Doc' Duvalier's rise to power which raised the game's profile, mainly due to the fact that he quickly began to pour money into it in the mid-1960s. A passionate follower of Italian and South American football, he fully understood that when it came to getting the populace on your side, football was arguably the most powerful mechanism of all, and when it came to the World Cup, the team and the nation – if conditions were favourable – could become one. With Haiti's notoriously primitive medical facilities, low literacy rate and high instances of rural famine, Papa Doc knew that a strong national football team could benefit him hugely in the long term and provide a ray of hope for the country's beleaguered populace.

He was lucky; after the team performed well at the 1965 Caribbean Youth tournament, the emerging attacker Roger Saint-Vil, goalkeeper Henri Françillon and future skipper Philippe Vorbe began to rise to prominence, attracting the interest of European club scouts. Papa Doc, determined to keep his emerging diamonds together and fearing that they might vanish into the mushrooming Haitian diaspora, banned all foreign transfers.

Saint-Vil, now a New York resident, recalls, "Our training facilities improved and whenever we played a rival Caribbean country we stayed in good hotels and were fed well. You have to remember our background. Many of us came from impoverished families and already François Duvalier had brought light into our lives. For us, he was a giver of life, a ray of hope and we'd do anything for him."

The team underwent serious training for the 1970 World Cup qualifiers and it's still a matter of bitterness that they failed to reach Mexico. The berth instead went to El Salvador (who'd earlier knocked out Honduras – thus sparking the 'Soccer War') who beat Haiti 1–0 in a play-off on neutral ground in Jamaica. The countries had played two games before that – Haiti losing 2–1 at home, before defeating El Salvador 3–0 away – but that was in the days before aggregate scores counted. "That was heartbreaking," recalls Joe Namphy, former Secretary General of the Haitian Football Federation, "because that vintage was easily as good as the one four years later. We really should have been in two consecutive Finals."

Under wily coach Antoine Tassy, Haiti's bold attacking play attracted the attention of English football journalist Brian Glanville, who remarked upon "the sheer tenacity and fluid movement of the gallant Haitians" in a *Times* article.

The Duvalier government issued a statement which read, "We pledge to our people that the football team will reach the 1974 World Cup Finals and that President Duvalier will continue to monitor his team's progress and to back the team, its players and manager to ensure that this dream becomes a reality."

Papa Doc had already interfered in the life of one-high profile Haitian football star, with devastating consequences. Before the golden generation emerged during the late '60s and early '70s, the nation's most famous player was Joe Gaetjens who opted to play for the USA rather than his homeland. The lanky striker's claim to fame came in the 1950 World Cup when his diving header squirmed under England goalkeeper Bert Williams to give the USA a highly improbable 1–0 win. Gaetjens's moment of glory made him a national hero back in Haiti and, after his football career ended, he returned to Port-au-Prince where his family still lived, and opened a dry-cleaning business. "Everyone loved Joe," explains local resident Roger Saint-Vierre, wearing the loudest of Hawaiian shirts and swigging beer with both fists. "And he loved both his family and his football. His life was rich and full. Little else mattered to him. He was really what you might call a salt-of-the-earth character." Gaetjens later organised a youth soccer league and, for a while, coached the national team where he was universally known as 'Gentleman Joe.' At no time, according to anyone who knew him, did he show so much as a passing interest in politics. But unfortunately for him, his brothers did.

When Papa Doc won the Presidency in 1957, and again in a sham 1961 election backed by money and guns, Gaetjens's brothers openly supported his opponent, an industrialist and close family friend named Louis Dejoie. Gérard Gaetjens was one of Dejoie's closest advisers. On the morning of 8th July 1963, two member of Papa Doc's secret police – the dreaded 'Tonton Macoutes' (taken from the Creole term for 'bogeymen') – showed up at the family's dry-cleaning business, got into Joe Gaetjens's car and, at gunpoint, ordered him to drive away. Three days later his blue station wagon was found parked in front of the police headquarters in Port-au-Prince. He was never seen again. The rumours continue to rage about exactly what happened to him. Twenty years after Joe's disappearance, a former Haitian senator claimed that he'd shared a cell with him, in Fort Dimanche military prison, and that Gaetjens was shot dead by prison guards.

During my time in Port-au-Prince, two drinkers in a decrepit downtown joint tell me they also came across the terrified Gaetjens at the prison shortly before his apparent murder at the hand of Duvalier's heavies. My fixer Jean suggests I, "treat these stories with caution. Everyone over 50 with a grudge against Papa Doc claims to have been in a cell with Joe Gaetjens in Fort Dimanche." Roger Saint-Vierre explains, "Haiti has got many dark secrets, and Joe's fate is just one of them, albeit one of the most infamous. You can be sure that there are still residents here in this street who really know what happened to him. Papa Doc's men didn't simply vanish when Duvalier died. They may have got older, but many are still here. At the time, no one discussed what happened to Joe, although most people probably surmised it. If you uttered the name 'Gaetjens,' you only did so with people whom you trusted with your life. Who is to say who was listening to you?"

The Duvalier regime always denied any knowledge of Joe's eventual fate, and he remains among the country's *disparus* (disappeared). Even Pelé, whilst at New York Cosmos, implored the Haitian government to open its files on Joe Gaetjens. In 1971, the Cosmos staged an exhibition game at the Yankee Stadium to raise money for Gaetjens's wife and three sons, who went into hiding for two years after his disappearance before emigrating to the USA for good.

Papa Doc also stands accused of fixing matches by Haiti's Confederation of North, Central American and Caribbean Association Football (CONCACAF) rivals. During the 1970 World Cup qualification tournament, an unnamed Dutch Antilles player claimed to have seen a Duvalier official disappear into the referee's room prior to their clash with Haiti, and emerge smiling minutes later. Duvalier's boys won 2–0, but the Dutch Antilles – according to a report from the game by a Jamaican journalist, had four blatant penalty appeals turned down. Haitian historian Jean Antoine explains, "One can view these stories in two ways. On the one hand, there may well be some truth to the Dutch Antilles player's claim, because Duvalier had a huge amount of power and wealth in those days when referees were paid a pittance. During the 1974 qualification round, his son Baby Doc clearly pulled some strings, so it would hardly be a surprise. On the other hand, it's too easy to claim that they won matches through foul means. You can just blame Duvalier for everything, and that detracts from the fact that Haiti were a bright, attacking side. One has to consider that rivals from El Salvador, Mexico, and Honduras – more established football countries – were jealous of Haiti's rise to prominence."

By 1964, Papa Doc had awarded himself the title 'President for Life' after securing 28 million votes (3,000 brave souls voted against him) in another sham election. A staunch advocate of *negritude* (black pride) he garnered much support from poor black people anxious to challenge the power of Haiti's *mulatto* (mixed-race) elite. Striker Manno Sanon, emerging as Haiti's star performer in the early 70s, explained, "Most of us guys came from very humble backgrounds but both Duvaliers pushed the idea of *negritude*, which made them very popular with the masses. It meant we were something worthy, rather than just another black person. Both Duvalier and the coach Tassy were very adept at inspiring all players. I knew that when I pulled on the orange shirt I was representing both Haiti and pushing the concept of *negritude*. But there were also a number of *mulattos* in the side. Some spoke French, some Creole. But Tassy spoke both languages and the squad was united because Tassy would have stood for nothing less. I firmly believe that the national football team was a beacon – a symbol – for what Haitian people should have aspired to."

As well as following Italian football closely, Duvalier was

also a fervent admirer of Mussolini's black shirts, and modelled his bodyguards, the Tonton Macoutes, on Il Duce's private army. Papa Doc's bogey men weren't directly paid for terrorising would-be opponents, but they were able to make their money from extortion and intercepting funds supposedly bound for social aid in Haiti's poorest areas. Sanon recalled, "It was the side of the regime that the players weren't aware of, although there were always guys hanging around the team, particularly when we travelled abroad. They smiled at us though, like friendly big brothers. We didn't see their ugly side, not until the 1974 World Cup, anyway."

Several Haitian stars decline to comment on their relation-ship with Papa Doc, which seems to confirm the fact that he ruled by fear and even now, as Sanon admitted, "The mention of his name still makes many Haitians shudder." Yet when asked to recount a Duvalier story, three members of the side trot out the tale of former Tonton Macoutes leader Clement Barbot. Sanon explained, "Papa Doc became convinced that Barbot was plotting against him and after he had him executed, he was told by a witch doctor that Barbot had been transformed into a black dog. Duvalier ordered that all black dogs on the island be shot on sight. Then he ordered that Barbot's head be packed in ice and sent to him. He spent several hours staring at the head, trying to connect with Barbot's spirit." Sanon laughed. "So many people know the story that it must be true, but he was still our benefactor nonetheless. I'm not always comfort-able with that," he added. Many of Haiti's 1974 team, directly or indirectly, for better or for worse, were affected by the Duvaliers' frequently uneasy mix of voodoo, oppression and negritude.

The vast majority of Haitian players continued to live in their homeland and they couldn't fail to notice the impact of the Tonton Macoutes in rural areas. Papa Doc's heavies seized much of the good quality peasant land, forcing huge numbers to flee to the increasingly dangerous and disease-ridden capital city. One member of the team, who ran a small electrical business in Port-au-Prince and who even now asked not to be named, explains, "I hated the Duvaliers with a passion. It was fairly easy to see what was happening if you used your eyes and members of my family disappeared at the time, and my cousins lost their farmland which they'd worked so hard to build up over the years. Yet as a footballer who wanted to do well I knew that my destiny lay with him. We were helpless but at that time you kidded yourself that what people were saying wasn't true. The propaganda claimed that the Duvaliers' enemies were responsible for the glut of disappearances – not Papa Doc. If you closed your mind, your eyes and your ears, you could just about believe it. Some days."

In April 1971, Papa Doc died, and his only son, Jean-Claude 'Baby Doc' Duvalier, became the world's youngest president at 19 years of age. Notorious for showing a complete lack of interest in domestic affairs and intent on pursuing a playboy lifestyle, Baby Doc nonetheless realised that unless he reduced the excesses of his father's autocratic approach, he would be toppled quickly, most probably by the CIA. In response to US pressure he blunted the harsher edges of his father's regime by releasing political prisoners, easing press censorship and initiating judicial reforms. As an act of good faith the US government restored its aid programme late in 1971. Through this injection of cash, Haiti was able to achieve its economic miracle – such as it was. Historian Jean Antoine explains: "Of course, much was still wrong with the country in the early days of Baby Doc, but many Haitians look back on the era with nostalgic pride. The numbers of lootings, murders and outbreaks of disease were significantly reduced, and the government made more of a concerted effort to ensure that children went to school. And the football team benefited enormously."

Baby Doc opened up his coffers to an even greater extent than his father had done, setting up a special bank account for the Haitian Football Federation. Joe Namphy explains: "He financed the whole show, including the national Sylvio

Cator Stadium, which was totally refurbished for the 1973 CONCACAF tournament, at the cost of one million dollars. He also built the Olympic Track and Centre Sportif de Carrefour and the Gymnasium Vincent for basketball. He was almost like Berlusconi at AC Milan. He was in complete control of things." Manno Sanon explained, "He made it clear that it was his team, and his money which got us to where we were. He was much more accessible than his father. He'd show up to training and regularly phoned me and several of the other players to check that we were OK. Some of the guys felt it was dangerous to have Jean-Claude too close to the team. Although he was young, he was still like an old-fashioned father, who gave us life but could also punish us if he wished."

The 1973 CONCACAF tournament doubled as a World Cup qualification competition and all games were played at the intimidating 30,000-capacity Sylvio Cator ground in Port-au-Prince, famed for its bear pit atmosphere during big matches. Manno Sanon admitted that home advantage helped Haiti massively. "The crowd made a huge noise, and intimidated the opposition. Games in Central America and the Caribbean can always be vocal, but this got fairly toxic at times, with objects thrown onto the pitch and at rival players, and there were stories of opposition players getting hassled in car parks. It wasn't something any of us would condone but it happened and I can't deny that it helped us."

Somewhat predictably, Baby Doc stands accused of malpractice, especially before a key match with Trinidad and Tobago, which Haiti won 2–1. Trinidad striker Steve David, who finished as the tournament's top scorer, alleged that "Dark arts enabled Haiti to get through that. You can't tell me that that game was fair and above board." David's misgivings about the match, which saw the Salvadorian referee Enriquez rule out four decent-looking Trinidad goals, seemed to be confirmed when Enriquez was banned from officiating a year later after accepting bribes.

Baby Doc also planted 'conductors' in the crowd to whip fans into a fervour. Bar owner Pierre Dierdiste, a well-known face at Haiti games in the 1970s, claims to have been approached by a government official and told to "turn up the noise" at games. "I was given a megaphone, surrounded by drummers and told to whip everybody up. There were several of us around the ground and it definitely worked out for us. That wasn't all. There were also witch doctors in the crowd conjuring spirits and casting spells on the opposition. It was unbelievable."

Haitian musician Bob Lemoine, now a New York DJ, penned a special song for the tournament, Toup Pou Yo ('Kick for Goal'), which was played prior to matches and remains the most famous football song to emerge from the country. Former Haiti midfielder Jean Herbert Austin recalls, "Those three weeks were the most incredible I can remember in Port-au-Prince. After every victory in the tournament there were carnivals in the streets and the whole place came to a virtual standstill. The crunch game was against Guatemala, and before the game Duvalier was in the dressing room urging us to 'Win, win, win for Haiti.' And we did just that." When the final whistle went at the end of the 2–1 victory, signifying Haiti's qualification for the 1974 World Cup Finals, Manno Sanon sank to his knees. Others were crying, or screaming like lunatics. The whole country was in uproar. When the players finally got away from the stadium after police finally dispersed the thronging crowd, they went to party with Baby Doc. "You're heroes, every one of you," beamed their benefactor. Controversially, he'd fulfilled his late father's dream.

The team flew to Germany two weeks before the tournament started and stayed at the Grunwald Sports Complex in Munich, where they would play their matches in a tough group which also included Italy, Poland and Argentina. For many of the players it was their first time in Europe and Jean-Herbert Austin recalls that "some of the players felt very isolated, away from what they knew. We simply weren't seasoned campaigners at this level."

Despite coach Tassy's attempts to stop the team from

feeling homesick, their feelings of detachment grew during the tournament although, as Austin admits, "We were all looking forward to playing Italy in the first game. They hadn't conceded a goal for 1,100 minutes – a world record at that time – but we felt they were an ageing team and we knew they were fighting between themselves. We knew there were some problems with their striker Georgio Chinaglia, who was making waves in the squad at that time."

As the Italy match approached, Tassy sensed that his players were getting a little blasé and, according to legend, he fired several shots from a starter pistol into the ceiling after a training session, causing masonry to fall on the players' heads. Austin and Sanon claim it never happened, although others explain it was "a wake up call with a hint of menace behind it before the Italy game."

Italy's *catenaccio* defence, with its resolutely negative sweeper and with goalkeeper Dino Zoff in superlative form, made them formidable opponents, and Manno Sanon claimed, "They justified their spot as one of the favourites, and there was always Riva to snap up the goals, and Rivera and Mazzola to help construct them." But it was Sanon who stunned the Italians shortly after half-time when, from an inch-perfect Philippe Vorbe pass, he galloped through the defence, rounded Zoff, and slammed the ball into the net. "I can remember it like it was yesterday," he claimed. "I always knew that with my speed, I could get at the Italian defence and that goal put Haiti on the map, whatever came afterwards. Psychologically, I don't think we were ready for it, and we got caught up in the goal and lost our concentration. But that moment was my greatest in football. Zoff's face – he was absolutely furious with his defence, and I was joyful too because I knew that back home everyone would be going wild."

Painfully, the Italians pulled themselves back to win 3–1, but their press made clear its disgust that little Haiti had broken the 1,147 minute record. Sanon and his teammates were the heroes of the moment and next morning in glorious sunshine, they strolled around Munich Zoo lapping up the attention of the press. Back home, Baby Doc, who rarely ventured outside Haiti, conveyed his congratulations by telegram.

The following day, Haiti's world collapsed. A routine dope test on Ernst Jean-Joseph, their red haired, *mulatto* centre half had proved positive. Jean-Joseph protested that he had to take pills for his asthma, only for the team doctor to inform a press conference that this was nonsense, stating that the player was "not intelligent enough to know what he was doing."

The world's press hovered as Jean-Joseph hung around wretchedly, waiting for the inevitable punishment. Haitian officials dragged the screaming player out of the Grunwald Sports Centre, beat him up in full view of the world's press, shoved him into a car, drove him to the airport and flew him back to Haiti.

Jean-Joseph's teammates were horrified. "I remember the look of venom in one official who'd always been all smiles previously," explains Miami-based Fritz Plantin, a former central defender." As successful footballers, we'd been protected from that side of the regime, but now we saw the dark side. We had a sleepless night before the game against Poland and, to be honest, I was only thinking about Ernst, not the game."

The same could probably be said for all Plantin's teammates, and they were thrashed 7–0 by the rampant Poles who were inspired by Grzegorz Lato. "We were 5–0 down at half-time," recalls Plantin, "and to be honest, they were kind to us in the second half because they only scored twice more. If they'd run up double figures it wouldn't have flattered them."

Later, back at the Sports Centre, skipper Phillipe Vorbe was called to the telephone. Jean-Joseph had been instructed by Baby Doc to telephone the team's headquarters to prove to the team that he was still alive. That had a calming effect and, in their final game, Haiti acquitted themselves well against Argentina, losing just 3–1 with Sanon once again on the score sheet.

Jean-Joseph, who had never previously spoken of the

dubious honour of being the first player to be banned from the World Cup for a positive dope test, made encouraging noises about an interview before I arrived in Haiti, only to vanish as soon as I arrive in Port-au-Prince, apparently on a fishing trip in the north. A family friend agrees to speak with me (after my fixer claims to have seen Jean-Joseph in a down town bar that afternoon), denying allegations that Ernst Jean-Jospeh had both arms broken by the Tonton Macoutes, before returning to football a year later after his FIFA ban ran out.

"He was lucky that he was one of Baby Doc's favourites, and he knows it," explains Jean-Joseph's friend. "One of the reasons he hates speaking about what happened is the shame he feels he brought to Haiti. He still has to live with it, but of course they roughed him up. His psychological scars are deep-rooted. He prefers to forget it ever happened."

Thirty-six years later, several of his teammates clearly feel the same way. Many leads go dead as soon as the Jean-Joseph affair is mentioned and Haitian historian Jean Antoine explains: "Culturally, that generation of Haitian men were encouraged to remain coy in conversation. To commit anything controversial in conversation, or to print, was a dangerous thing. Many have remained that way."

For Manno Sanon, did Jean-Joseph's punishment take the shine off Haiti's brief World Cup adventure? "Perhaps to a slight degree," admitted Sanon, "but Ernst returned to the national team and resumed his career eventually. So there isn't a tragic ending, or anything like that. 1974 was our moment, our time, when Haiti was more stable than it had been for a long time."

On the face of it, the passage of time appears to have washed away any lingering bad taste left by Jean-Joseph's treatment at the hands of Baby Doc, and in these parts Haiti's tangerine shirts continue to glow brightly in the memory – unblemished and unsullied. The '74 World Cup wasn't all about Holland's brand of brilliant orange. According to the UN, Haiti remained the poorest nation to qualify for the World

Cup Finals until Angola travelled to Germany in 2006, making the Caribbean state's achievement even more remarkable.

In Port-au-Prince, Sanon in particular has enjoyed a deification similar to that of Diego Maradona in Naples and Gigi Riva in Sardinia. Pictures of him adorn assorted cafés and bars and on the rickety buses – the *tap-taps* – Bob Lemoine's song still blares out at regular intervals.

"That was the time, my friend, that was the time this place was alive," the bus driver claimed. Unlike the sad plight of many Zaire players in the wake of their solitary appearance at the World Cup in 1974, many Haitian stars subsequently prospered in their football careers. Joseph Namphy recalls, "The exposure many players received in Germany enabled them to land contracts abroad. Sanon played in Antwerp, the goalkeeper Françillon played for Munich 1860, and players like Jean-Joseph, Matthieu and Antoine played in the NASL for Chicago Sting. As a promoter, I brought the Cosmos and Tampa Bay Rowdies, as well as European sides like Borussia Mönchengladbach, to Haiti as well. Most of the team remained together for the 1978 qualification tournament, where we finished second in the days before two sides qualified from our region."

Although several Haiti players from the era are now back in their native country, a significant number have drifted abroad. For the last 20 years of his life, Manno Sanon lived in Orlando and from his American base often expressed his despair about his native country's ongoing economic upheaval and occasionally attracted faint criticism from teammates who returned to Haiti and reckoned he'd taken the easy option by living in the States.

The class of 1974 rarely keep in touch. A notable exception came after Sanon succumbed to prostate cancer early in 2008 and all the surviving members of the squad acted as pall-bearers at the funeral in Port-au-Prince. Haiti ground to a halt, all TV channels ran coverage of the event and the solemn ceremonies which followed, and the squad was awarded lifetime pensions by the government.

One significant absentee from the funeral was Baby Doc.

Now exiled somewhere in Paris (he changes address at least three times a year due to continued fear of assassination) he struggles to make ends meet after squandering his fortune. After embezzling an estimated $150 million from Haiti, he lost much of his loot during a costly divorce and described himself as "penniless" last year. That didn't prevent him from pledging $5 million to Port au Prince's earthquake victims, although he demurred from explaining how he planned to access the money. He occasionally makes noises about returning home, although the fear of arrest for crimes against his countrymen prevents him from actually doing so. Ousted during a military coup in 1986, there are still ardent Duvalierists who claim, despite the economic hardship, the tales of torture and Baby Doc's appalling waste of public funds, that the '70s was a golden age for many Haitians. There are several footballers who wouldn't disagree.

15
LENGTHENING SHADOWS

Now distinctly unsteady on his feet, former junior sprinter and long-jump champion Giovanni Meifredi is largely reliant on his son Enzo to ferry him around Rome. It's an arrangement which constantly irritates Maifredi Jr, especially as his ageing father insists on carrying his Young Fascist black shirt (unworn for more than 60 years) and a photograph of the preening Il Duce, with jaw tilted at an outrageous angle, around with him, which he shows to passers-by. The pair spend most of the time arguing, not always in a good-natured way either. The situation isn't helped by the fact that Giovanni's blind and incontinent Labrador continually yelps during our conversation.

"The dog should be put down, and my father is a crazy old man," Enzo tells me before adding, with deliberate volume for his father's benefit, "but he'll be dead soon, like his dog, I suppose." Enzo's cheek earns him a clout around the ear from Maifredi Sr. Seventy years ago, Giovanni was an enthusiastic member of Mussolini's Young Fascists when Italy hosted the second World Cup Finals tournament and he keeps his black shirt as a reminder of the time when, "Italy felt like it was aiming for the stars. The national team was Il Duce's football soldiers."

Giovanni has plenty of time to think about his life, and

football in particular. "Italy has won the World Cup four times," he says. "Twice, in the 1930s, there were strong links with fascism. And in 1982 and 2006, both triumphs came as scandal [*Totonero* which saw Paolo Rossi suspended for a year before the tournament and the *Moggiopoli* bribery and match-fixing scandal which broke during the 2006 World Cup] engulfed the domestic league. Whenever Italy wins on the grand stage, there is trouble. Whenever we don't win, conspiracies fly around. Always, there is trouble, whatever happens. This is Italy," he shrugs. His biggest regret is being ill on the day he was supposed to parade in front of Mussolini in Rome. "I had food poisoning," he laments. "Others in my regiment saluted him, and he met some of them individually and shook their hands. It still gives me sleepless nights."

Father and son are in the midst of packing for their annual excursion to the Museo del Calcio in Florence. Giovanni insists on travelling there every April to see the *Coppa del Duce*, the bronze trophy awarded to the victorious Italian side in 1934 by Mussolini, and taking his son with him. "My father is just a crazy old fascist," grumbles Enzo. "Couldn't he just have died in the war like most of the others?"

After seizing control of Italy in 1922, Mussolini stated his intention to make the country "great, respected and feared." During the 1930s, he embarked on a series of lightning fast invasions of Libya and Ethiopia in a bid to build his "new Roman Empire" and gain respect as an international statesman. He needed football in order to mobilise the masses at home but, added to his military success, if the national team gained plaudits in the World Cup, it would confirm his standing, official party propaganda claimed, as "our new Julius Caesar."

Under Mussolini's regime, the country embarked upon an ambitious construction programme and sporting facilities and stadia were right at the top of the list. Sports buildings, often with marble statues nearby glorifying the beauty of the human body, were designed to showpiece strength and athleticism and act as a signpost to a new, vibrant Italian youth that the country was in the ascendancy.

"Mussolini had a desire to propagate his image of the 'new Italian' as courageous, physically attractive, vigorous, sporting," explains Angela Tegy of Rome University. "He liked to think he could lead from the front on this." Newsreel footage regularly showed a bare chested Italian leader skiing or horse riding. He loved flashy demonstrations of raw Italian power and sponsored Major de Bernardi's successful attempt to break the water speed record. Before the Schneider Cup race in Norfolk, Il Duce sent him a telegram saying, "All Italy prays for your success," as Bernardi prepared to fly a Macchi Fiat Monoplane. In front of 60,000, he reached a maximum speed of 246 mph. Mussolini was thrilled, describing the feat as "further evidence of Italy's emergence into genuine power."

Mussolini revelled in the 'glory' of war, and in the '30s, football was an entirely new ideological battlefield. By 1932 there were sufficient modern stadia for Italy to launch a successful bid for the World Cup. Il Duce was thrilled at the prospect of his country hosting the tournament and not only did he seek to use it as a propagandist tool but he also demanded nothing less than an Italian victory. With backing from Comitato Olimpico Nazionale Italiano (CONI), he challenged the nation's foremost sculptors to create a special trophy (to be presented to the triumphant Italian side, obviously), which would "reflect the glory of the nation."

The result was the *Coppa del Duce*, which consisted of a group of footballers fixed in an action scene in front of the *fasces* – a central bundle of rods carried by magistrates in Ancient Rome. It was carved in bronze by the sculptor Grazes, who had been responsible for the winged statue of *Victory* on the roof of the Littoriale's Marathon Tower. Standing at almost six times the height of the Jules Rimet trophy and laden with fascist iconography of pure physical power it was the ultimate statement of intent by Mussolini. One official press release announced: "Besides the World Cup offered by FIFA, the football world championship is blessed by some of the richest prizes among which, unique in moral value, is that offered by Il Duce, who wanted to recognise the exceptional importance of the event in such a way." Shortly before the Finals, Mussolini had informed Italian journalists: "Good kicking is good politics," and it quickly became clear that Mussolini had no intention of presenting the trophy to any other team but his own.

Giovanni Meifredi still marvels at the *Coppa del Duce* because it reminds him of "when football and fascism entwined. It was a very powerful, occasionally intoxicating combination," he explains. "It reflected the zeitgeist of the time. It summed up the moment." His son loathes the trophy. "Self-absorbed, vulgar, vain and ridiculously over the top. Like Mussolini himself," insists Enzo, who isn't old enough to have any memory of Il Duce. Opinion may be split as to the aesthetic merits of the trophy, but Italian players quickly saw it as a trophy that was worth fighting for.

Mussolini's influence was felt everywhere across Italy during the 1934 World Cup and even non-fascists were quietly impressed by the organisation. Foreign tourists were actively encouraged to come to Italy and support their national teams and the Italian Football Federation offered to subsidise their travel by anything up to 70 per cent. Internal travel was also massively discounted for supporters travelling between host cities.

"As everyone knows, Mussolini did indeed get the trains running on time," Enzo mutters darkly. Giovanni delves inside one of his living-room drawers and pulls out a smartly designed match ticket for Italy's semi-final clash with Austria. It doesn't look over 70 years old but Il Duce insisted that no expense was spared when it came to the marketing of the '34 World Cup. Giovanni has, in addition, a full set of commemorative stamps which show images of the Italian team and Mussolini. There were also badges, pennants and keyrings on sale which, as well as carrying the image of the players, bore Il Duce's image.

"The view was that visitors would travel back home and show their family and friends this form of Italian merchandise and that it would show the world that apart from succeeding on the pitch, everything else about the tournament was very high quality," explains Giovanni.

The tournament was an almost exclusively European affair. There are two possible reasons why holders Uruguay declined to travel to Europe to defend their title in 1934. One is that in the wake of the Wall Street Crash the Uruguayan Government didn't consider it a worthwhile use of their funds to send a team around the world to compete in a tournament they felt would be controlled by biased European officials. The other is that the Uruguayans hadn't forgiven European sides as a whole for (largely) snubbing their 1930 fiesta and were returning the insult in kind. The truth probably lies somewhere in the middle.

Runners-up Argentina were present in body in 1934, but the fighting spirit was lacking. Three of their leading stars, including Luis Monti, were now naturalised Italians and when the *Albiceleste* faced Sweden there wasn't a single survivor from their 1930 team in the line-up. A late goal from Kroon meant that Argentina were eliminated after the first match. Brazil were also sent packing by Spain after just one game in '34. On the 12-day boat trip to Italy their four black players had been banned from mixing with other passengers by both the Brazilian FA and the shipping line and the squad was divided when the World Cup began. Brazil would only emerge as a genuine force four years later so it meant that, in the continuing absence of the Home Nations, leading European lights Italy, Hungary, Sweden, Germany and Czechoslovakia largely had the field to themselves.

At the draw for the Finals in Rome, the *Coppa del Duce* had stood in the middle of the room and, flanked by fascist black-shirted henchmen, had taken centre stage. Mussolini attended most of Italy's games. He took both his sons to the opening game against the USA in a bid to stress the importance of family life to the populace and he made a huge show of paying his way at matches in a bid to end the "immoral system of complimentary tickets." *La Nazione* stressed that those who expected to receive such tickets were an example of "a bad moral attitude that they believe can be justified by their social position, sporting connections and other means that are condemned in the fascist regime."

Giovanni Meifredi explains: "If members of the Fascist Party were using their contacts to get into football matches for free it would have hampered Mussolini's aim to use football to gain the support of the working classes. He had to make a stand. He had to set an example." Many of the arriving teams paid their respects to Il Duce, some sending telegrams of admiration and the Argentine squad even visited Mussolini's parents' tomb and laid a wreath. Small wonder that after the World Cup, Jules Rimet questioned whether it was FIFA which had controlled the tournament, or Mussolini. Events on the pitch would give further credence to the view that, on home soil, Italy couldn't fail to win the trophy.

Italy manager Victor Pozzo was not a fascist, although as Brian Glanville later wrote: "He was an authoritarian. He did profit from the tenor of the time." It appears that Mussolini gave him free reign to select the squad, although Pozzo later claimed he'd been instructed to select only Fascist Party members in 1934. Nonetheless, the support of the Fascist Party's top brass enabled him to introduce a more professional set-up for the national team. He introduced tough training schedules for the players and Italian training camps were closed off to visitors in order to prevent would-be spies stealing information.

At a mountain retreat near Lake Maggiore, Pozzo had a full six weeks to work with the team prior to the Finals and opted for a 2-3-2-3 formation which would facilitate quick counter-attacking. Pozzo was also able to recruit Monti, Orsi and Guaita, three Argentine oriundi (foreign players of Italian extraction) who now plied their trade in Italy.

Italy hammered the USA 7–1 in their opening match, but a great deal of attention in the Italian media was also afforded to Germany, now controlled by Adolf Hitler. The Italian press had labelled Germany as one of the weaker teams in the tournament, even though they hadn't lost a match in 16 months and modelled their play on Herbert Chapman's 'WM' formation, deployed with great success at Arsenal. Giovanni Meifredi explains: "At that point, Adolf Hitler was still only the German Chancellor. Not the Führer. We viewed ourselves as the bigger, elder brother both in politics and on the football pitch. Mussolini had been in charge of Italy for nine years, and we had the better football team, too." In fact, Il Duce had even dared to threaten Hitler with war in 1934 if Germany invaded Austria to create a 'Greater Germany.' When Hitler actually proceed to do so four years later, Mussolini did nothing.

Defeated rivals suggested that Mussolini bribed referees as the tournament went on. Against Spain, Italy drew 1–1 thanks to a controversial goal scored despite Italian striker Schiavio appearing to impede the Spanish goalkeeper. Initially the referee disallowed the goal before a mass of Italian players persuaded him to change his mind. A Spanish goal was also ruled out for offside during the game, even though striker Lafuente had beaten four opponents all by himself before slipping the ball into the net.

The following day Italy won the replay 1–0 after two perfectly legal-looking Spanish strikes were disallowed. Referee Rene Mercet was suspended for his performance by the Swiss FA upon his return home. Just two days later, in the mud of the San Siro in Milan, Luis Monti marked Austria's star player, Sindelar, out of the match in the semi-final, as his team squeezed past the *Wunderteam* to reach the final.

Austrian striker Josef Biscan later described the Italians as "little cheats," and suggested that the Swedish referee Ivan Eklind overlooked constant fouling by the Italians during the game. In 1998, Czech football writer Miloslav Jensik alleged that the night before the match Eklind and Mussolini had had dinner together, where the pair of them "discussed tactics." When Austrian manager Hugo Meisl discovered what had happened, according to Biscan, "he realised the referee had been bribed." "Come on. That's nonsense. What home side doesn't have a huge advantage in the World Cup?" asks Giovanni Meifredi. "Look at England in '66 and Argentina in '78. Even South Korea had officials on their side."

Despite the allegations of foul play, Italy faced Czechoslovakia, conquerors of Germany, in the World Cup Final on 10th June 1934. In an unprecedented manoeuvre, Mussolini insisted that Eklind be referee for the final as well. Shortly before the game, Eklind was summoned to meet fascist dignitaries. "It's an extraordinary episode," explains Miloslav Jensik. "No one will ever know for sure the exact nature of the conversation between Eklind and the dignitaries, but it appears highly suspicious. If it had been both captains summoned by Mussolini, that would have been different, but not the referee!"

The final was played at the recently refurbished Stadio Nazionale del Partito Nazionale Facista in Rome, Mussolini's showcase stadium. Made out of stone, the grand arches carved into the exterior of the 55,000-capacity ground were designed to evoke memories of antiquity and the Colosseum and to highlight the fact that this was a new age of prosperity. It was the perfect fascist finale.

Three years before, Mussolini had urged Education Secretary Renato Picci to "reorganise the youth from a moral, physical, social, and military point of view." For Giovanni Meifredi, it was the most memorable afternoon of his youth. "It was a beautiful day in Rome," he explains, "and we knew it was a showpiece for the nation. My father, my brother and I had tickets for the match. There were so many young boys walking towards the ground in black shirts, and you knew you were walking towards a collective experience. We practically marched in, and sang our marching songs on the way into the ground. Inside, the noise was huge – of epic proportions. Surely it was a throwback to the days of gladiators in the Colosseum? Mussolini always knew how to make a grand entrance and when he appeared in his white suit the entire crowd sang 'Duce, Duce' and gave the Roman salute. There were Italian flags everywhere and banners with 'Mussolini Is Always Right' around the ground. Like the Berlin Olympics for Hitler two years later, this was surely the highpoint for Mussolini. And I remember it [he touches his black shirt] like it was yesterday."

Antonin Puc put the Czechs ahead after 71 minutes, but Raimondo Orsi equalised with just eight minutes remaining and in extra time, with Pozzo struggling to make his voice heard above the din, Schiavio netted Italy's winner. Il Duce and the legions of his Fascist Youth in the crowd had fulfilled the national dream.

"For that day in particular," explains Meifredi, "football, like politics at that time, was almost a lay religion. Everything came together on that glorious afternoon." Clearly moved by his recollections, Giovanni offers to give me a fascist salute. Enzo grabs his father's arm to stop him: "You're not Paolo Di Canio," he reminds his father.

"Ten years later, everything went to shit in Italy at the end of the war, and many cursed Mussolini and forgot what he had achieved. I saw fellow Italians take pot shots at his statue and curse him. In the end he was strung up on a meathook and his corpse abused and ridiculed. His name became filth. But I never forgot him, and remember him still, and nothing resounds quite like the team winning the 1934 World Cup," recalls Giovanni.

Italian captain Giampiero Combi received the World Cup trophy and gold medals from Il Duce, as well as the *Coppa del Duce*, and signed photographs of Mussolini in recognition of the team's efforts on the pitch. Both sides saluted the fascists in the stand, and the Italians went off to pose for pictures with their leader.

In typically grandiose fashion, Mussolini claimed the events of 10th June 1934 "rivalled the achievements of previous Emperors of Rome." Questions remained about how complicit referees had been on Italy's behalf during the World Cup, and home advantage had clearly played a huge role in their success.

Four years later in France, there was a sense of impending doom hanging over Europe and the list of withdrawals mirrored these unsettling times. Spain, torn asunder by civil war, pulled out and Austria, annexed by Germany earlier that year, did likewise. Demonstrating how sport and politics were enmeshed at that time, the Austrian *Wunderteam*, which had bewitched European crowds by playing a daring 2-3-5 formation under Hugo Meisl, had been subsumed by Germany in March, and a raft of their leading players were railroaded into playing for a 'Greater Germany.' Neither of the River Plate nations showed up in '38; there was a riot in Buenos Aires when it was announced that the AFA, slighted by missing out on hosting the World Cup, had decided not to send their team to compete. For champions Italy, only Meazza and Ferrari survived from four years earlier, as Pozzo drew upon his resources from the winning 1936 Olympic football squad.

France had been chosen to host the tournament at the 1936 FIFA congress in Berlin, as it was believed that under the auspices of the competition's pioneers, Jules Rimet and Henri Delaunay (heads of the French Football Federation), there would be no repeat of the overt propaganda displayed by Mussolini in Rome four years before.

Despite the Italians' victory in 1934, a FIFA report in 1934 had concluded that "Austria, England and Scotland are in the super class of international football teams." In November 1934, the *Azzurri* had taken on England in a match which became known as the 'Battle of Highbury.' On the day before the game, Mussolini had claimed, "The only beautiful thing in life is war."

The English press claimed the Italians had been offered £150 a man and an Alfa Romeo car if they defeated England, whose team contained seven Arsenal players. In a slug fest which ended 3–2 to the home side, five England players later needed hospital treatment and Italian hard man Luis Monti was taken off after suffering a broken foot. The English media believed it had all the evidence needed to claim they were the moral world champions. However, England passed on the opportunity to prove the fact for real by declining a late offer to take up Austria's place in 1938.

Political tension crackled through the 1938 World Cup from beginning to end. Before the opening game at the Parc des Princes between Germany and Switzerland, anti-fascist demonstrators in the crowd threw bottles and booed loudly as the Germans gave the Nazi salute. The neutral Swiss kept their hands pinned to their sides. Then, with Pozzo's Italy side preparing to face the unfancied Norwegians in Marseilles, they faced the wrath of an estimated 10,000 Italian political exiles in the crowd before the match.

In 1999, I spoke with Padua-based Mario Perazzolo, the Italian right half who spent the entire World Cup warming benches. Perazzolo, having played in the matches leading up to the tournament, may have missed the final cut, but clearly he spent much of his time observing the political machinations of the late '30s – as well as keeping a close eye on teammate's Giuseppe Meazza's nocturnal activities. "It was very hostile towards us in Paris. There were many Italians living there who felt they had an axe to grind, having left Italy because of their political beliefs. I couldn't tell the exact political affiliations of the team, but I know that Pozzo most definitely was not a fascist. Nonetheless, he was dictatorial with us and he insisted on togetherness and everyone treading the same path. When the team lined up for the Norway game, they did the salute. The atmosphere got really aggressive. I thought it was disappointing that they should boo their own countrymen but knowing what I know now, and having lost family in World War II, I fully empathise with their feelings. The stewards had to prevent the anti-fascists running onto the pitch. The team quickly put their hands down, but then Pozzo made them salute again, to show that they had no trepidation and wouldn't be corralled into changing their ways in the face of pressure. It's very difficult – given the circumstances and what came next – to explain to you that Pozzo didn't regard the double salute as an overtly fascist gesture, or an aggressive one, more a gesture of intent and solidarity. Our knowledge of what happened during the war means the salute now has totally negative connotations, whereas back then it didn't." The Italians won 2–1 after extra time.

Pozzo later told Brian Glanville that his approach with the team was, "Kind, but with a firm hand. If I let them make mistakes, I lose my control." Mario Perazzolo suggests that even Pozzo was powerless to stop the colourful Meazza enjoying life to the full even in the midst of the World Cup. "Giuseppe did what he liked to do. Outside observers, picking up on the political angle, would lazily suggest that we were a 'fascist football team,' and that everyone blindly followed Pozzo's orders like soldiers. Meazza didn't. After the Norway game he asked Pozzo, on behalf of the team, if the players might be allowed the night off. Pozzo acquiesced but insisted we maintain our discipline. With that Meazza disappeared, but the squad later found him in his room with two young French ladies and plenty of wine. Actually, a few of us had wine that night. So you see, we didn't blindly follow orders, and there was room for a degree of individuality. At least if you were Giuseppe Meazza there was, anyway."

In the quarter-final, Italy faced hosts France at the Stade Colombes near Paris. Both sides normally wore blue, and Italy were instructed to change. At this juncture, Pozzo and Mussolini disagreed. Pozzo expected the team to wear their customary white change strip, but Il Duce intervened, ordering them to wear black in order to provoke the anti-fascists. Perazzolo recalls, "Pozzo resented any kind of interference in the team and he wasn't happy about the change because whereas the double salute had been designed to show the crowd the team's solidarity, this was supposed to stir up and annoy the crowd. It was a fascist gesture and the crowd were savage towards the team. In one sense it bound the team together and they won 3–1, but the Italy team never played in black again. Fortunately it was a one-off. General Vaccaro, the President of the Italian Football Federation, was the only one who really stood up to Mussolini, insisting they never wore black again. Early on in the tournament, Pozzo was told by Mussolini to play Monzeglio in defence, not his preferred choice, Foni. Vaccaro intervened, and Mussolini was instructed to back out of interfering in football."

Italy went on to beat Hungry 4–2 in the final, with two goals apiece from Piola and Colaussi. Huge amounts of controversy had surrounded Italy during both the 1934 and 1938 World Cups but now, on foreign soil, they had proved themselves to be the best team, and to this day Pozzo is the only coach to have retained the trophy.

For Perazzolo, the triumph was an Italian one, not a victory for fascism. "Although Mussolini had his picture taken with the team afterwards, and he used it for his own ends, for the team it was all about the nation. They did it for Italians at home and themselves, not Mussolini. He couldn't control the Italian players' thoughts and opinions."

Two years before the World Cup in France, Adolf Hitler had taken Mussolini's penchant for self-publicity to its ultimate extreme and ensured that the 1936 Berlin Olympics, with the construction of the Olympic Stadium and the German team finishing top of the medal table, were a propaganda triumph for Nazi Germany. However, the Führer didn't have it all his own way. Firstly, Jesse Owens was the star of the games, winning gold medals in the 100 metres, 200 metres, long jump, and 4 x 100 metres relay, destroying the myth of Aryan superiority. Hitler stormed out of the stadium in a rage.

Two days later, he watched Germany take on Norway in an Olympic football match. "The Führer is very agitated. I can barely contain myself. A real bath of nerves," was how propaganda chief Joseph Goebbels described Hitler's mood as Germany struggled against, and eventually lost to, the Norwegians, before the Führer once again stomped off in disgust. That should have been a warning to Hitler that football, with its myriad variables, is nigh on impossible to control.

The German team wasn't a patch on Il Duce's Italy in the 1930s, but after the annexation of Austria in 1938, the absorption of the Austrian team seemed set to guarantee the Greater Germany's domination of European football, given the quality of the Austrian team of that time. Fluid, artistic and subtle, the star of Austria's *Wunderteam* was Matthias Sindelar, known as the 'Mozart of Football,' or *Der*

Papierene ('Paper Man') for his slim build and his uncanny ability to glide and float around opponents with the minimum of effort. By 1938, Sindelar was 35 years old and, what's more, he disapproved strongly of the Nazis and their annexation of his homeland. He'd openly declared his disgust at the way in which Jews had been dismissed from jobs at his club side, Austria Vienna, by leading Nazis, and there had long been a Gestapo file on the player. In it, he was described as "a Czech national, pro-Jewish, and a social democrat." Sindelar refused to play for the newly constructed Greater Germany, and instead bought himself a coffee house in Vienna in preparation for his retirement.

In April 1938, the Austrian team played Germany in the Prater Stadium in Vienna, its final match as an independent Austrian side. The match, later known as the *Anschlusspiel* ('Anschluss Game') was attended by thousands of leading Nazi dignitaries and was expected to finish in a diplomatic draw. For 70 minutes Austria seemed to allow an inferior Germany side dominate the game. Sindelar uncharacteristically missed several gilt-edged chances before he, and teammate Karl Sesta, scored late on to give Austria a 2–0 win.

Subsequent match reports claimed that the pair danced a jig of delight in front of the senior Nazi figures after their goals. From this point onwards, Sindelar's cards appeared to be marked, especially when he once more refused to leave his home country and rejected the chance to play for Germany in that summer's World Cup, citing old age and injury as his excuse. Before the tournament, Germany was rated as one of the favourites, but Sindelar's absence hampered the new team's performance, and they lost 4–2 to Switzerland after a first-round replay.

Back in Vienna, Sindelar settled into life as a café owner, and was widely regarded as an extremely approachable ex-footballer, despite the aura which surrounded him. Fritz Polster's father used to drink and gamble with 'Sindi' in his café and recalls what it was like to be in the presence of the 'Paper Man.' "He was what I would call and old-fashioned superstar. There wasn't the kind of hysteria which surrounds players these days, more a quiet reverential hush. My father took me to meet him several times. He was a very trim, almost frail-looking man, who looked like he might blow away at any time. You wouldn't have thought it possible that he could destroy defence almost single-handedly during the 1930s. He was always very gracious and polite to us kids, although I'm sure he grew tired of our unceasing questions. He was a very generous host at his café, and many of his circle, including my father, had drinking and gambling sessions until dawn, much to the annoyance of my mother. I remember my father saying that it was a shame that Sindi didn't play for Germany in the 1938 World Cup, not for football reasons, but because by not playing it opened him up to suspicion from the Nazis."

A year after he refused to play for Germany in France, Sindelar was found dead at the apartment he shared with his girlfriend, Camilla Castagnola. The official verdict cited carbon monoxide poisoning as the cause. Two days later, Austrian newspaper *Kronen Zeitung* ran a story suggesting "everything points towards this great man having become the victim of murder through poisoning." "My father was convinced that Sindi had been murdered by the Nazis. Others claimed he'd committed suicide. Having met the man and seen how vibrant and full of life he was, I've always doubted that," argues Polster. The suicide story has been referred to in several written works. The poet Friedrich Torberg, in his poem *Auf den Tod eines Fussballspielers* ('On the Death of a Footballer') claimed he'd killed himself because he felt disowned on account of the new order. The 1994 *Cassell Soccer Companion* claimed he "was of Jewish descent, and committed suicide by gassing himself after the Nazis took over." Other works have suggested that his girlfriend was also Jewish, and this brought them to the attention of the Nazis.

"Sindi wasn't Jewish. He came from Moravia, and his girlfriend wasn't Jewish either. She was a staunch Italian Catholic. So was he. Sindi had bought a café, and his girlfriend a bar. If they were Jewish, they would have been banned from doing so. Any 'undesirables,' as the Nazis described them, would never have got their hands on property," explains Polster. In 2003, the BBC screened a documentary entitled *Football and Fascism*, on which one of Sindelar's friends, Egon Ulbrich, claimed a district official ("a Nazi but a nice guy . . . he said 'I know Sindi deserves a state funeral'") had been bribed to record Sindi's death as an accident, which ensured he would receive a state funeral. "According to Nazi rules, a person who had been murdered or who has committed suicide cannot be given a grave of honour. So we had to do something to ensure the criminal element in his death was removed," explained Ulbrich.

"My father only died a couple of years ago," explains Polster, "and up to his death he never believed any of these rumours. He got to hear what Egon Ulbrich had said and he still didn't believe it, because everyone who gave a damn about Sindi found out that the malfunctioning chimney which pumped out carbon monoxide had made his neighbours ill the previous week. The simple truth was that no one unblocked the chimney quickly enough and if Sindi and his girlfriend knew about the problem, they were too slow to call anyone in to sort it. There was nothing suspicious about it."

Sindelar's funeral was attended by over 15,000 Viennese, many of whom were convinced that the man who would be voted the best Austrian footballer of the 20th century and Austria's sportsman of the 20th century would still be alive but for the Nazis. Alfred Polgar wrote in his obituary, "The good Sindelar followed the city, whose child and pride he was, to its death. He was so inextricably entwined with it that he had to die when he did." In 1978, Friedrich Torberg wrote, "[Sindelar] had no system, to say nothing of a set pattern. He just had . . . genius."

Fritz Polster explains: "So much was written, so much was said, when Sindi died, and at the risk of sounding cynical I think that too many people have read too much into what happened. Sure, on the field, he was an iconic figure, but he himself told us youngsters that by 1938 he was getting too old to play football, and he showed us the scar on his ankle which Luis Monti had given him at the last World Cup. Tactically, things had altered in the 1930s. Austria had been successful playing a 2-3-5 formation, but such a bold approach was starting to bear less fruit at the highest level. 'Football is changing. Italy are physically and mentally stronger than us now. Our time is up,' he told us. He despised the Nazis as well, and so much the better, and he freely socialised with Jews, but I think that romanticising his death in the way people have done wouldn't sit easily with him.

"One thing which is undeniably true, however, is that under fascist leaders, football was supposed to be a means of instilling loyalty to the regime and reflecting the sense of fanaticism felt by mere mortals for the demigods who led them. In the case of Sindi, football became a means of resistance to the Nazi hierarchy. That at least would have pleased him, in light of the atrocities which were about to be committed in Europe."

16

KEEPY UPPY WITH IDI AMIN

In the late 1940s, with the British poised to leave Uganda, which had been a "region" under the jurisdiction of the British East African Company since 1888, stories began to drift around concerning the larger-than-life Lieutenant Idi Amin, erstwhile of the King's African Rifles, a regiment of the British Army. There were strange rumours that in distant frontier villages, trussed-up captives were being bayoneted under the orders of a big, happy, laughing officer with a particular line in sadism. One of his fellow officers described him thus: "Not much grey matter, thick from the neck up, but a splendid chap to have about." Others spoke of his prowess in the boxing ring, and on the rugby pitches (he was an unused substitute when Uganda played the British Lions in the 1950s). Maybe his superiors in the regiment should have investigated those bayoneting claims a little more closely but by then, with a raft of African states declaring their independence, the British had other issues on their minds. Some 20 years later, as he crushed Uganda within his mighty fist, Amin began to view football in the same way Mobutu had in Zaire: as a pathway to immortality and demigod status in Africa.

When Ugandan Prime Minister Milton Obote departed for a Commonwealth Conference in 1971 Amin, using his feral cunning, struck, and after a short coup he assumed power and promptly began slaughtering those whose loyalty was uncertain. Military officers were appointed to senior civil service posts and Amin's particular brand of 'justice' was brutal. He realised that two things were required to survive beyond the short term; a strong and loyal military to protect him in his plush Kampala pile and sportsmen who could bring glory and prestige to his regime at home and abroad. He quickly got lucky. John Akii-Bua won a gold medal in the 400-metre hurdles at the 1972 Munich Olympics, and the athlete was rewarded with a car and a city bungalow and both a street and a sports stadium were named after him. However, his position as a national icon didn't prevent Amin's 'State Research Bureau' murdering three of Akii-Bua's brothers.

It was football which began to dominate Amin's attentions by the mid 1970s and, in line with his foreign policy, getting one over on arch-rivals and neighbours Tanzania. The 2006 film The Last King of Scotland, although only partly based on the truth, shows Amin (played by Forest Whitaker) kicking a ball around with his sons on the grass within his Kampala compound. The truth was that he was more of a boxing man, but he'd later use his pugilistic experiences to make a point to the football team. Although Amin had met Uganda's two star footballers – Philip Omondi and Stanley 'the Tank' Mariba privately before (the pair were treated to luxury shopping trips in Tripoli after flying there on Amin's private jet), his first face-to-face meeting with the entire squad happened in the early part of 1976, with Uganda poised to embark on a World Cup-qualifying session.

In the run-up to the campaign the six foot four, 18 stone Amin had begun to shower gifts on his star players and terrify journalists who dared to pen disparaging headlines about 'the Cranes', the national symbol of Uganda since imperial days. "My dreams always come true," he informed the assembled Ugandan squad, "and I have foreseen that you will not only be Kings of Africa, but that you will also reach the World Cup Football Finals. You will be part of the new Uganda which will stun the world. You must reach the Finals at all costs."

Amin had always insisted that his boys were fed green vegetables and red meat in order to build up there strength prior to an international match. One of the cooks, Dennis Oboda, who worked with the team in the late '70s, recalls the sense of expectation as the squad prepared to welcome Amin to their training camp outside Kampala: "The whole party would form a guard of honour to welcome him, because he believed that everyone – players, cooks, trainers and administrative staff – were a unit. Amin was always a notoriously bad timekeeper. Then, in the distance, you would hear the convoy of jeeps approaching, a cloud of dust would fly up in the air and the vehicles would hove into view. Amin would be flanked by gun toting guards and he liked a grand entrance. He visited the training camp several times and he was usually dressed casually rather than in his military uniform with all the medals which clanked around as he walked. He'd usually head straight for Omondi and Mariba and embrace them before he set about advising us on how we should play. We generally only ever saw his playful side. He'd challenge the team to see if they could drop-kick the ball further than him. He always won! He was a powerful man and I think the players never knew whether they were expected to beat him or whether they should politely lose.

"'Is anyone as strong as me?' he'd bark. He'd walk around most of the squad, and shout at individuals 'You – are you stronger than me?' The players were usually open mouthed with the power of his personality. 'You must play with both beauty and ferocity' was one of his main phrases. He'd also repeat endlessly that he could see into the future. He'd close in on players until his nose touched theirs, and say, 'I foresee your destiny. It is glorious, like that of Uganda.' On one occasion, he challenged the players to a keepie-uppie competition. It was actually very funny, watching this great ox of a man trying to keep a heavy leather ball in the air in his leather shoes and his trousers. He was happy to act like a buffoon in front of people he felt comfortable with. That time he did lose, but he saw the funny side anyway and contented himself with setting up a competition to see who could kick the ball highest into the sky. 'I think I can hit the sun,' he'd joke. He won that high kicking competition, although he never actually hit the sun, to my knowledge."

Amin's main concern appeared to be whether the football team was physically strong enough on the pitch to see off opponents. He was once an East African heavyweight boxing champion and in 1974 he entered the ring at Lugogo to fight Peter Sseruwagi, the then national boxing coach, in an undercard fight that Amin won with a knockout. During his regime the national boxing team, 'the Bombers', was ranked third in the amateur boxing world. Stars like John 'the Beast' Mugabi and Cornelius Boza Edwards ('Bother Edwards') terrorised the boxing world after turning professional and Amin would use them in his lectures to the football team.

"One time, Amin turned up with 'Bother Edwards' in tow," recalls Dennis Oboda. "We were in awe of him, but we wondered why he'd been brought along. Amin explained that his boxers used to complain to him that white judges were biased against them and they didn't know what to do about it. 'I told them to knock out their opponents,' barked Amin. 'Then there is nothing to debate. The fight is won. That is what you must do on the football pitch. Do not be afraid to be physical, to knock out opponents' teeth or break their limbs. Show them that the Ugandan man is the strongest man of all.' Then he growled at us like a lion. Later many of the squad laughed, as these words suggested Amin knew little of football's rules."

In 1976, Uganda was drawn against neighbours Tanzania in the first round of qualifying for the 1978 World Cup. This time Amin appeared at the training camp in full military regalia. The relations between both nations were complex. Although the Soviet Union supplied both nations with arms, Amin's major ally was Libyan leader Colonel Gaddafi. The socialist regime in charge of Tanzania was pushing through its grand socialist plan, which involved destroying existing farms and villages and forcing all agricultural workers to live in collectivised farms. From 1976 onwards there were sporadic uprisings throughout the region as workers, many of whom were now starving, protested about what was happening. Amin seized upon this and announced that Tanzania's Kagera province would soon belong to Uganda.

"'You are my football soldiers,' he told his assembled squad," recalls Dennis Oboda. "'You will crush them. You will destroy them,' he went on. He told the players that we would surpass what Mobutu had achieved with the Zairean national team at the last World Cup. Then he trotted out some well-worn clichés. 'Uganda is a paradise in Africa. If you have a shirt and trousers you can live in Uganda for years.' He was ignoring the fact that by then he had expelled around 100,000 Muslims who had been the backbone of Ugandan business and that the country was about to slide into anarchy.

"Around that time, as stories of atrocities within Uganda spread, his team-talks grew more serious. We were told not to make any sudden movements. His guards had their weapons permanently cocked in our direction. He was still friendly, but more tense. We presumed it was the pressure of his job, although I later heard it was due to the impact of prescription drugs. But he made the team chant in unison about killing Tanzanians and off he went in his jeep."

A week before the showdown was due to kick off – the talk in Kampala was of little else – the match against Tanzania was abruptly called off, as Uganda's neighbours descended into civil chaos and were forced to withdraw from the qualifying rounds.

Amin was on the one hand delighted, citing Tanzania's "cowardice" as their reason for pulling out, but he knew that he'd lost out on a golden propaganda opportunity. The

Cranes received a bye to the next round and, in February 1977, they faced Zambia in a two-legged play-off which they lost 4–3 on aggregate.

According to Dennis Oboda, Amin was relatively magnanimous in defeat, suggesting his team turn its attentions to the forthcoming African Cup of Nations. There are numerous stories of him terrorising journalists who dared to pen critical commentaries of his team's matches. *Voice of Uganda* (the government newspaper of the time) sports editor Sam Katerega fled to Kenya without even bothering to clear his desk after discovering he'd been fired while listening to a 1pm news bulletin. The story went that star player Denis Obua complained directly to Amin about Katerega's acidic pen. Obua claimed that by criticising the national team, Katerega made himself a sworn enemy of the national team. Amin promptly announced Katerega's sacking to the team before moving onto other business. A scout was dispatched to the radio station to inform them of the newspaper editor's dismissal.

"On the whole," explains Dennis Oboda, the majority of players realised that Amin was their benefactor and that through their position in the football team they enjoyed privileges which were deprived to others in the country at that time. How could they dare challenge him – without putting themselves at enormous risk?"

Milton Asamba played twice for Uganda in the late 1970s and recalls the mixture of respect and terror which Amin stirred within the players. "One of the initiation ceremonies for young players who seemed gullible, was to get them to shout 'Down with Amin,'" he recalls. "It was considered that this would test whether a player really had the stomach to play for Uganda or not. Some would-be debutants agonised for hours about whether or not to say it. After all, it only took one grass and that player would be dead. Several young payers opted not to play for Uganda at all rather than put their lives at risk in such a manner."

In 1978, Amin's sporting officer, Major Nasur Abdallah, disbanded Express FC, one of the country's leading clubs. He accused it of having connections with Tanzanian exiles and two national team players, John Ntensibe and Mike Kiganda, were jailed at the infamous Makindye military barracks. When word filtered back to Amin that two of the Cranes' leading stars were languishing behind bars, he ordered their immediate release. "Many of Amin's men were football fanatics," explains Milton Asamba, "and although they could be barbaric, there are countless examples of lives being saved simply because potential victims played football. There are many former footballers who continue to see the positive side of Amin, even if the majority of Ugandans view him as a devil."

In 1979, Tanzanian-based Ugandan exiles began to close in on the dictator and his regime and Amin fled into the arms of Colonel Gadaffi. As the economy collapsed and the whole nation descended into chaos the football team also disintegrated and Uganda was forced to withdraw from the qualifying rounds of the 1982 World Cup on the grounds of internal instability.

To this day, an East African side has never reached the World Cup Finals, or indeed produced a world star of note, and in a region beset by conflict, (Uganda v Tanzania, Ethiopia v Eritrea and Hutus v Tutsis), widespread corruption and political infighting, the chances of any of these sides doing so in the near future appear as remote as ever.

Milton Asamba is convinced that but for Idi Amin's manic sabre-rattling in the late 1970s, which hurried the onset of the Tanzanian war, Uganda's Cranes could have been the best of an admittedly bad bunch. "But then," he admits, "if he hadn't opened his bank account for the team back then, the Cranes would never have taken off in the first place."

SELECTED BIBLIOGRAPHY

Books

Abbott, Elizabeth, *Haiti: Duvaliers And Their Legacy* (Robert Hale Ltd, 1991)

Beck, Peter, *Scoring For Britain: International Football And International Politics 1900 – 1939* (Frank Cass, 1939)

Bellos, Alex, *Futebol, The Brazilian Way Of Life* (Bloomsbury, 2002)

Bosworth, RJB, *Mussolini's Italy: Life Under The Dictatorship, 1925 – 1945*, Penguin, 2006

Breen, Michael, *Kim Jong Il: North Korea's Dear Leader* (John Wiley & Sons, 2004)

Briggs, Simon, *Don't Mention The Score: A Masochist's History Of The England Football Team* (Quercus, 2008)

Castro, Roy, *Garrincha: The Triumph and Tragedy Of Brazil's Forgotten Footballing Hero* (Yellow Jersey, 2005)

Chyzowych, Walt, *The World Cup* (Icarus Press, 1982)

Dawson, Jeff, *Back Home: England And The 1970 World Cup* (Orion, 2001)

Douglas, Geoffrey, *The Game Of Their Lives: The Untold Story Of The World Cup's Greatest Upset* (Henry Holt and Company Inc, 1996)

Downing, David, *England v Argentina: World Cups And Other Small Wars* (Portrait Books, 2003)

Downing, David, *The Best Of Enemies, England v Germany* (Bloomsbury, 2000)

Foer, Franklin, *How Football Explains The World* (Arrow, 2004)

Foot, John, *Calcio, A History of Italian football* (Fourth Estate, 2006)

Galeano, Eduardo, *Football In Sun And Shadow* (Fourth Estate, 1997)

Glanville, Brian, *The Story Of The World Cup* (Faber and Faber, 2001)

Goldblatt, David, *The Ball Is Round: A Global History Of Football* (Penguin, 2006)

Hawkey, Ian, *Feet Of The Chameleon, The Story Of African Football* (Portico, 2009)

Hesse – Lichtenberger, Ulrich, *tor! The Story Of German Football* (When Saturday Comes books, 2002)

Hunt, Chris, *The History Of The FIFA World Cup: World Cup Stories* (Interact Publishing, 2006)

Inglis, Simon, *Sightlines: A Stadium Odyssey* (Yellow Jersey, 2000)

Jawad, Hyder: *Four Weeks In Montevideo: The Story Of World Cup 1930* (Seventeen Media, 2009)

Jenkins, Garry, *The Beautiful Team: In Search Of Pele & The 1970 Brazilians* (Simon & Schuster UK, 1998)

Kang Chol – Hwan & Pierre Rigoulot, *The Aquariums Of Pyongyang: Ten Years In The North Korean Gulag* (Atlantic Books, 2001)

Kapuściński, Ryszard, *The Soccer War* (Granta, 1990)

Kyemba, Henry, *State Of Blood: The Inside Story Of Idi Amin* (Corgi, 1977)

Lever, Janet, *Soccer Madness: Brazil's Passion For The World's Most Popular Sport* (Waveland Press, 1983)

McKinstry, Leo, *Sir Alf: A Major Reappraisal of the Life and Times of England's Greatest Football Manager* (Harper Sport, 2006)

Mailer, Norman, *The Fight* (Penguin, 1975)

Martin, Simon, *Football And Fascism: The National Game Under Mussolini* (Berg, 2004)

Mason, Tony, *Passion Of The People? Football In South America* (Verso, 1995)

Miller, David, *World Cup, The Argentina Story* (Frederick Warne, 1978)

Motson, John, *Motson's World Cup Extravaganza: Football's Greatest Drama 1930 – 2006* (Robson Books, 2006)

Murray, Scott & Walker, Rowan, *Day Of The Match, A History Of Football In 365 Days* (Boxtree, 2008)

Pele, *The Autobiography*, Pocket Books, 2007

SELECTED BIBLIOGRAPHY

Perryman, Mark (ed), *Going Oriental: Football After World Cup 2002* (Mainstream, 2002)

Robinson, Adam, *Terror on the Pitch: How Bin Laden Targeted Beckham and the England Football Squad* (Mainstream, 2002)

Robinson, John, *The World Cup 1930 – 1986* (Marksman Publications, 1986)

Schott, Ian, *World Famous Dictators* (Constable and Robinson, 1992)

Seddon, Peter, *The World Cup's Strangest Moments: Oddball Characters and memorable matches from over 75 years of football's greatest tournament* (Robson Books, 2005)

Tomlinson, Alan & Christopher Young, *German Football: History, Culture, Society, And the World Cup 2006* (Routledge, 2005)

Twentieth Century Day By Day (Dorling Kindersley, 2000)

Ward, Andrew & Williams, John, *Football Nation: Sixty Years Of The Beautiful Game* (Bloomsbury, 2009)

Ward, Colin, *Steaming In: Journal Of A Football Fan* (Sportspages, 1989)

Weiland, Matt & Wilsey, Sean, *The Thinking Fan's Guide To The World Cup* (ABACUS, 2006)

When Saturday Comes, The Half Decent Football Book (Penguin Books, 2005)

Wilson, Jonathan, *Inverting The Pyramid: A History Of Football Tactics* (Orion, 2008)

Winner, David, *Brilliant Orange: The Neurotic Genius Of Dutch Football* (Bloomsbury, 2000)

Wrong, Michela, *In The Footsteps Of Mr Kurtz: Living On The Brink Of Disaster in Mobutu's Congo* (Harper Collins, 2002)

Documentaries/Films

Futebol: The Story Of Brazil's Obsession With The Beautiful Game And Its Stars (Verve Pictures, 2001)

History Of Football: The Beautiful Game (Freemantle Media, 2002)

The Game Of Their Lives . . . The Greatest Shock In World Cup History (Very Much So/Passion Pictures, 2002)

The Last King Of Scotland (Twentieth Century Fox, 2006)

Magazines/Periodicals

Four Four Two

When Saturday Comes

DEATH OR GLORY

So Foot
Hard gras
Elf Freunde
La Prensa
La Gazzetta Dello Sport